—— Ray Farabee ——

Ray Farabee

MAKING IT THROUGH
THE NIGHT AND BEYOND

A MEMOIR

ISBN 978-0-615-25762-4

Contents

Introduction

*Each of us is all the sums he has not counted . . . Each moment is
the fruit of forty thousand years. The minute-winning days, like flies,
buzz home to death, and every moment is a window on all time.*
—Thomas Wolfe, *Look Homeward Angel*

L IKE THOMAS WOLFE'S NOVEL based on his family and early life in
North Carolina, this book is an account of my family and life. It is a
"moment" about the lives of Farabees who started in North Carolina, came
to Texas by way of Georgia, survived the Civil War, and commenced the
history reported in this book.

Much like the Gants in *Look Homeward Angel*, my life has been "touched
by that miracle of chance that makes new magic in a dusty world"—particularly dusty in Wichita Falls at the time of my premature arrival in 1932.
The doctor didn't think I would make it through the night. With some
luck, love, and help of family, friends, and others, I made it through the
night and beyond.

This memoir is a window to my origins, life, and times past—the Great
Depression, growing up in the 1930's and 40's, working my way through
college and student leadership experiences in the 1950's, practicing law
and raising a family in the 1960's and 70's, politics and public policy in the
1970's and 80's, higher education law and health policy in the 1990's, and
finally retirement with the turn of the century.

I commenced this effort in 2004 in preparation for a family reunion,
writing four chapters about Farabee family history and my life through
public schools in Wichita Falls. When my wife edited the first chapters, she
observed that I wrote "like a lawyer." She was correct, and I have worked

hard to shed my "wordy ways." It has been a learning experience—about myself, family, writing, and navigating the computer.

This book is not written for commercial publication, but rather for family, friends, and inquiring minds who may wonder where I came from and what has happened along the way. Hopefully, it will encourage others to record some of their history and memories for future generations.

Acknowledgments

I T HAS REQUIRED A "VILLAGE" of family and friends to get me
through the project of writing this book. My wife Mary Margaret Farabee has been patient and helpful with research (tromping through grave-
yards and courthouses in search of facts about long-deceased relatives, and
translating the handwriting in old letters), editing, proofreading, and giving encouragement. Son Steve Farabee helped throughout the task, consulting and educating me about the computer and its programs, which
made it technically possible to produce the 15 chapters.

Lynda Farabee, Nephew Edd's wife, edited the early chapters and made
valuable suggestions from afar—the High Plains near Littlefield, Texas.
Lia Clarkson reviewed several chapters, and was always available to answer
technical questions about the computer. Bill Hobby read the three chapters about my State Senate experiences and gave helpful advice, as did Patsy
Spaw, the current Secretary of the Senate, in connection with Chapter Ten:
The Senate Years: 1975–1988.

Prior to her death 15 years ago, Cousin Frances Putnam of Ft. Worth
sent me copies of twelve letters from my great grandmother Mary Frances
Lanier Farabee and others, which was helpful in giving insight into my father's family. Cousin Hazel Beighley (now deceased) spent several hours
answering question about my mother's family. Other friends and relatives
have also been generous in furnishing pictures and information.

This book has more images than most, many from my collection of family snapshots. I wish to thank the Texas Senate Media Services, the *Wichita Falls Times Record News*, the *Daily Texan*, the United States Student Association, the Wisconsin Historical Society, *Texas Monthly*, and others who have given permission to use photographs, newsclips, and segments from articles.

Thanks to friends and family members who read portions of this book and have given encouragement and suggestions. I would never have completed the project without their help.

Some Family History and Stories

In every conceivable manner, family
is link to our past, bridge to our future.
—Alex Haley, *Roots*

M Y PARENTS were Jack Wortham Farabee and Annie Lee Sneed Farabee. My life began with them and is bound up with their families before them—my roots. In 2004 I wrote two chapters for a family reunion about "History of the Farabees in America" and "An Unlikely Pair: Jack and Annie Lee." I have combined and shortened those chapters for this book, but I think it's important to share some information and recollections about my family before getting on with my own life.

The Caleb Mystery

The most comprehensive history of the Farabee family is found in *Genealogy of the Farabees in America* (the Genealogy) compiled over the period of 1906–1914 by Louis Thomas Farabee and published in 1915. The 341-page book outlines several thousand Farabees as of early 1914. L. T. Farabee devotes only one page to the history of the Farabees prior to my great-great-great grandfather Benjamin Farabee. On the first page of the preface he states:

> The antecedents of the Farabees recorded in this volume resided in the northwestern part of England and were of Scotch-Irish origin.
> There appears to be no record showing when the first Farabees in

America arrived here. The earliest record that I have found relative to the Farabees in America shows that in 1758 Caleb Farabee was captain of a company of Kent County, Delaware, militia. He is the ancestor of all the Farabees recorded in this volume. . . .

No subsequent Farabee genealogists have found records of Caleb Farabee, but there are records about Caleb Furbee that seem to match those in the Genealogy. He is buried in the cemetery of Barratts Chapel in Murderkill One Hundred, Kent County, Delaware, southeast of Dover. Murderkill is the name of an area river flowing into the Delaware Bay, and a "One Hundred" is a colonial land measurement.

In 2001, my wife and I visited the first Methodist Church in North America, Barratts Chapel in Frederica, Delaware, (Barratts@aol.com). Though no longer an active church, it is a heritage landmark of the United Methodist Church and a museum. We were fortunate to arrive at the Chapel as a wedding ceremony concluded. A local Methodist minister assisted us in finding the tombstone of Caleb Furbee. Though difficult to read the carved name and date on the two-hundred-year-old gravestone, it reflected the death of Caleb Furbee in 1796.

So the question remains: Was the first "Farabee" in America really a "Furbee," or a Farabee or some other similar sounding name? No Farabees have been located in northwest England, but there are Furbees, Ferebees, et al. In any event, the "Farabees," whether Furbees, Ferebees, Furbys, etc.,

Barratts Chapel: the resting place of Caleb Furbee, 2001

apparently arrived in this country prior to 1760, when Benjamin Farabee was born, quite possibly before 1700, if they were initially Furbees.

Benjamin, the Great, Great, Great

Although some doubt remains as to whether the Farabees descended from Caleb Furbee, there is no doubt that my family line came from Benjamin Farabee, who spent most of his life in Davidson County, North Carolina. Benjamin was born in 1760; whether in Kent County, Delaware, or elsewhere, the date is confirmed by his tombstone in the Bethany Reformed and Lutheran Cemetery near the Walburg Community, north of Lexington, North Carolina.

The oldest of the seven children, Benjamin had five brothers and one sister. His siblings migrated west to Ohio, Pennsylvania, and Indiana. In fact, so many Farabees settled in Southeastern Indiana that a town, now listed as a settlement, was named for them: Farabee, Indiana.

Benjamin married Mary Cook circa 1785 in New Jersey, and their first two children, John and Joseph, were born there in 1786 and 1788. Benjamin and Mary had nine children in all. They moved to Davidson County, North Carolina, in approximately 1790, where the rest of their children were born.

Benjamin died in Davidson County on September 15, 1836. Approximately one month before his death on August 13, 1836, he wrote a will that was probated and filed in Lexington, North Carolina. This fascinating will gives us a view of rural Southern life at the time. Benjamin left his "beloved wife Mary" the right to the following:

> [to] occupy & possess the dwelling room in the N. part of the dwelling house where I now have my residence next to the well & also the loom house joining that room during her natural lifetime or in other words her widowhood—I likewise will & bequeath to my wife during her whole lifetime two bed steads & furniture, the clock & desk & chest and as much of the dresser furniture as she may deem necessary for her accommodation & likewise two choice cows, two fattened hogs & four head of sheep & I likewise bequeath wife the upper garden & privilege to the well for her necessity.
>
> I will that my executors sell my homestead tract of land on a reasonable credit & the money arising from such sale to keep in their hands

for the maintenance of my wife & Cloe, my black woman, during their natural life or in other words during Cloe's lifetime and my wife's widowhood.

The residue of the sale was to be distributed: $500 to each of his four sons, and $300 to each of his four daughters. We know from the Genealogy and from my examination of her gravestone that my great-great-great-grandmother Mary Cook Farabee died in 1850 in Davidson County. We have no record of Cloe's death, age, or relationship with Benjamin, though she would have been freed in 1864, if she lived so long and was not previously set free.

Joseph Farabee

Joseph Farabee, my great-great-grandfather, was born on September 22, 1788. He married Mary Harvey. They had six children; the oldest was my great-grandfather, George Washington Farabee. After Mary's death in 1854, Joseph remarried but had no additional children.

In September 2002 my wife and I visited Davidson County. We spent the night in Lexington, the Davidson County seat. After researching the genealogy in the local library, we went to the courthouse, where I found copies of the wills of Benjamin and Joseph Farabee. With that information, we located Benjamin's and Mary's graves in the Bethany Cemetery. After that success, we went in search of Joseph and Mary in the Bethel cemetery.

Mary High Farabee, a Davidson County historian, reported that Joseph gave the land, "from the edge of his plantation for the Bethel Church and Cemetery." His will left money in a trust fund for upkeep of the cemetery. When we saw a road sign near Tyro, North Carolina, that read "Farabee Homestead Road," we knew we were near Joseph's "plantation" and the Bethel Cemetery. The plantation is no more. Now rural homes on one-acre tracts are scattered along the country lane named for him and members of his family who had remained in the area.

We found the grave of Joseph Farabee and more Farabee gravestones than I have witnessed anywhere. This was not surprising because I saw more Farabee telephone listings in Lexington than I have observed in the phone books of other cities, including New York, Chicago, Los Angeles, Houston, Denver, and London.

4

The will of Joseph Farabee, dated April 20, 1860, reflects the growth of his estate, as compared to that of his father. Part of the growth was apparently achieved with slave labor. After giving his second wife Isabella 200 acres of land, buildings, a garden, a well, one Negro man, one Negro woman of her choice, one two-horse wagon, one buggy or carriage, four head of cattle, four head of sheep, a spinning wheel, and other items of personal property, Benjamin directed his executor to sell the rest of his property—including slaves—and divide the proceeds between his four living children, including my great-grandfather George Washington Farabee, a Methodist minister who had recently moved to Texas with his wife and family.

On August 26, 1863, Joseph added a codicil to his will of 1860 because of "circumstances having now changed." The circumstances were probably related to the Civil War, its effects on the North Carolina economy, and the emancipation proclamation by Abraham Lincoln on January 1, 1863. His wife Isabella was given a life estate instead of outright grant of land and two Negroes of her choice. He expressed his preference that "my Negroes shall be equally divided between my four children instead of being sold as directed in my will . . ."

Three other circumstances were to affect Joseph's will and codicil. First, his son George Washington Farabee had died in Galveston, Texas, on July 30, 1863. Apparently he was not aware of the fact that he had only three living children at the time of the codicil because he still made reference to

Farabee Homestead Road

"four children." This was understandable, considering the poor communication in 1863 and the war. Second, his son Joseph Columbus Farabee, to whom he had willed his silver watch in the 1860 will, was to die on June 14, 1864, in Lynchburg, Virginia, in the service of the Confederacy. Third, the Union would win the Civil War with the surrender of Robert E. Lee at Appomattox on April 9, 1865, ending slavery.

Joseph died on November 25, 1865, five months after the end of the Civil War. He no longer had slaves. Four of his six children had preceded him in death, two during the "Great War." His plantation was in all likelihood diminished, but he left his mark on Davidson County, including hundreds of descendants (many still residing in Davidson County), the Bethel Cemetery, Farabee Homestead Lane, and the surrounding real estate development carved from what was once his plantation.

George Washington Farabee

George Washington Farabee, my great-grandfather, was born in Davidson County on August 5, 1811, the first child of Joseph and Mary Farabee. We know very little about his childhood or education, which would have been sparse in the early 1800's. His five siblings were born two to five years apart. Unlike his brothers and sisters, who stayed in Davidson County for the duration of their lives, George left the farm/plantation, became a minister of the Methodist Episcopal Church, South, and moved to Georgia, where he was a circuit rider preacher working out of Athens. He later preached at Methodist churches in North Carolina and Texas.

The September 29, 1843, issue of the *Southern Advocate,* a regional Methodist newspaper, reported that "George W. Farabee of the Georgia Conference was married to Miss Mary F. Lanier, Talbotton, Talbot County, Ga, on August 2d (1843) by Rev. J. F. Steagall, P. E. of the Fort Gaines District." George and Mary had three children: Cecil Fauntleroy Eugene (Leroy) Farabee, born on September 10, 1846, in Athens, Georgia; Julia May Waters Farabee, born January 21, 1855, in Brunswick County, North Carolina; and James Victor Farabee, born January 12, 1857, also in Brunswick County.

James Victor died in Carthage, Panola County, Texas, on October 3, 1859, before reaching his third birthday. Four years later, his father George Washington Farabee died in Galveston, Texas, on July 30, 1863, at the age of 52. We don't know whether George had a church in Carthage or was traveling through Panola County with his family on the way to Galveston or elsewhere in Texas.

MARY FRANCES'S STORY—
AT LEAST THE LAST CHAPTER

Twelve remarkable letters, written between 1865 and 1867, tell a poignant and dramatic story about my great-grandmother Mary Frances Lanier Farabee. Copies of the letters, given to me by a cousin, help us know more about the last five years of Mary Frances's life—and about her and her husband's family, including my grandfather Leroy.

As the wife of a Methodist preacher, Mary Frances experienced a more transient, structured, and economically limited life—at least as compared to her in-laws, who had a plantation, slaves (until 1865), and relative wealth for the time. The pace of her life began to change in 1859 when the family moved to Texas; she lost her infant son James Victor during the same year; and the Civil War began in 1861. By that time the family lived in Galveston, then the largest city in Texas.

In 1862 her remaining son Leroy, age 15, did what he perceived was his patriotic duty. He joined the Confederate Army in Texas, serving at Sabine Pass as a drummer boy until discharged at the request of his mother because of his age. In 1863, Mary's husband of twenty years died; she was left destitute, with two children, in the middle of a civil war, far away from her family in Georgia. The family headed back home to Georgia or North Carolina, but on the way, her son reenlisted in the Confederate Army in Kentucky. Shortly thereafter, he was captured and imprisoned for the balance of the war.

You may think that things could not get worse for Mary Frances, but they did, as letters documented. The letters from Mary Frances to her son Leroy were written between 1865 and January 1867, and the five subsequent letters are to Leroy from a friend and family in 1867 and 1868, after his mother's death near Columbus, Kentucky, in 1867.

Mary Frances developed health problems, which required hospitalization. Treatment included morphine and opiates; like many people of the time, she became addicted to opium and similar medications. In her letter to son Leroy from Norwich, Connecticut, on October 17, 1865, she wrote,

"My health is on the mend—I have touched neither Morphine or Opium in 2 months and begin to look more like my former self."

Mary Frances was in Connecticut, spending the summer with Emma Gardner, who, in her words, was "the same lady who crossed the Potomac with me, and who gave evidence in my favor when I was taken a prisoner at Washington [D.C.]." Mary Frances had gone to Washington to secure the release of her son, but was imprisoned as a spy or enemy combatant. In her last letter to Leroy dated January 20, 1867, Mary Frances said, "I have [to] go to Washington City in April. I have sued Stanton [Edwin M. Stanton, Secretary of War] for damages for my imprisonment."

In her efforts to secure Leroy's release, Mary Frances met Colonel Martin, a Union officer. A personal relationship ensued, and although we have no documentation, she may have married him. Mary Frances signed the letter of October 17, 1865, "Your Mother, M F Martin." There were other references to "Colonel Martin," like the one expressing her intention to meet him in Savannah in October 1865, but she never used his first name.

There is no indication that Mary Frances was living with Colonel Martin during the time from October 1865 to January 20, 1867, nor is there expression of affection for him. In fact, her last letter stated, "I am going to Cairo Ill[inois] to see Col Martin die. He will leave me a very pretty property (sic) and the time will come and that before spring when I will come to Wash's house and prove to him that I have been unfortunate ..."

Mary Frances's relationship with, and/or, marriage to the Yankee Colonel created stress, if not alienation from her son, southern in-laws, and relatives. For example, in the January 1867 letter to her son, she wrote, "Your Grand Mother had told me how contemptuously you treated my very name in her presence. It sank deep. It brings tears to my eyes now." Ironically, it was on her trip to Illinois that a tragic accident occurred.

In a letter to Leroy, written from Forsyth, Georgia, and dated February 11, 1867, E. C. Phelps writes:

It is painful to tell you that we rec'd a letter from Capt [Colonel?] Martin informing us of the death of your dear mother. She was drowned on the 1st of Feb. in crofsing [crossing] from car (railroad); her foot slipped and she fell into the river [Mississippi] among the ice, her body had not been recovered. Your____ sister Julia is in Columbus, Ky, alone and among strangers.

1860's Mississippi River Boat

In a letter to Leroy dated March 1, 1867, his grandmother Lanier further confirmed that his mother drowned on February 1 in Columbus, Kentucky, at ten o'clock at night, when she slipped and fell into the river amid floating ice. Mrs. Lanier stated that it was public opinion that the owner of the boat should be sued for damages. The letter said that Julia was apparently walking behind her mother when the accident occurred, and was "inconsolable for a long time but was improving," though still in Kentucky.

There is no record of a lawsuit or recovery of damage for the tragic death of Mary Frances, but Julia finally returned to Georgia. She then moved to Meridian, Texas, to join her brother Leroy. She married James Marcellus Gandy, had three children, and died in 1889 in Allen, Texas. Since my grandfather Leroy married a Gandy, you will hear more about the Gandy family in the next segment of this chapter.

LEROY FARABEE

By the end of the Civil War, my grandfather Leroy had experienced the varied life of a minister's son in Georgia, North Carolina, and Texas; drummer boy for Company B, Likens Battalion of heavy artillery at Sabine Pass, Texas, Confederate States Army (CSA); private in Company B, 1st Kentucky Cavalry, CSA; a prisoner of war in Mt. Sterling, Kentucky, McLean Barracks in Cincinnati, Ohio, and Johnson's Island, near Sandusky, Ohio, on Lake Erie. He was released from prison upon his oath of allegiance to the United States. Union war records show that Leroy was

Confederate Memorial Johnson's Island, Ohio

age 18 when released, his place of residence was Galveston, Texas, his complexion and hair "light," his eyes were gray, and he stood at a height of 5 feet, 6 inches. This was only the first quarter of Leroy's life.

Like most Confederate veterans, Leroy was bitter and disappointed at the end of the "Great War." Not only had the Confederacy lost the war, but his father died two years earlier in Galveston. His mother had taken up with a Yankee officer and had become a drug addict while trying to secure her son's release from prison. He was unemployed and far away from his former home in Texas and his relatives in North Carolina and Georgia.

Mary Frances's letters indicate Leroy returned to Georgia, where he found a place to stay with his cousin Delaney ("Lanie") and her family in Athens. According to one letter, he went back to school. His mother advised him to "gratify yourself to write and to cipher well, to understand book keeping" and that he would "not long be dependent upon any one."

In addition to the value of education for Leroy's future well-being, Mary Frances gave abundant "motherly advice," including: 1) to marry well, saying, "get a rich old lady in law to give me a nice home.... There are rich girls in Harmony Grove, or there use to be"; 2) to pursue his rightful inheritance from the estate of his grandfather Joseph Farabee in Davidson County; and 3) in her last letter, that she "will do all I can for you and Mollie (but) I would prefer your marrying Ruth."

After the death of his mother on February 1, 1867, Leroy continued to get on with his life. We do not know whether Leroy received any inheritance from his grandfather Joseph Farabee's estate. However, he went to North Carolina and tried to get what he could from his uncle Samuel, the executor of the estate. He didn't marry Mollie, Ruth, or Mary. Aunt Genie (sister of Mary Frances) on March 26, 1868, wrote:

You know as well as I do that Mary is true & that she loves you & I know she had refused good offers on your acct. and I believe you will prove true to her. Why don't you write her; I will get it safe to her if you will mail to me. I think where a Gentleman promises to marry a lady that he should let nothing but death prevent, and I do not think is right or kind for any one to interfere & I would not be the means of breaking up a match for the world, let every one do as they please; then they must suffer the consequences.

In the same letter his aunt refers to Leroy's intention to "go out west." It is unclear whether he went "out west" to Galveston or Meridian, Texas, where he married Susan Elizabeth Gandy on September 18, 1870. Leroy's sister, Julia, found her way to Bosque County and married James Marcellus Gandy, a brother or cousin of Susan Elizabeth.

Leroy and Susan had five children, all born in Meridian: Fannie Lee Farabee born November 12, 1871; James Victor Farabee (named for Leroy's little brother who died at age two and a half and was buried in Carthage, Texas) born August 26, 1873; Jack Wortham Farabee (my father) born November 7, 1875; George Edwin Farabee, born November 3, 1877; and Lenora Farabee, born October 25, 1879. All married and had children except George Edwin, for whom one of my brothers was named. According to my father, George was shot and killed by a local gunslinger in Walnut Springs, Bosque County, Texas, on May 31, 1901, at age 23.

Susan Elizabeth died on August 24, 1881, in Meridian. Leroy's entry in the family Bible states that Susan "departed this (life) in the full trust of the Lord," setting out the exact hour of her death at 2:15 a.m. The cause of her death is unknown, but we know she was relatively young, at age 37; her children were quite young at the time; and the oldest child, Fannie Lee, helped raise her brothers and sister.

Leroy remarried on February 3, 1883. His new wife was Georgia Jamison (possibly Jimmerson). Georgia and Leroy had one child, Mark Farabee, born January 3, 1885, in Meridian. Leroy and Georgia were divorced on January 21, 1899. Leroy stated in the family Bible that Georgia "Died to me Sept 30, 1897." We can only speculate about the meaning of these words, but Uncle Mark, the son from Leroy's second marriage and my favorite uncle, was always on good terms with his half brothers and sisters.

Leroy was a carpenter by trade, but suffered from rheumatism in his later years, preventing him from work. In 1909 he made application for a Confederate veteran's pension, which was granted. In his last years, Leroy lived in Austin, Texas, with his daughter Fannie and her husband E. B. "Eph" Robertson, an able and distinguished attorney, originally from Bosque County. At the time the Robertsons were living in Austin, Uncle Eph was First Assistant Attorney General of Texas. They lived at 2510 Guadalupe, north of the University Methodist

*Cecil Fauntleroy Eugene
Farabee (Leroy)*

Church, an area I frequently walked while attending the University of Texas as an undergraduate in 1952–1955. According to his death certificate, Leroy died on January 14, 1914. He is buried next to his wife Susan Gandy Farabee in Meridian, Texas.

AN UNLIKELY PAIR: JACK AND ANNIE LEE

My parents, Jack Wortham Farabee and Annie Lee Sneed, were an unlikely pair for marriage in December of 1912. Jack was 37 years old—20 years older than Annie Lee; he was a well traveled "city boy," a worldly Methodist who smoked, drank whiskey, and had various girlfriends along the way.

Annie Lee was a "country girl" at 17 years of age, and had never traveled much beyond Eastland County, Texas. She was a Baptist and believed it "sinful" to smoke and drink—let alone dance. It was not a marriage made in heaven . . . or was it?

Jack's Story

My father, Jack Farabee, was born in Meridian, Bosque County, Texas, on November 7, 1875, the third child born to Leroy and Susan Gandy Fara-

Jack Farabee with mustached office workers, Galveston, circa 1890

bee. Jack's mother died before he reached his sixth birthday. His oldest sister Fannie helped raise him. Since his father Leroy was a carpenter, Jack grew up in a well-maintained house in Meridian and attended the limited public schools available to Texas children in the 1880's.

I have fond memories of my father telling me about fishing on the Bosque River when he was a boy. Jack's early boyhood in Bosque County was similar to that of John Lomax, another native of Meridian. Lomax wrote in *Adventures of a Ballad Hunter* (1947), "I hunted and fished, went swimming [in the Bosque] and lived with my kind—Frank and Tom Gandy, et al." In Jack's case it was probably first cousins Sam and Lula Gandy whom he played with, since his Aunt Julia had moved to Meridian and married Samuel Marcellus Gandy.

Young Jack learned the "three Rs" well, that is, reading, 'riting, and 'rithmetic. He did not go to college, nor did his brothers or sisters. In about 1890, he went to Galveston, then the largest city in Texas, where he apprenticed as an office boy in one of the larger businesses of that city, probably a cotton exchange or shipping company.

For reasons unknown, Jack left his office job, and went to work for the railroad. Prior to 1900, Galveston was the largest seaport in Texas, as well as a major railroad terminal. Jack worked as a brakeman and traveled west to Arizona, Nevada, and California. He traveled back and forth from Galveston and had a girlfriend there who worked for a local opera house. According to family stories, they were seriously involved and considering marriage.

Galveston Flood

On September 8, 1900, a great hurricane and flood struck Galveston. An estimated 6,000 persons perished; it was the largest natural disaster in the history of the United States. Jack Farabee was in Arizona and saved from the devastation of the hurricane and flood; but his girlfriend was drowned and washed away. His clothing and other belongings in Galveston were destroyed. The city's railroad terminal and shipping business was seriously impaired, and it was never the same after the hurricane of 1900. Jack moved to Douglas, Arizona, and worked for the Atchison, Topeka & Santa Fe Railroad.

When Jack went to work for the Santa Fe Railroad, he joined the Brotherhood of Locomotive Firemen and Enginemen trade union. He worked for the railroad long enough to receive a small pension, which helped sustain our family in the Depression when he could no longer work and had no benefits except a small state pension for aged poverty level persons not qualified for Social Security.

After working for others for 20 years, Jack Farabee was ready to try his luck at business for himself. He observed mineral wealth at the Phelps Dodge mining operations in Arizona and heard of oil booms at Spindle Top, Sour Lake, and elsewhere in Texas. He pulled stakes in Arizona, left the security of the railroad, and returned to Texas in 1910.

It's unclear what first brought Jack Farabee to Eastland County, Texas.

He met Annie Lee Sneed in the latter part of 1912 in either Ranger or the Lone Cedar area where she lived with her parents. Whether it was love at first sight, we do not know; but the relationship progressed quickly, and Jack and Annie Lee were married on December 13, 1912, in Eastland County. From Ranger they headed north to Petrolia, Texas, to start a family and seek their fortune.

Annie Lee's Story

My mother was born March 10, 1895, on the family farm near the Lone Cedar community in Eastland County, Texas, approximately seven miles south of Ranger. Annie was the fourth of five children born to William Marshall Sneed and Mollie Woods Sneed. William ("Bill" or "Paw" to the family) was born in 1856 in Flintville, Tennessee. Mollie ("Maw" to the family) was born in 1866 in Mt. Vernon, Illinois. Grandma Woods was part American Indian.

Farm life was hard when Annie was growing up. Except for staples like flour, sugar, salt, and coffee, most of the food consumed was raised on the farm. Livestock was slaughtered and preserved in the smokehouse. The

Annie Lee Sneed, circa 1912, in Ranger, Texas

cows were milked and butter churned. Fruits and vegetables were dried, preserved, or canned in jars and kept in the storm cellar. There was no running water, gas or electric lights, indoor plumbing, or other niceties of life that city folks were more likely to have in the 1890's and early 1900's.

Bill Sneed was a good farmer and an able butcher. He raised additional livestock to help get the family through droughts and depression years. To earn extra money, he helped other farmers slaughter and butcher their livestock. Mother told me about going to town (Ranger) on the wagon with her father and mother. The round-trip and limited shopping took the better part of the day, but Annie experienced such rare delights as getting a piece of candy, a banana, or an orange. Nearly all of the children's clothes were homemade by Mollie. Maw once made the girls special dresses out of her house curtains so that they would be better dressed for a funeral in Burleson, Texas. That trip was one of the few times that Annie ventured out of Eastland County before her marriage.

Annie and her siblings walked a mile or more each day to the small one- or two- room school in Lone Cedar. On Sundays, Paw would hitch up the mule and take the family to the Merriman Baptist church near Lone Cedar. The church and school are gone, and Lone Cedar can no longer be found on the map. Paradoxically, the Lone Cedar Country Club is near the former community. As country clubs go, the Lone Cedar club is sparse on amenities, with only a nine-hole golf course and no clubhouse or swimming pool. The Club and the Sneed farm are located off Eastland County Road 570, north of Lake Leon, which was completed in early 1960.

Annie contracted tuberculosis at an early age. She attributed it to drinking raw, unpasteurized, cow's milk. (TB, also called consumption, can be transmitted by raw milk.) Cousin Hazel, for many years a registered nurse in Ranger, told me that significant numbers of children of that era contracted TB from each other because it was a highly contagious disease. Annie's lung problems dogged her all of her life. She spent months in TB sanatoriums and lived with her two oldest sons in El Paso in 1920–1921 because it was higher and drier than Wichita Falls and thought to be better for her lungs.

One of the more important influences on mother's life was the Baptist church. She told me about going to revivals, camp meetings, and singing conventions and witnessing people being "saved" and having profound religious experiences—including "shouting," speaking in unknown tongues, and fainting. Annie was baptized in Colony Creek near the Merriman Baptist Church. My grandparents and most of my mother's family were baptized in the same creek and buried in the Merriman Cemetery.

Annie Lee's favorite song from those camp meetings and singing conventions was the following: "I am bound for the Promised Land; Oh, who will come and go with me? I am bound for the Promised Land!" When she married Jack Farabee and headed to Petrolia in Clay County, Texas, it wasn't exactly the "Promised Land," but it was a far different land and life than that of Lone Cedar—and held more promise.

THE PETROLIA YEARS

Petrolia was originally known as Oil City because of shallow oil discoveries in 1901–04. This historic fact, reported in the *Handbook of Texas Online*, explains why Louis Thomas Farabee stated that Jack and Annie Lee lived in "Oil City, LA," when in fact they lived in Petrolia, Clay County, Texas, not Louisiana. By 1905, Petrolia was a booming town located on the Wichita Falls and Oklahoma Railroad, and it continued to grow with the discovery of natural gas that was sold to communities as far away as Dallas and Ft. Worth.

When Jack and Annie Lee got off the train in Petrolia in 1913, the population was approximately 500, and the community had five churches, a bank, a theater, waterworks, telephone connections, a newspaper, several oil field supply stores, and other retail businesses. Housing was in short supply, and mother told me they lived in a half dugout house for a while before moving into a small frame home. In any event, if it had running water and electric or gas lights, it was better than the farm near Lone Cedar.

Leroy and Edwin Farabee

My parents' first child, Jack Leroy Farabee, was born in Petrolia in 1914. He was named for his father and grandfather. The picture of baby Leroy on a white horse (identified on the back as "old Bessie"), with Jack holding the baby and Annie Lee holding the horse, tells us a lot about their early life in Petrolia. My dad was not an oil man, but an oil field worker, probably what is known as a tool pusher or pumper, operating some of the shallow wells of the area for others, and learning the oil business. When we were looking at this picture in the family album, mother told me that Jack traded Old Bessie for an interest in an oil lease, and that was the beginning of their oil business.

Baby Leroy on Old Bessie in Petrolia, 1914

Better times in 1916

The second child, Edwin Burnet Farabee, was born on June 28, 1916, either in Petrolia or Wichita Falls. He was named after Jack's younger brother George Edwin, who was shot and killed in Walnut Springs in 1901, and Jack's brother-in-law, Ephraim Barnett Robertson, who was married to Fannie.

A 1916 photo of a better dressed Jack and Annie Lee with a child (identified as Leroy on the back) indicates that times were changing. Although some pictures from the Petrolia era suggest Jack was still doing part of the dirty work, this picture, showing him in with suit, tie, gold watch chain, and his wife and child dressed nicely (it was still common practice to clothe little boys in dresses) signaled that the Farabees would soon be moving to Wichita Falls, where Jack would be an oil man—rather than a pumper or tool pusher.

OIL BOOM YEARS

By 1916, it was apparent that Wichita County was where the oil and gas future for north Texas was located. There were over 1,130 producing wells in Wichita County, yielding more than 7.8 million barrels of oil by the end of 1916. Joseph Kemp and Frank Kell, both from Bosque County, were developing everything from real estate to railroads, including a flour mill, lakes, irrigation systems, oil, and gas. The population of Wichita Falls was over 37,000 and growing.

2313 Ninth Street

On January 25, 1917, Jack Farabee purchased the house and lot in Wichita Falls at 2313 Ninth Street for $2900. The two-bedroom, one-bath house, with kitchen, dining, and living rooms, was located in the Floral Heights addition, and would remain the home place of the Farabees for over 55 years. A garage and attached servants quarters would first house Cora Belle Sanders, a black woman who helped care for the young Farabee boys in the good times, and later provide living quarters for Edwin and Janelle Farabee after their marriage, and then rental income in the hard times.

Leroy, Jack, and Edwin on a new car, circa 1922

Jack was beginning to make enough money to afford the purchase of the 2313 Ninth Street house and a car to reach places not available by train. Annie Lee once told me, in a derisive manner, that Jack boasted "there would never be a day when he couldn't earn $1000 dollars making trades." As it turned out, the boast was pretty accurate for the eight years from 1917 to 1925. Jack bought, sold, and traded real estate and other property, but was primarily an oil man, sometimes referred to as an oil operator. His offices were in the First National Bank Building in Wichita Falls, and his office manager or secretary was Fred Sehmann, Jr., who later became Executive Director of the North Texas Oil and Gas Association. Although Jack's fortunes changed dramatically in the late 1920's, Sehmann remained a friend until Jack's death in 1958.

Wichita Falls was the place to be for an oil operator in 1918 and several years thereafter. Oil production increased in 1917, but its growth exploded in 1918 with the oil booms in Burkburnett, Ranger, Desdemona, and Breckenridge. In 1919, oil booms followed in Thrift, Newtown, and Bridgetown along the Red River in Wichita County. Jack was involved in much of the boom activity in Wichita and Eastland Counties. He bought, sold, and traded oil and gas leases in counties across North Texas.

The Ranger oil boom was important not only for the Farabee family, but to Annie's family, the Sneeds. Oil was found on the Sneed farm near Lone Cedar, and Bill and Mollie Sneed moved to Ranger, purchasing a new house with running water, indoor plumbing, a bathroom, gas stoves, and gaslights. Paw was skeptical about electricity, and the house was not converted to electrical power until after his death in 1937.

William Marshall Sneed was known for his generosity after he came into oil money. One of the first things he did, after buying a Model T Ford, was to give each of his children $1000. Annie Lee related that he would loan friends some of his new money. Although he had friends when he lived back on the farm, Bill found a good many more with his easy credit. According to my mother, many of his new friends found "Uncle Billy" and didn't always pay their debts to him.

Annie Lee dressed for a night at the Wichita Opera House, circa 1922

The Wichita Opera House

On June 6, 1919, J. W. (Jack) Farabee and W. R. Priest acquired Lots 8 and 9 of Block 182 of the Original Town Site of Wichita Falls for $100,000 (Vol. 143 Page 81, Deed Records of Wichita County). This tract is identified as the Wichita Opera House, which later became the Wichita Theater. Jack owned two-thirds of the lots and Priest one-third. It is unclear to me who ran the Opera House/Wichita Theater when Jack and his partners owned it, but it was a popular place in the 1910's and early 1920's. Annie Lee told me about the vaudeville shows and the stars who came to the Opera House while they owned part of it.

In November 1924 Jack and Annie, together with O. L. (Ollie) and Della Rahl, conveyed their interests in Lots 8 and 9 to the Wichita Theater. I don't know whether Jack and another partner named W. L. (Bill) McAllister owned the Wichita Theater Company, but McAllister was always identi-fied by my parents as Jack's partner in the Opera House venture. The ad-vent of movies, particularly "talkies," replaced vaudeville, and a plunge in oil prices and decline of Farabee fortunes took the Farabee interest in the Wichita Theater Company. By the time of my arrival in 1932, all that was left of the Farabee investment on the northeast corner of Scott and Tenth Streets of Wichita Falls was a theater lobby ashtray stand; it stood in the en-trance hallway of 2313 Ninth Street until the house was sold. I now have the restored stand, which we use for an indoor planter and curiosity piece.

Jimmy Farabee

Annie Lee gave birth to their third child, Jimmy Wortham, on December 22, 1924, in Wichita Falls. Jimmy—not James—got his name from Jack's brother; his middle name came from Jack's middle name. When Jimmy was born, Brother Leroy was ten and Edwin was eight. Faithful servant Cora Belle Sanders and Jimmy's big brothers helped take care of the new arrival.

Leroy and Edwin giving Jimmy a bath
on back steps of 2313 Ninth, May 1925

THE OIL BUST AND BEGINNING OF HARD TIMES

Shallow oil wells in Burkburnett and other boomtowns had a short life because of the lack of well spacing, over production, and lower prices. Oil discoveries in East, South, and West Texas accelerated the downward spiral for the price of oil to ten cents a barrel. Jack Farabee either didn't seek production elsewhere or have any luck finding oil in areas further away from his home base in North Texas.

Although the Farabees had a better house, a bigger automobile, and more money to spend on clothes and travel, there were problems. Jack was away from home on business travel; Annie Lee felt he was drinking and smoking too much and she was having more problems with her lungs, periodically hemorrhaging, cough-

ing, and spitting up blood. As her tuberculosis became more acute, Annie Lee was required to spend time in TB hospitals during the 1920's, 30's and early 40's. On the back of one picture taken of her at a TB sanatorium, she wrote "all dressed up & no place to go." That was a fact in more ways than one; persons with active tuberculosis were quarantined and could not freely travel or make visits to their homes.

Annie Lee at TB hospital:
All dressed up and no place to go

Jack's health was also declining, as he developed chronic coughing problems diagnosed as bronchiectasis, which he and mother called "bronchialectus." Although Jack's problem was related to smoking, Annie, a non-smoker, was diagnosed as having bronchiectasis in her later years when her tuberculosis was inactive, and this was a primary cause of her death.

Both Leroy and Edwin contracted spinal meningitis. The disease left Leroy with one leg shorter than the other and Edwin later deaf in one ear. This is why Leroy and Edwin were 4-F for World War II and worked in the Houston shipyards.

The Internal Revenue Service filed liens in 1925 asserting claims for the year of 1920 for approximately $40,000. In January 1925 Jack mortgaged the house and lot at 2313 Ninth Street to the City National Bank to secure two notes for approximately $12,000. In 1931 and 1935, Jack gave additional mortgages to the City National Bank for $1500. Because of limitations on mortgaging homesteads in Texas, all of these bank loans were probably for the purpose of paying tax liens against 2313 Ninth Street.

In 1926 the Wichita County Water Improvement District No. 1 sued Jack for failure to pay property taxes on 2313 Ninth for the years of 1923 and 1924 in the amount of $65.41. The Water District suit proceeded to judgment on January 14, 1927, for $68.54 plus costs and foreclosure of its lien on the home. The Wichita County Sheriff sold 2313 Ninth on July 3, 1928, to the highest bidder for $83.04 plus costs. Thankfully, J. W. (Jack) Farabee was the highest bidder and the homestead was saved.

The Great Depression of the 1930's arrived early in Wichita Falls and other parts of Texas because of slipping crude oil prices and drought that created the "dust bowl" in Oklahoma and West Texas.

Practically everything Jack had acquired in the good years was sold to pay debts and taxes. What was not sold was foreclosed by the bank. Liquidations included their interest in the Opera House/Wichita Theater, real estate, and producing oil and gas properties. The only exception was the house, furnishings, a few non-producing mineral interests, and an old Model A Ford. Jack and Annie Lee came close to losing the house for back taxes. Jack tried to make oil deals or find other work, but none of his efforts materialized.

The toll of newly found poverty was not only hard on Jack and Annie Lee, but also upon Leroy and Edwin. Jimmy was too young to have experienced the perks and status of wealth, but Leroy and Edwin knew what it was like to have the best cars in town, new clothes, and travel with the rich kids. They would have been in junior high or high school when the Farabee finances hit bottom and their mother was in the San Angelo State TB Hospital.

One traumatic event in Edwin's life occurred in high school when he took a local girl one evening for some friendly "necking." A masked male, wearing a black cape, came up to the car and held a gun on the couple, making Edwin get out of the car. The masked man tied up Edwin and raped the girl. The rapist then fled, leaving the girl to untie Edwin. The couple reported the crime, and it turned out to be one of several similar crimes committed by the same person. Shortly thereafter, Wiley Culbertson, the son of a wealthy family, was apprehended, jailed, and convicted of the rapes.

Although Leroy and Edwin finished high school, they did not go to college, but sought work in the oil fields, roughnecking or doing what other little work was available during the Depression. Edwin graduated from high school into the worst of the bad times. He joined the Civilian Conservation Corps (CCC), a New Deal program of the Roosevelt administration to give young men work involving forest and park conservation.

Jimmy dropped out of high school in the late 1930's and never received a high school diploma, though he had a fine mind, as did his older brothers. Unless you had family money, opportunities were extremely limited in the 1920's and 30's. I have always felt that the contrast of wealth experienced in

Jimmy Farabee, circa 1939

their early lives, followed by sudden poverty, contributed to my brothers' problems in later years.

If things weren't bad enough for the Farabees at 2313 Ninth Street, another mouth to feed was on its way in 1932. Jack and Annie's fourth child, Kenneth Ray, was born on November 22, 1932. Having no personal recollection of my birth, I have tried to find out about this "blessed event," since I was rather intimately involved. This and recollections of my early childhood are the subject of the next chapter.

Early Childhood in Wichita Falls and Ranger

Solomon Grundy, born on a black and beastly Monday
Christened on a stark and stormy Tuesday
—Nineteenth century children's nursery rhyme

Help me make it through the night . . . 'cause tonight I need a friend.
—Kris Kristofferson song, 1970

MY CONCEPTION, birth, and survival seem as unlikely as Jack and Annie Lee getting together for marriage. November 1932 was the middle of the Great Depression; my parents had no money, no work, very little income, and three children to feed, though Leroy had graduated from high school and found sporadic work in the oil fields.

Also, the health of both my parents was poor. Mother was afflicted with tuberculosis, and my father had bronchiectasis. They spent a good deal of time coughing and spitting up phlegm, Annie's sometimes laced with blood.

Jack and Annie Lee didn't get along very well. They frequently argued about a variety of matters, but mostly religion. Jack was a Methodist, Annie a Baptist. Their most profound theological arguments involved the relative merits or shortfalls of "sprinkling," the Methodist form of baptism, and "immersion," the Baptist way. It wasn't that a Methodist couldn't be "saved," and go to heaven. However, according to the Baptists, a few drops of water on the head, usually when one was a child, was not a sure thing, as compared to "getting salvation and being saved" when one was old enough to "accept Jesus as your personal Savior," usually at a revival, and then being fully immersed by the preacher in a creek, river, or pool of water.

I was conceived by my parents—not an Immaculate Conception or otherwise; however, I suspect my parents had not intended to have another child. Annie Lee's pregnancy was unexpected and depressing to her, in light of the dour circumstances described above. At least she had one last hope, that of finally having a daughter, after having three rambunctious boys.

HELP ME MAKE IT THROUGH THE NIGHT

I was born on November 22, 1932, "on a black and beastly" Tuesday. Signs of an early arrival prompted mother's sister, Allie Faircloth, to come from Ranger, Texas; her eldest daughter, Billie, a recent graduate as a registered nurse at the Wichita General Hospital Nursing School, was also present.

When my birth became more imminent, the family physician, Dr. Bailey Collins, was summoned to our home. Dr. Collins, with the assistance of Cousin Billie and Aunt Allie, a practical nurse, delivered me in the back bedroom at 2313 Ninth Street in Wichita Falls.

Dr. Collins was not optimistic about my chances for survival; I was six weeks premature and underweight. He told Aunt Allie and Billie, "Put him over there, out of the way. He won't make it through the night; we've got to save Annie."

Fortunately, Aunt Allie and Billie were more optimistic. They took charge by removing a small dresser drawer, lining it with a towel, and putting me in it. I was then placed on the open door of the kitchen oven in my makeshift cradle/incubator to keep warm. Annie Lee and I made it through the night. Unlike Solomon Grundy, I was not christened on "a stark and stormy Tuesday" since Annie was skeptical about any sprinkling or christening of infants who were not fully cognizant of the theological implications of baptism.

When advised that I was a boy, Annie Lee was depressed beyond words. According to my aunt, Annie Lee said she didn't want me; she wanted a girl; she already had three boys! During the two days of maternal rejection, Aunt Allie named me Kenneth Ray—"Kenneth" for Aunt Maude's oldest son Kenneth Falls, and "Ray" for her son Rayford Faircloth.

Within a few days, my mother's disappointment about my gender subsided, and she took me back. In fact, she showered me with more love, advice, and protective care than needed, at least in my boyish opinion. Thankfully, she didn't clothe me in a dress, as was the custom—at least that I can remember.

Aunt Allie Faircloth, circa 1938

Billie Faircloth Redd, circa 1932

EARLIEST MEMORIES

Some early childhood memories are more vivid than others. Those recollections involving place, anxieties, fear, and other emotions are the first to spring from my mind.

The place was 2313 Ninth Street in Wichita Falls. By 1932 it was well-worn, and no money was available for paint or repair. The roof leaked and stained the wallpaper on the ceilings. After I graduated from a baby bed in my parents' bedroom, I slept in the double bed with my father. My mother slept in the same room, but in another bed because of her tubercular condition. The front bedroom was rented, whenever possible, to provide a small amount of income. My brothers slept in what was designed for the dining room, but was never, in my time, used for that purpose. We ate in the kitchen.

When it rained and the roof leaked, we put buckets and pans around the house to catch the water dripping from the ceiling. Awakening in the morning or sick in bed, I stared at the stains on the ceiling wallpaper above me. I saw outlines of elephants, clouds, and other imaginary figures. The wallpaper, and the canvas under it, sagged downward, and I was afraid it would fall on me. Daddy patched the roof to stop most of the leaks, and the ceiling paper never fell. The wallpaper was replaced in 1939 by a paper hanger from the Works Project Administration (WPA), a New Deal program to help people return to work during the Depression.

2313 Ninth in the 1920's

Winters were windy and cold in North Texas, summers dry and hot. Our home was not energy efficient by any standard. To keep utility bills low, my parents heated only the back bedroom, front bedroom (if rented), kitchen, and bathroom (on Saturday night when we took our baths). The house was heated by natural gas—space heaters and the kitchen stove. Electricity was used sparingly; we had no air conditioning. Someone gave us a used black Westinghouse oscillating fan, which helped move the hot air around during the heat of summer. Even though I can now afford higher energy bills, I still go around turning off lights, just like Annie Lee taught me. Back then it was not for conservation of energy, but to save a dollar or two and be able to pay the electric, gas, and water bills.

The one use of electricity that my mother did not scrimp on was a small radio next to her bed. I would awake in the middle of the night, and Annie Lee would be listening to her radio—usually Dr. E. F. Webber, bringing the "old time gospel" from Oklahoma City. (E. F. Webber, who died in 1957, founded the Southwest Radio Ministries in 1933, which continues and is the oldest, longest running Christian radio program in the United States.) Dr. Webber, sometimes referring to himself as "Brother Webber," opened and closed his nocturnal messages with the phrase "God is still on the throne and prayer changes things." As poor as we were, mother would occasionally send a dollar to Dr. Webber, who then showered her with mailings for more of the "widow's mites." Taking Brother Webber's suggestion, I prayed for my own room, and the prayer was answered when I graduated from my father's bed to the back porch. It was small and very cold in the winter, but free of the nighttime sermons of Brother Webber.

We raised chickens in the backyard for eggs and a limited amount of meat, usually for Sunday dinner about once a month. I remember gathering eggs, which my mother would fry for breakfast and sometimes for dinner. In the spring, Dad went to Central Feed and Seed and bought baby chicks. Dad and I would go to the General Mills Elevators and get waste wheat to feed the chickens, along with scraps from our table. Someone gave me a baby white Peking duck that I raised until the time came for its sacrifice in the name of Sunday dinner. I protested and cried, but eventually joined the family in eating my pet duck.

My father was a member of the Floral Heights Methodist Church, located only a block from our home. Because of her health, mother seldom went to what she considered her church, the First Baptist. Dad regularly

Floral Heights Methodist Church, circa 1939

took me with him to Floral Heights. We both attended our respective Sunday school classes, and then I joined him for the church service. I slept through the sermons with my head on dad's lap, but I enjoyed the choir, paying particular attention to a tall, lanky man with a big Adam's apple, whose name was Sam Gose.

When I tell stories of my adolescence, I will recount how I was swept away from Methodism at a Baptist revival, to the joy and delight of my mother.

As a child, my health was not very good. I frequently suffered from sore throats, bronchitis, and low-grade fever. One of my problems was diagnosed as tonsillitis. When enough money or charity was available, my mother took me to Dr. Collins office in the Hamilton Building for the stated purpose of "taking out my tonsils." The nurse put me to sleep by placing an ether-soaked bandage over my nose, and the operation began. When I awoke, my tonsils were removed, and I was also circumcised. Dr. Collins apparently decided to finish up the job he started with my delivery. Since he didn't anticipate my survival when I was born, he didn't worry about circumcision. Many years later, after the doctors moved out of the Hamilton building, I was a partner with the Sherrill & Pace law firm located in the same building. Thankfully, the law practice was not as traumatic as the tonsillectomy/circumcision that caused pain on both ends of my body.

Christmas is a special time for children, and it was for me as well. However, I remember more than one "hard candy" Christmas. My folks had little money for gifts, but Aunt Allie, cousins Hazel, Billie, and others made up for it with new clothing that supplemented the "hand-me-downs," a few toys, and games. My namesake cousin, Kenneth Falls, gave us a blanket each Christmas, which helped keep us warm through the cold winter nights. We received an occasional charity fruit basket, turkey, or ham. Like other children, I hung the largest stocking I could find in anticipation of Santa Claus. We had no fireplace or chimney for Jolly Ol' St. Nick to traverse, but I placed the stocking in the most practical location. As I became older, I noticed that the apple, orange, and nuts in my stocking looked like those from the fruit basket, and my belief in Santa began to falter.

RANGER TIMES AND STORIES

My mother and I somehow got to Ranger each year to visit her family or go to a funeral. Grandpa ("Paw") and Grandma ("Maw") Sneed slept in the front bedroom, Aunt Allie and Aunt Maude shared the back bedroom, and Uncle Charlie lived on one end of the closed-in back porch. We ate breakfast, dinner (lunch), and supper on the other end of the back porch. Maw and Paw were quite old by that time, and each had a rocking chair in what would have otherwise been the dining room. When Mamma and/or I visited, we slept in the living room, which was called the "parlor."

Maw used Garrett snuff, and Paw chewed Redman tobacco. Each had a stained blue Chase & Sanborn ("Good to the Last Drop") coffee can, for the purpose of periodic spitting. Lights and heat were furnished by natural gas, so we had no radio. Maw and Paw hardly ever spoke to each other or

Grandma Sneed (Maw), circa 1935   *Grandpa Sneed (Paw), circa 1934*

to the rest of us. They just rocked, chewed, and spit, from morning into the early night. This was particularly eerie at night because the gaslights made a hissing sound, the floor creaked under the rockers, and there was very little conversation by anyone.

An old, ornate pump organ sat in one corner of the parlor. Paw bought the organ for Aunt Allie, and she learned to play music on it from a mail-order instruction book. She was the only person in the family who knew how to play the organ, and she would play and sing hymns. I tried to play the organ, but my feet couldn't reach the pedals that pumped the air into the bellows that made the music. As my legs grew longer, I finally managed to pump the organ and make discordant sounds, but I never learned to play it.

Aunt Maude Falls, circa 1938

Aunt Maude was the gardener and principal cook for the family. An adjoining vacant lot provided fresh fruits and vegetables during the growing season and dried peaches and canned goods in the winter. In addition, Aunt Maude raised a front yard full of petunias, phlox, periwinkles, and other flowers each year. With Maude's tender care and encouragement, all of the flowers emerged each spring as volunteers from the prior season. People stopped and admired the multiple colors and varieties of flowers.

Three occurrences at 1001 Desdemona Road stand out in my memories of Ranger days: Grandpa Sneed's death, my grandmother's death several years later, and Uncle Charlie's occasional epileptic seizures, generally referred to at the time as "fits."

I was five when my Grandpa Sneed died. Killingsworth Hardware Store, then located on Main Street in Ranger, served as the town undertaker, and the hardware store embalmed Paw's body and returned it to the parlor of the home. The body laid in state for a couple of days so that friends and family could come by, see Bill, and express condolences to the family before the church service and burial at Merriman Cemetery. This was the first time I had seen a dead person. If that wasn't traumatic enough, I had to sleep in the parlor with Grandpa, who was all laid out in a very nice casket. The first night I could barely sleep. Later, at age nine, death was easier to handle when my grandmother died and I went through a similar experience.

In 1938, I was six years of age and my mother had a bad spell with her lungs. She returned to the state TB hospital in San Angelo, which had treated her before. Aunt Allie and Aunt Maude took care of me in Ranger for much of the time during her absence, including Christmas of 1938. It was the longest period of time I was ever away from home and my parents before leaving for college in 1952.

No children of my age lived in the Ranger neighborhood, and I was lonely—not that I had an abundance of friends back in Wichita Falls. As a result, I created an imaginary friend whose name was JB. We rode the range all around 1001 Desdemona on our imaginary horses, mine an old broomstick and JB's one more layer of my imagination. I don't recall our exact conversations, but we talked a lot and were good friends. I liked JB so much that I took him back to Wichita Falls with me when I returned home.

Mr. Moore lived on about 15 acres across Desdemona Street. I never knew his first name; he was just "Mr. Moore." He was an older, big man who smoked a pipe, had a mule, a milk cow, and some chickens. JB and I frequently visited Mr. Moore's "ranch." In the spring Mr. Moore plowed his field behind the mule, which pulled an old-time steel plow. JB and I followed along each new furrow. After a hard morning's work, Mr. Moore would have a light lunch, smoke his pipe, and lay down on the floor for an afternoon nap. Sometimes JB and I would join him, but I wasn't too much on naps.

On Tuesdays, Aunt Allie would drive us over to Eastland, the county seat, for what was called "Bank Night" at the downtown movie theater. I don't recall ever winning any prizes, but I enjoyed most of the films, particularly the ones about swashbuckler pirates and cowboys. These would provide additional adventure opportunities for JB and me, as we roamed up and down Desdemona, the woods across the street, and Mr. Moore's ranch.

On one occasion, we went to Eastland early and visited the courthouse where I first saw Old Rip. Rip was a dead horned frog, encased in glass, on an elaborate granite pedestal located in the center of the first floor hallway of the courthouse. Legend has it that Old Rip was placed in the cornerstone of the new county courthouse in 1897, along with a Bible, newspapers, and other artifacts. The cornerstone was opened in 1928, and various witnesses claim that Old Rip was still alive, apparently in hibernation for 31 years without food, water, or fresh air. Although horned frogs (we called

Kenneth and Alma Falls, Ranger, circa 1935

them 'horny toads') are now rare in Texas and on the endangered species list, lots of these small, spiny critters were all around 1001 Desdemona in 1938. Of course, JB and I preferred the live ones better than the dead ones like Old Rip.

On practically every visit to Ranger as a child, we would drive out to the "Home Place," which was the old Sneed Farm near Lone Cedar. Cousin Kenneth Falls and his family lived on one side of the road and Uncle Gene and his wife on the other. Uncle Ernest also lived on the farm with his family. Cousin Joann Sneed and second cousin Betty Jean Falls were the closest to my age, and I always enjoyed visiting with them. On one occasion, I spent a summer night at Cousin Gene's house. The windows were up, and I could hear the pump jacks struggling to get the last of the shallow oil from beneath the Home Place. Coyotes would make distant howls throughout the night. It was a lonely place, and I was ready to go home.

RETURN TO WICHITA FALLS AND
THE BROTHERS THREE

In July of 1939 I returned home to start school in September. Mamma wasn't home yet but would soon return. Brothers Leroy and Edwin were married. Each had a child and lived at or near 2313 Ninth Street. Brother Jimmy lived at home. As compared to Ranger, there was a lot of activity. I barely had time for my imaginary friend JB, but he stuck with me.

My oldest brother Leroy married Maxine Polson from Alvord, Texas, in 1936. They were married in a double wedding ceremony with Cousin Billie Faircloth and Guy Squirrel Redd. All of my brothers were married in Oklahoma, where weddings were faster, cheaper, and just as valid as those occurring in Texas. Leroy continued to find work as a roughneck in the oil fields around Wichita Falls. Their first child Margot was born December 16, 1937, a little more than five years after my birth. Leroy and Maxine followed the oil patch first to Freer in South Texas, and then on to Houston, where their second child Mark was born on August 3, 1942.

Brother Edwin married a high school classmate, Janelle King, in 1937. They lived in the garage apartment at 2313 Ninth Street. Edwin worked for a dental laboratory, learning the trade of making dentures and bridges for area dentists. Edwin and Janelle had their first child, Edwin Thomas Farabee ("Eddie," now "Edd") on January 29, 1939, and a second child, Deanne Farabee, on June 3, 1940. Shortly after Deanne's birth, Edwin and Janelle separated and later divorced. Janelle and Deanne moved in with Mr. and Mrs. King, Janelle's parents. Edwin moved to Houston to seek new employment. Jack and Annie Lee took Eddie and raised him for much of the next ten years. Because of the proximity of our ages, my nephew Eddie is much more like a brother than my real brothers, who were significantly older.

My brother Jimmy, a good mechanic and technician, was still at home and working nearby at Willard Stehlik's filling station. He purchased a Model T Ford with his earnings. Jimmy enjoyed driving his friends through area pastures and over country roads. Although the Model T required considerable work to keep it running, Jimmy took me for several rides, which were memorable because the top was open and his driving adventurous. By that time, my parent's Model A was never used, either because they couldn't afford license plates or because of mechanical failure.

Jimmy traded the Model T for a yellow Indian motorcycle that was more reliable and faster. On occasion, he let me ride with him on it. I would hang on for dear life, with the roar of the engine beneath my legs and the wind in my face. This was the most exciting experience yet. "More, more, take me for a ride" was my frequent request, but Annie Lee would not hear of it. She was convinced that both Jimmy and I would be killed, or at least maimed,

Model T Ford

on the nefarious yellow Indian motorcycle. Although she could not stop Jimmy from riding his motorcycle, she severely limited my exciting experiences as a passenger.

During the 1930's, my brothers helped out with a few dollars here and there to keep food on the table at 2313 Ninth. Leroy was the most generous, perhaps because he had a better job; but as the oldest, he also felt more responsibility for the struggling family. Although they were older, I have fond memories about each of my brothers. They were good to me, providing loving kinship throughout their respective lives. They and their wives gave Annie Lee and Jack seven fine grandchildren, providing me with two nephews, five nieces, and multiple great-nieces and -nephews—even some great-great ones.

One memory of that period in Wichita Falls before the return of my

1930's Indian motorcycle

mother from the TB hospital was the freedom I had under supervision—or lack thereof—by my father and brothers. All of them smoked cigarettes, mostly homemade using Bugler tobacco or sometimes Prince Albert. The cigarettes were made with a small hand-operated device. You placed the cigarette paper in the machine, filled the paper with tobacco, and pushed the lever over a hump, which "rolled" it into a cigarette. Then you licked the open edge of the paper, secured a tight fit around the tobacco, and lit up.

It didn't take me very long to try my hand at making cigarettes with Bugler tobacco. Once I learned to make cigarettes, I quickly moved to the next step and lit up by myself. I don't remember smoking in the presence of my father or brothers, but I do recall two older neighborhood kids coming over when I was having a smoke on the front porch. They commented that I was sure young to be smoking and asked if they could have one of my homemade smokes. At the ripe old age of six, I advised them they were too young and shouldn't smoke. Annie Lee returned from the TB Hospital soon thereafter and put a stop to my smoking and any other "sinful" activity she could identify.

Inspectors from the Wichita County Health Department periodically visited our home after mother returned from the TB hospital. They required mother to sterilize her dishes and eating utensils in boiling water. I was required to get a lung X-ray each year until I was in high school. All of this caused me anxiety and embarrassment, but it was good to have Mamma back home, even if she wouldn't let me smoke. I never smoked cigarettes thereafter, contracted tuberculosis, or developed lung cancer.

Public School Years and
Turning Points: 1939–1952

What are YOU going to do right now to lift yourself out of the
crowd and make something significant out of your life?
—William H. Danforth, *I Dare You*

WHEN I ENTERED public school in 1939, no one asked me the above
question, and if they had, I would not have known the answer—
or even what they were talking about. Over my thirteen years in public
schools, I reached important turning points that greatly influenced what I
would do with my life. I began to ask questions and find some answers.

An African proverb says that it takes a village to raise a child. My "village" progressively grew larger from family to neighborhood schools, city,
and beyond. Some dedicated teachers, work experiences, church and youth
organizations, friends, and family helped expand my village and vision—to
dare to make something significant of my life.

GRADE SCHOOL, OR "REMEMBERING THE ALAMO"

In September 1939 I entered the first grade at Alamo Public School, which
was five-and-a-half blocks from 2313 Ninth Street. Mother walked to school
with me. My clothes were not new, and I felt embarrassed that my mother
was older than the other mothers. Miss Polly was my first grade teacher. Not
knowing any kids in my class, I was scared and shy, and lacked the enthusiasm about going to school for the first time that I witnessed in my own chil-

dren and grandchildren on such an important day.

No free-lunch program existed in 1939, but an arrangement was made that year and several thereafter for me to receive a free meal ticket. The customary cost of a meal ticket at the time was one dollar a week. I doubt the other kids knew the difference, but I was embarrassed about receiving a "free lunch." I walked to and from school each day. Since neither of my parents were able to work, they were always home when I arrived, and that was a plus.

Alamo Elementary School

When I arrived home on Mondays, Mom and Dad would be washing the sheets and our clothes in a black kettle over a wood fire in the backyard—that was our "washing machine." The dryer consisted of a series of wires strung up in the backyard, upon which the sheets and clothes were hung out to dry. The linens in the wash included those of any renter in the front bedroom, since the seven dollar weekly rent included clean sheets at least once a week.

Age 6, 1939

Bacon drippings and other cooking greases were saved to make homemade lye soap. This soap-making project occurred once or twice a year in the same black kettle, fired by pieces of wooden crates from grocery trash bins and anything else that would burn. I hated lye soap; not because it didn't smell good—which it didn't—but because my dad would cut it into big squares, too large for my small hands. Thankfully, we usually had storebought soap for my Saturday night bath. Though I didn't care too much for bathing, at least I could hold the bar of soap.

The most important thing I learned in the first grade was to spell and write my name. I had trouble writing "Kenneth," so Miss Polly suggested the use of my middle name "Ray." Three letters and one syllable being easier than seven letters and two syllables, I quickly mastered "Ray" and thereby became better known by my middle name than the first. My family continued to use "Kenneth Ray," and the folks at the church settled for "Kenneth."

In December of 1939, I developed a cough, which turned into whooping cough and progressed to pneumonia in January. About the same time, I had a light case of small pox. As a result of these health problems, I missed several months of school in the first grade. When I returned to school in early spring, I was behind everyone else. Since I was spoiled by all the attention my illnesses brought me at home and felt insecure and unappreciated on the few days that I was back in school, I returned to the security of home and bed. As a result, I failed the first grade and had to do it over in 1940–1941. This also meant that I was forever one year older than most of the kids in my classes.

I made it through the first grade on the second try, but I was sick and out of school for much of the second grade. Fortunately, a lady named Miss Annabelle Farquhar ran a kindergarten two blocks from 2313 Ninth. Miss Annabelle, for little or no money, came to our home about one hour a day during my sickly period of 1941–1942 and imparted enough knowledge for me to pass the second grade under Miss Carter and move on to Miss Vigas in the third grade.

Suffice it to say, I was not feeling good about myself by the time I got to the third grade. I was a year behind, sickly, skinny, and not very quick with numbers, reading, or other aspects of elementary education. Miss Vigas had taught my older brothers, knew my distant cousin Ethel Farabee (who taught in high school), and took an interest in me, though I was by no means the teacher's pet. Another kid named Jesse was also a year behind, and he befriended me. I made a few other friends. All of this helped, but I owe the most to Jesse—at least in the third grade—for my academic improvement.

Miss Vigas used flash cards as a learning tool, particularly for arithmetic. Jesse told me that I should get a seat in the front row, and from that vantage point, I could see the answers on the back of the card as the teacher displayed the card to the other side of the room. With this helpful hint and the good teaching of Miss Vigas, my grades moved up to A's and B's.

More important, I quickly learned the answers to the math questions presented by the flash cards and didn't need to cheat. I also developed some confidence in myself. Of course, it helped to be present in class and not miss school because of illness. The last time I heard of Jesse, he was a Methodist minister in Callahan County, Texas. I suspect he's still suggesting that folks sit in the front row—but for a more noble purpose.

After graduating from the third grade, if not with honors, at least in one year and with respectable grades, I "went upstairs" to the fourth grade. It was a very big deal to be on the second floor of Alamo School, and I was beginning to like school. Brother Jimmy had dropped out of high school, worked in the construction of Sheppard Air Force Base after December 7, 1941, and then joined the Army to become part of the Army Air Corps as a radio communications specialist for the balance of World War II. Brothers Leroy and Edwin went to work in the shipyards in Houston to help the war effort. I traveled by bus to visit them in the summers of 1943 and 1944. Houston was very different from Wichita Falls and Ranger. Most notable to me at the time were the larger five-and-dime stores, frequency of sirens downtown, and proliferation of movie theaters.

In the fourth grade at Alamo, I made friends with DB Pattillo, who moved into a duplex on Eighth Street with his mother and sister, just one block from my home. We quickly became fast friends and remain so to this day. I'm not sure which of us was Huck Finn or Tom Sawyer, but our river

Alamo School fourth grade class, 1943. DB Pattillo is on the right end of top row next to me.

was the Wichita rather than the Mississippi, and our adventures, though not as dramatic as those of Huck, are memorable.

DB and I played "kick the can" on Eighth Street, wrestled, threw ball, and fantasized about our great sports capabilities. In early wrestling matches, DB always won, but later I occasionally pinned him down. Through this process I developed my first competitive senses and confidence that I could win, at least some of the time. We found a leaky sheet metal canoe on one of our adventures to the river and drug it home to DB's garage. We scraped tar from the brick paved street, melted it, and tried to caulk the leaks. With great expectations, we carried the repaired boat to the river and put it in the water, and with my newfound confidence, I climbed into the canoe, which promptly filled with water and sunk to the bottom of the river.

One day after school, classmate Tommy Gribble suggested that DB and I visit the Riverside Cemetery with him. The cemetery is located on a high bluff above the Wichita River, completely surrounded by a tall iron picket fence. It was in the fall of the year and darkness came early while we were still exploring the cemetery. We soon discovered the gates were closed and locked at dusk. We were locked in!

Tommy was not much help with his talk about ghosts and the suggestion that the fence might be electrified, but we finally got over the fence without being electrocuted or impaled. We trudged home. It was dark and I was a couple of hours late for dinner. Earlier, when Mother heard we were last seen headed for the river, she became highly alarmed, called the sheriff's office to report us missing, and feared that I was either drowned or kidnapped. Annie Lee was not known for her optimism or positive attitude. To say the least, I received lot of "what for" and hysterics when I did get home, but I finally got my supper—after mother calmed down enough to call the sheriff's office and let them know the prodigal son had returned.

My academic skills were better than my boat repair capabilities or judgment of time, and I matriculated on to the sixth and seventh grades in Alamo, where I made other good friends, including Jim Hobbs and Bob Smith. I joined Troop 18 of the Boy Scouts

Age 14, 1946

and made additional friends like Lee Hite, Larry Robinson, and Jim Cochran. I also learned some of the skills that would be helpful on bigger rivers than the Wichita, like swimming.

MORE WORK AND LESS PLAY

My parents had very little money to give me for such luxuries as picture shows, soda pop, candy and comic books—though the cost of such indulgences was modest by today's standards. For example, movies for kids cost eleven cents, soda pop a nickel, candy one to five cents, and comic books a dime. Children could ride the bus for a nickel, and downtown they could buy a chili dog or hamburger for ten cents. My only way to afford these niceties on a weekly basis was to find gainful employment.

My first job was helping my mother clean the house on Saturday mornings; for these labors I received a weekly allowance of 25 cents. This was during World War II, and I took my quarter and, with any other money I could earn, bought "defense stamps." Over a period of a couple of years, I had enough stamps to get a savings bond. I was convinced that this rigorous thrift plan helped defeat Japan and Germany, and bring my brother Jimmy home from the war.

In the fifth grade, I secured my first paper route, delivering the *Wichita Falls Daily Times* to houses on ten to twelve blocks of Taylor and Fillmore streets, near my home. A year later I got a larger paper route on Ninth and Tenth streets, which paid more money—a whopping four dollars a week. About the same time, I took a second summer job at the Kemp Public Library (now the Kemp Center for the Arts) shelving books each morning for 25 cents an hour. Not only did I learn the Dewey Decimal System backwards and forward, I got my first library card and started checking out books. My favorite books were by Zane Grey and Jack London. On occasion, I would sneak a peek at medical books that had clinical pictures and diagrams of female anatomy. Jim Hobbs, who also worked at the library, was much more sophisticated; he read some of the more interesting segments of *The Decameron* by Boccaccio.

Hobbs and I mowed yards in the summer with his mother's lawn mower. The green Montgomery Ward push mower was not "user friendly," particularly in the typical Wichita Falls summer heat of 90–105 degrees. I was motivated to find cooler working conditions at the neighborhood grocery stores. I usually worked on Saturdays as a sacker and helped customers get their groceries to the car. I worked for A&P, E Z Grocery, Safeway, Day and Night Food Store, and finally six days a week during the summer of 1948 for Parker Food Store #17 on Monroe Street. At Parker #17, I worked in all departments, including the meat market as a butcher boy, scraping the butcher block, cleaning display cases, and waiting on customers. When the bacon or hams became a little moldy or the chickens a bit slick, I washed them off. It was all a part of our consumer protection plan.

One of the more interesting jobs I had while in junior high school was as an "inserter" for the Sunday newspaper. At that time, printing was done by linotype machines that set print from molten lead. Between the clanking noises of the linotype machines, the smell of molten lead, and the roar of the presses, it was something to experience. Our job was to put all of the sections of the Sunday paper together, inserting one into another by four a.m. Work was done on a piecework basis. With scraps of rubber inner tubes on our hands, we shuffled the comics and other sections together as fast as we could. Although the piecework was grueling, it was strangely mysterious to be working when the rest of the city was sleeping.

In 1949, my friend Larry Robinson landed several of us Sunday afternoon work at the Wichita Falls Gun Club. Mamma didn't like me working on Sunday, but I had already crossed the line by dancing on Friday and Saturday nights. Wealthier folks would come and shoot hundreds of clay pigeons in a form of sport called skeet and trap shooting. Someone had to load the clay pigeons and keep scores, and those were our jobs. Although it was boring to work in the trap pit or skeet houses, it was interesting to watch the rich folk and learn about the sport. Some of the shooters drank a goodly amount of whiskey, but we were safe in the bunkers of the trap pits and skeet towers. No one was ever hit by stray buckshot, though DB once had a close call while keeping score.

My last summer work while in high school was loading boxcars and trucks with sacks of flour at the General Mills flour mill in Wichita Falls. Larry Robinson's dad was the general manager of the mill. Larry worked at the grain elevator unloading wheat, and I worked in the mill loading everything from five-pound bags of Gold Medal flour to 200-pound bags of export flour. I was required to join the union, which worked out well for me because I earned more money per hour than I had ever made before.

1937 Chevrolet Sedan—my first car

The mill operated 24 hours a day, and my work rotated every two weeks between the day, swing, and midnight shifts.

At first I encountered some resentment because everyone knew the boss had hired me because of my friendship with his son. I weighed about 100 pounds at the time, and others doubted whether I could pull, or in this case push, five or six times my weight on a large two-wheel dolly. The two- or three-hundred-pound loads were no problem, but I lived in fear of the six-hundred-pound loads and getting them into the boxcars. But I did it and finally earned the respect of my fellow union members, though they still called me the "pup."

In the process of working these jobs, I saved enough money to buy Uncle Charlie's 1937 Chevrolet, purchase some new clothes, help my mom and dad with expenses, and save something for college. More important, my work experiences taught me a lot about people, problem solving, and financial independence. I even learned to shoot craps on the evening shift at General Mills.

FIRST BAPTIST YEARS: TO BE OR NOT TO BE . . . BAPTIZED

When I was thirteen my mother took DB and me to a revival at her church, the First Baptist. I had visited the church with her before, but only for a few Sunday night services. The pastor in 1946 was Jimmy Landes, and the revival preacher was W. H. Criswell of Dallas. The lower floor was packed, and we sat high up in the balcony for the morning service. Dr. Criswell was a powerful speaker and ended his moving sermon with the traditional Baptist invitation to "walk down the aisle, be saved, and commit your life to Jesus Christ."

As the choir and congregation sang "Just as I am, without one plea, but that Thy blood was shed for me," I was so emotionally moved that I walked all the way down from the balcony to the front of the sanctuary, before more than a thousand people, and I was "saved." Considering my shyness and being in a strange place, it was remarkable that I did it; but the experience and resulting consequences had important influences on my life.

After the morning service, many church members came and shook the hands of those of us who had been saved, joined the church, or simply re-committed their lives to Jesus. Those of us who had not been baptized were told that we could join the church and be baptized. Since I only came down the aisle to be saved, I was undecided about membership or baptism. I was already attending Sunday school at the Floral Heights Methodist church.

My mother and father were patient with my indecision, affirming that I didn't have to be baptized or join the First Baptist Church, and it was my decision to make. The important thing, particularly with Mamma, was that I had been "saved," and under the Baptist doctrine, "once saved, always saved." After an emotional afternoon and some tears, I talked to the only person of my age that I knew at First Baptist, Lee Hite. Lee en-couraged me to join and explained that his parents could pick me up on their way to church that night, which they did. I was baptized in a white robe, fully immersed, neither in a river nor creek, but in a white marble baptistery by Jimmy Landes. I joined the First Baptist Church of Wichita

First Baptist Church in Wichita Falls, 1940's and 1950's

Falls and commenced one of the more important aspects of my youthful development.

Lee Hite became, and remains, one of my best friends. For the next several years, Lee and I participated in all the activities available to us at the church—morning and evening Sunday services, Sunday School, Baptist Training Union (BTU), Wednesday night prayer meetings, revivals, choir practice, and church socials for the young folks. Lee's parents, Vic and Bertha Hite, provided transportation for this multitude of activity, except when Lee and I would walk home on spring and summer evenings, having long philosophical discussions and stopping for an ice cream cone at the Dairy Queen.

The First Baptist, particularly the Sunday evening BTU youth group, gave me opportunities to exercise leadership and make talks before small groups. When selected as a group leader of my training union class, I assigned parts of the evening lesson to various members for delivery of a talk and group discussion. I came to enjoy making short speeches so much, that I assigned myself several parts on occasion. For the first time in my life, I became a leader, and I learned to involve others in the group process, despite my early tendency to take more than one part of the speech making and discussion.

Most of the young people in my BTU and Sunday school classes were several years ahead of me in public school. Nevertheless, I was elected president of my BTU and Sunday school classes and given additional responsibilities. These were the first times I was elected to anything. Church activities also led to another group of friends.

ZUNDY JUNIOR HIGH SCHOOL AND
THE "I DARE YOU" AWARD

It was exciting to move up to junior high school (now called middle school). My junior high was Zundelowitz, better known as Zundy. Zundelowitz students came from other grade schools, as well as Alamo. With my newfound confidence from church, work, and the Boy Scouts, I easily made new friends from the other grade schools comprising our class. My grades were good, and I sang in the church choir, a quartet, and the Zundy Glee Club.

Zundy Junior High, 1948

Sports were important at Zundy, particularly football. I was too skinny to play football, but I went out for the basketball team. My basketball career didn't last long for two reasons: I wasn't very good, and I needed to work after school, rather than stay over for practice. My old imaginary friend JB and I tramped up and down Ninth and Tenth streets delivering newspapers. I shot baskets behind Floral Heights Methodist Church and Lee Hite's garage. Sketchy entries in my diary indicate that my focus was turning to extracurricular activities such as church, singing, scouts, some sand-lot sports, and girls.

Dorothy Blankenship attended the First Baptist Church. Dorothy was blonde and beautiful. She lived with her mother and older brother H. B. nearby in a large house on Tenth Street. Lee Hite and I both developed a crush on Dorothy. Despite the fierce competition for her affections, neither of us won Dorothy's heart. Helen Harris, a classmate, was another girlfriend during junior high years. Skipper Truly and I vied for her affections. I won, but she moved to Waco, leaving me with a broken heart.

The most traumatic event during the Zundy years was not my failed love life, but the death of my brother Leroy. As recounted in Chapter Two, Leroy was a good and generous person, but he had a bad drinking problem that led to a divorce and ultimately caused his tragic death. After the divorce in 1946, Leroy had returned home to 2313. An entry in my diary for November 7, 1946, reads:

> Made an A in math. When I got home, Leroy was drunk. The house needed cleaning and mother can't do any work. Jimmy was as cross as a bear, and he got mad at me. I got pretty disgust[ed] and down hearted. Mamma feel[s] bad.

Shortly thereafter, Leroy took a job in the oil fields of Kuwait. He made good money and sent some of it home, but I suspect that he spent much of

his pay on booze. Leroy lasted about six
months in Kuwait, then came home to
2313 Ninth. He had lots of interesting
stories about his experiences abroad,
but he continued to drink heavily.

On September 25, 1947, the principal of Zundy came to my room and
asked me to come outside. He told
me that something had happened, to
get my things and he would drive me
home. When I arrived at 2313, Mother
was crying, and Dad told me that Leroy
was dead. In my diary I wrote, "Leroy

Leroy Farabee, 1914–1947

was killed—murdered. I got out of school at noon." On the next day the
entry read, "We had the funeral today." Newspaper articles and evidence
presented at a murder trial in 1948 indicated that Leroy was drinking at a
bar and got into an argument with a man named Hubert. They went outside and may have had a fight. Leroy was robbed, sustained serious blows
to his head (probably from being kicked), taken on a country road, and
thrown into a ditch, where he died. His body was found by someone the
next morning and reported to the sheriff.

Hubert Phillips, an ex-convict, was found, charged, and convicted of
murder, but the jury determined it was "murder without malice." I attended the trial, which took several days. Mother and Dad wasted part of
the life insurance money they received for a special prosecutor to assist the
District Attorney, hoping for a death penalty or life imprisonment. The
jury was more persuaded by the defense counsel that the murder was not
intentional, just a drunken brawl. Hubert served five years or fewer. Annie
Lee never got over the death of her firstborn.

At the final school assembly in May 1949, seventeen awards were presented to students at Zundy. To my great surprise, I was selected by the
principal and faculty to receive the Danforth Foundation "I Dare You"
Award for being the best all-around boy in the graduating class. The book
that came with the award challenged me to "dare to be bigger than I was,
dare to adventure, dare to do things, dare to be strong, dare to think cre-
atively, dare to share, and dare to launch out into the deep." And I did.

HIGH SCHOOL YEARS

In 1949 Wichita Falls had two high schools: Wichita Falls Senior High (WFSH) for white students and Booker T. Washington for African American students. WFSH was one of the largest high schools in the state and a football powerhouse with its Coyote team. Although football was king, WFSH had a well-rounded curriculum, some excellent teachers, and an abundance of extracurricular activities.

Uncle Charlie died during my sophomore year. I took my hard-earned savings and bought his 1937 Chevrolet sedan for $250. In 1949 you could get a driver's license at age sixteen, and I had attained that age, with one problem—I didn't know how to drive. Someone brought the car from Ranger to Wichita Falls. Lee Hite, friends, and relatives taught me to operate the old-fashioned car with its stick shift rising out of the middle of the floor. I got my Texas Driver's License, and drive I did. My "new" old car solved many problems. Not only could I drive to school, church, and work, I could pick up girls for dates. This was a substantial improvement over riding the bus.

Although Lee Hite and Larry Robinson were about the same age, they were three years ahead of me in school and graduated from WFSH. Lee suggested that I consider joining school clubs like the Hi-Y (The Hi-Y was the YMCA club in high schools across Texas and the United States—even in communities that didn't have a local YMCA. The Tri-Hi-Y was the YMCA club for high school girls, though WFSH didn't have a Tri-Hi-Y club). Larry Robinson, a debater, suggested that I take speech classes so I could participate in debate tournaments. Lee and I took up tennis before I went to high school and enjoyed it. I signed up for tennis class and went out for the tennis team at WFSH. Though I was never very good at tennis,

Wichita Falls Senior High School (WFSH), 1951

I played in some tournaments and lettered in the sport. The advice from my friends had a significant impact on my high school and college years.

SPEECH AND DEBATE

The first elective course I selected at WFSH was speech, and I entered various speech and debate tournaments throughout my high school years, as Larry Robinson had suggested. My first speech contest was the Voice of Democracy, sponsored by the Wichita Falls Junior Chamber of Commerce. I came out strong for democracy, placed second, and won a small radio. I would listen to that radio late into the night, with dreams of going to the far-off places broadcasting from New Orleans, Nashville, and Chicago.

The next contest was in Dallas at the Adamson High School Speech Tournament. I had never attended a speech tournament. I didn't have a suit of my own, so I wore an old, wool, gray tweed suit that my brother Jimmy had left at home. It was scratchy, and didn't fit very well. The pants were too long, so I wore a cheap pair of Acme cowboy boots to keep the cuffs from dragging on the floor. In addition to debate, I entered the extemporaneous speaking part of the tournament.

In extemporaneous (sometimes referred to as "extemp") speech, each contestant draws a subject for the speech, has eight minutes to prepare, then delivers a talk before one or more judges. The well-dressed kids who regularly attended such contests had never seen me and barely heard of Wichita Falls, except for its football team. To my surprise, and even to the greater surprise of the other competitors, I won the contest and received my first gold medal. It wasn't exactly the Olympics, but it was an important high school tournament. I was on my way to bigger contests, more speeches, and larger cities. But first, I took some of my savings, bought a non-scratchy suit that fit, a "lucky tie," and a pair of new shoes.

After my Adamson conquest, I participated in a number of speech contests and debate tournaments. I was not as good at debate as I was at extemporaneous speaking, but I won my share of medals and made some new friends in other cities. I became a member of the National Forensic League, won the Texas-Louisiana Regional tournament, and went to the national tournament in Boston, where I made the finals. On our way to Boston, we stopped in New York City and visited the Empire State Building, saw

*With Mrs. Moss and Marilyn Boren
at State Finals, UT Austin, 1952*

the Radio City Rockettes, and rode on the subway—the first of many times in the Big City. During my last two years of high school, I participated in the University Interscholastic League (UIL) extemp and debate contests. Our team won in the regional contest and went to the finals in Austin, where I placed but did not win.

The experience of standing before others and expressing ideas, thoughts, and facts was more important than winning or losing the contests. Sometimes I tried the patience of my fellow students who had to listen to me practice on them. I recall one instance, about which I still feel embarrassment. It arose from one of my speeches condemning racial prejudice and criticizing the use of racial epithets. I told the group how ignorant it was to use words like "nigger," "spic," "kike," and "Jew," (Epithetical use of such words was common at the grocery stores and flour mill where I had worked.) I gave the talk on several occasions, and a classmate finally pulled me aside and explained how offensive my inclusion of the word "Jew" was to Sandra Weiss, a Jewish student, causing her to leave the classroom in tears. Though my intentions were good, I was the ignorant one and the justified criticism reduced my growing ego by a couple of notches.

On June 5, 1951, at a time when the South was segregated and racial discrimination was prevalent throughout our country, I was invited to speak at a plenary session of the Centennial International YMCA Convention in Cleveland, Ohio. A surprise, the invitation was likely due to my "Y" activities and speech experience. I was one of four youth speakers; each of us spoke for approximately twelve minutes to more than 6,000 persons from all over the world. I was the only one to receive an ovation during the talk, when I called for the YMCA to "get into the forefront of battle against racial prejudice, or we should change our name [the 'Christian' of YMCA], for there is no place in our democracy for ignorant beliefs of this kind."

HI-Y AND THE PATH TO THE
UNIVERSITY OF TEXAS AND POLITICS

During my first year in WFSH, I joined the Hi-Y Club sponsored by the local YMCA, as Lee Hite had suggested. Jim Hobbs and I also joined the downtown Y and started playing handball. I was elected President of the Good Fellowship Hi-Y Club at the beginning of my junior year. In 1950–1951 I participated in the Hi-Y Youth and Government Program, going to the District meeting at Texas Tech and the Model State Legislature in the Capitol building at Austin. Delegates from our club drafted a bill regulating insurance companies, and we secured passage of it at the state meeting. It was my first trip to Austin and the State Capitol, but not the last.

In November 1951, I was selected by the Northwest Texas District Hi-Y's to be their nominee for Hi-Y Youth Governor of Texas. After a vigor-

Governor Allan Shivers confers with "Governor Farabee" in the real Governor's office at the State Capitol, December 1951

ous campaign in Austin at the old Driskill Hotel, with "Elect Farabee for Governor" banners strung across the pillars on the first floor, I was elected Youth Governor of Texas for the three-day session, December 14–16, 1951. I occupied one of the offices of Governor Allan Shivers and was privileged to discuss legislative processes with him. I made a State of the State Address, signed and vetoed legislation, and consulted with my cabinet. On the last night, I presided over the Governor's Ball and Banquet. Texas Secretary of State John Ben Sheppard spoke, and I met Dr. Read Granberry, Parliamentarian for the Texas House of Representatives and Vice Chancellor of the University of Texas System. Granberry invited me to visit him when I was next in Austin. This invitation led to my decision to attend the University of Texas at Austin.

SOCIAL LIFE AND THE WESTERNERS

When I started high school, much of my social life was centered at the First Baptist Church with activities such as picnics, hayrides, and roller skating parties. More social functions were available at WFSH, and I made new friends who had attended Reagan Junior High School. Having my own car, old as it may have been, was a big asset.

Jim Hobbs and I became very good friends and sang together in a quartet at Zundy—Jim a tenor and I a bass. I had an old guitar, but never progressed much beyond the chords of G, C, and D. Hobbs, on the other hand, applied himself, and with the help of a correspondence course by Roy Smeck, mastered guitar playing. During the summer before high school we got together with Jim Cowles and Skipper Truly to sing and play songs from the Sons of the Pioneers, like "Cool Water," "Tall Timbers Calling," and "Just a Closer Walk with Thee." A new band was born, and we called it the Westerners.

The Westerners (from left to right) Jim Hobbs, Bob Nimmo, Skipper Truly, Jon Dell Brashear, me, and Jim Cowles

Skipper Truly was leader of the band, and Jim Cowles was our lead guitarist and singer. I played the harmonica on occasion, sang bass, and served as the announcer. Bob Nimmo joined with his accordion. As time went by, two more voices were added with Edgie Donnell and our class president, Jon Dell Brashear. On occasion, Bernie Adair played the trumpet and Louis Bartosh the fiddle.

The Westerners frequently played and sang at school events, parties, and social gatherings. Skipper arranged for a live weekly radio program on KTRN at the early hour of 6:45 a.m. each Saturday before the farm report. A big guy, Skip played a bass fiddle that was even bigger than he was. At 6:00 a.m. or earlier, he put his bass in the car and picked up the band, with one or two of us hunkered beneath the bass fiddle. Our radio show provided my first opportunity for broadcast experience. As the emcee of the show, I announced the songs, introduced the players, and issued an invitation for "all you folks out there in radio-land send us your cards and letters." Amazingly, we got a few cards and letters, and I enjoyed the experience of talking into a radio microphone.

We were sufficiently popular to move up to a Saturday 10:00 a.m. show on radio station KFDX. When television came to Wichita Falls, KFDX-TV invited us to do a live weekly program. Very few people in Wichita Falls had television sets at that time. TV broadcasts were in black and white and seen on very small screens. Local shows were more frequent because there was less network programming than we now have. It was a new medium. Skipper's little brother David prepared artful slides to break the monotony. For the first time, I learned to speak before a camera, look into its eye, and say, "Hello folks, welcome to another evening with Skipper Truly and the Westerners!"

The Westerners did not achieve the fame and fortune of other West Texas groups like Buddy Holly, the Crickets, or the Flatlanders, but we had a great time and helped others to do so. We were picking, singing, and harmonizing right up to graduation day, when we all went our separate ways to college.

GIRLS AND GRADUATION

When I got to high school, my dating expanded beyond the girls at the church. I dated classmates, and in my junior and senior years I dated several girls in the classes under ours. I will always remember a date with a girl from the Country Club Addition, an exclusive Wichita Falls residential area, in my 1937 Chevrolet. We drove up to Lester's Minute Inn, the best steak house in town. My date rolled her window up, and the glass fell out. Fortunately it didn't break. I rushed around the car, picked up the window, put it in the back seat, and took her in for a hamburger.

Whether it was my old car or serious demeanor, I never went "steady" or dated any local girl for a long period of time. As I attended speech contests and meetings in Dallas, Lubbock, Cleveland, and elsewhere, I met many girls that I found bright and attractive. Several of these meetings on foreign turf led to an exchange of letters and sometimes dates.

I met one girl from Highland Park High School at a Junior Red Cross Retreat. After our "love at first sight" romance at Camp Grady Spruce on Lake Possum Kingdom, Claire invited me to visit her in Dallas for several dates. I drove my '37 Chevrolet right up to her family's mansion, met her parents, and took her on a date. Unfortunately, we had a minor fender bender on Oak Lawn Avenue. The police could not determine who was at fault, so they gave both me and the other driver a ticket. Luckily, a lawyer in the car behind us rushed up to my car and said he witnessed the whole thing. In his opinion, the other driver was on my side of the street. He gave me his card.

I was to appear three weeks later in Dallas traffic court, which was a good excuse for another date with Claire. She drove me to the court, where we found my new friend, the lawyer/witness, who explained it all to the judge. The traffic ticket was dismissed, justice done, and we had another good date.

One of the most attractive girls I met during my high school years was Joan Kimes from Newport Beach, California. We met at a national Hi-Y meeting in Washington, D. C. I don't recall our having a date, but we talked and visited during the meeting. With an exchange of letters and class pictures, I became quite taken with her.

Joan Kimes, 1952

I wrote to her about my upcoming graduation at the end of May 1952 and off-handedly invited her to come to the graduation prom as my date.

To my utter shock and amazement, Joan accepted my invitation and said she would be arriving from Los Angeles by train. Where would she stay? What would she think about my aged parents, dilapidated home, and ancient car? Although I didn't know much about Newport Beach, I suspected it was more exciting and scenic than Wichita Falls. Joan arrived and stayed with my good friend Marilyn Boren. Marilyn's father was president of the local college, and they lived in the Country Club Addition. Joan was my date to the senior prom where the Westerners performed, and Joan and I danced. After the prom we drove with Marilyn and her date to Scotland (Texas, that is). We turned around and came back home. I think we kissed three times, once in Scotland, good night at Marilyn's home, and good-bye when she boarded the Zephyr for California. We wrote a few more letters, but I never saw her again, even when I finally got to California in 1957.

After the prom festivities, I graduated from Wichita Falls Senior High School with honors, received a $200 scholarship to the University of Texas, and delivered one of the student speeches at the commencement. Marilyn Boren and I were selected as outstanding students of the class and received gold wristwatches.

1952 senior class picture

College Years: 1952–1955 and 1956–1957
A World of Discovery and Possibility

For a little time the student lives in a world of discovery and of
possibility where nothing is yet completely settled, where everything,
including the achievement of greatness, is still actively possible.
—Dr. Harold Taylor, President, Sarah Lawrence College,
Keynote Address to USNSA at the University of Michigan, 1956

M Y "LITTLE TIME" as a college student was longer than most. I spent
eight years in one kind of higher education or another before graduating from law school and joining the adult workaday world: three years as
a pre-law undergraduate; two years as a student leader visiting more than
200 colleges and universities; and three years as a law student. Those eight
years, intertwined with getting married and serving in the United States
Air Force, provided a world of discovery and possibilities that I could not
have imagined when I graduated from high school in 1952.

Neither my parents nor brothers attended college, except for several
courses Brother Jimmy took through the G.I. Bill after World War II. I
was the first person in the Jack and Annie Lee Farabee line to secure a college degree.

By my senior year in high school, I knew I wanted to go to college and become a lawyer, just like my friend Larry Robinson. Larry was a pre-law student at Midwestern University (now Midwestern State University), where
he was student body president and an outstanding debater. Midwestern
seemed the logical choice for me, and I was ready to follow in Larry's foot-
steps, or at least try. I was offered a scholarship by Midwestern to cover my
tuition and books. I planned to live at home, to avoid room and board expenses. My parents were not able to help out with any of my expenses, so it
was clear that I needed to work and pinch pennies.

While participating in the University Interscholastic League state finals of extemporaneous speech at the University of Texas in Austin (UT) during the spring of 1952, I followed up an invitation to visit Read Granberry, Vice Chancellor of the University of Texas System (UT System). The UT System offices were on the second floor of the Main Building, adjoining the very impressive UT Regents Room, which had large beams and a high ceiling with the names of world-famous scholars painted on it. Little did I know that later in life I would become a Vice Chancellor of the UT System and legal advisor to the Board of Regents.

UT Main Building—the Tower

Granberry welcomed and introduced me to Judge James Hart, Chancellor of the UT System. Granberry suggested I attend UT Austin as an undergraduate. He assured me a scholarship to cover the costs of books and tuition, a room in an inexpensive dormitory, and part-time employment. It did not take long to make one of the more important decisions of my life—to attend UT in Austin. Midwestern would have provided a good undergraduate education, but UT opened a new world of discovery, and the possibilities seemed unlimited.

UNDERGRADUATE YEARS AT THE
UNIVERSITY OF TEXAS

I entered UT in September 1952, and comparisons of the institution then and now are dramatic. Student enrollment was 12,842, whereas now it's 50,000 students. Undergraduate admission was much less competitive, as were graduate programs like business and law. No Black students were admitted to UT except in the law school, where the U.S. Supreme Court had ordered the admission of Heman Sweatt. Computers and Internet for registration and quick dissemination of information were non-existent. Most undergraduates lived and ate their meals in dormitories, boarding houses, co-ops, and fraternity and sorority houses. Women students were

strictly supervised and required to return to the dorm or boarding house by
10 p.m. on weekdays and 11 p.m. on the weekends. Student organizations,
including fraternities and sororities, were more important than now.

Despite these significant differences, UT was and remains the principal flagship university of the state, attracting more of the best and brightest than any other Texas institution of higher education. (However, Texas
A&M University—then segregated and all male—has become more competitive. Rice University— then Rice Institute—has always had a higher
academic rating, though with a much smaller student enrollment.) UT was
and is the largest university in the state. Size, then and now, presents problems, but it also provides rich and diverse opportunities not available at
smaller colleges.

During my first year and a half as a college student, I lived in Dorm B, a
World War II reconditioned wooden barracks located on San Jacinto, adjoining Waller Creek and directly across from Memorial Stadium. Rent
was ten dollars a month with clean linens furnished each week. During my
freshman year, I shared a room with Joe Shaddock from Wichita Falls. In

the first semester of my second year, I
shared a room with fellow Westerner
Jim Cowles. Jim completed his first
year of pre-law at Midwestern. Dorm
B was demolished in 1964, and the UT
Ex-Students' Association headquarters
now occupies that space.

Three influences dominated and
contributed to my educational experience at UT: academics, which includes the courses, faculty, assignments, homework, and research that
resulted in the award of my academic
degrees; part-time work in a series of
diverse jobs; and extracurricular activities involving time spent outside
the classroom in student organizations and activities, particularly student government and the Phi Gamma
Delta fraternity. Balancing academics

*Dorm B, 1952, on Waller Creek; now
site of UT Ex-Students' Association*

with work and extracurricular activities was difficult but worth the long hours and sacrifice of some grade point average.

ACADEMICS

Although I originally contemplated doing my pre-law work as a government major, I chose a three year pre-law program in the UT College of Business. The course requirements were better coordinated with my employment schedule. Most of my elective courses were in the College of Arts and Sciences; my favorites being economics, sociology, world literature, and philosophy.

The business college had the reputation of "run and play with BBA"; yet it is now one of the top business schools in the United States with entrance requirements stricter than those of the College of Arts and Sciences. Business courses were not easy and later proved beneficial in my law practice, particularly statistics, insurance, marketing, accounting, and business letter writing. Most of my classes were moderate in size with about thirty-five students. My geology course was an exception; lectures were held in an auditorium filled with approximately 250 students, but the related lab, taught by graduate students, was much smaller. At any rate, I learned a great deal about geology, which continues to be of interest.

One of the best of all my college teachers was Professor A. F. Edwards (Prof), who taught my government and history classes at Midwestern, where I took four courses during the summer of 1953. Prof was controversial in some quarters of Wichita Falls because of his outspoken support of Democratic candidates and officeholders. Although a committed Democrat, Prof was a good friend of John Tower, who also taught government at Midwestern until he was elected to the U.S. Senate in 1961. Years later, in 1994, I flew to Wichita Falls with then-

Professor A. F. Edwards (right) with Governor Mark White, 1983

Governor Ann Richards for Prof's 100th birthday celebration, where he was recognized as the oldest and longest serving County Democratic Chairman in Texas. Prof died at the age of 103.

My coursework included eight semesters of Air Force Reserve Officer Training Corps (AFROTC). The United States was at war in Korea, and I was subject to the draft. I signed up for the Air Force ROTC to assure four years of uninterrupted college before entering the armed services. My eyesight disqualified me for pilot training and later for being navigator, so when I received my commission as a Second Lieutenant in the U.S. Air Force in 1957, I was classified as an intelligence officer. I did well in my AFROTC classes and was selected in 1955 for membership in the Arnold Air Society, an organization that recognizes academic achievement and leadership.

Courses in law school were taught by the Socratic method, requiring students to stand and recite information about the law cases assigned, as dramatically and realistically illustrated in the television show *Paper Chase*. I was fortunate to have some of the great UT Law faculty legends including Dean Charles McCormick, George Stumberg, Dean Page Keaton, Leon Green, and Charles Alan Wright.

College courses required much more thought and study than those in high school. I was fortunate to have competent professors, but their assignments had to be balanced with employment and extracurricular activities. College courses demanded time for reading, research, and writing. For the first time in my life, I became a serious reader—and remain so to this day.

I completed my education at UT with a solid B average and received a Bachelor of Business Administration degree in 1957 and a law degree in 1961.

WORKING MY WAY THROUGH COLLEGE

My first part-time job at UT was alphabetizing 3″ × 5″ index cards at the Student Union. It was temporary work, and upon completion I returned to the Student Employment Office to seek another job. Although night work at the Austin State Mental Hospital was available, I opted for an afternoon job at Burton's Laundry & Cleaners (now Jack Brown's), located on Martin Luther King (MLK) and San Jacinto streets, because it was within walking distance of the campus. Burton's clients were students and upper-middle-class Austinites, but dirty laundry is dirty laundry. As customers drove up and honked their horns, I rushed out to retrieve their soiled clothing and return freshly cleaned items.

Thinking that a Hi-Y Youth Governor should do better, I checked with the office of Attorney General John Ben Sheppard, citing our acquaintance through the YMCA Youth and Government program. The AG's office had no vacancies but referred me to the Secretary of State's office with a strong recommendation from John Ben. I landed my first job in the Capitol building working part time for then–Secretary of State Jack Ross for the rest of my freshman year. The offices were on the first floor of the Capitol, across from where my State Senate offices would be 22 years later. Most of my work was done in a vault, filing corporate charters, but I did other work as needed. I recall working with Harold Jones's mother (you will meet Harold in the chapter about my law practice in Wichita Falls) processing franchise tax checks, which then came to the Secretary of State rather than the Comptroller. I remember the check from Humble Oil & Refining Company (now Exxon) for more than a half-million dollars.

My sophomore year brought a big upgrade in employment. I secured a part-time position with John Ben Sheppard as an Assistant to the At-

torney General—not to be confused with the lawyer jobs, which are "Assistant Attorney Generals." The AG's office was still in the Capitol building, but at the other end of the first-floor hallway from the Secretary of State. I did everything from research and writing speeches to addressing Christmas cards. On occasion, I drove John Ben's new Ford. (I still have the credit card for Sinclair gasoline!) I came to know Sheppard well and soaked up experience and information about statewide officeholding, as well as political campaign organization.

Texas Attorney General John Ben Sheppard—
Texas Heritage Foundation book cover, 1954

I attended my first State Democratic Convention while working for John Ben. It was conducted in the remote town of Mineral Wells to assure Governor Shivers's control of the state's dominant political party at the time, far away from his detractors on the Gulf Coast.

Two high-profile cases occurred during my year at the AG's office. One involving George Parr in Duval County was a meritorious inquiry into corruption and election fraud in South Texas. The other case was more dubious; it alleged corruption and communist infiltration of a labor union in Port Arthur. The star witness against the union was Harvey Matusow, a former member of the American Communist Party. He became a professional informer for the U.S. government, riding the wave of anti-communist feeling during the Cold War. I knew something wasn't quite right when I observed him stealing a handful of John Ben's cigars while waiting to be called as a witness. As it turned out, he was a false witness who was later convicted of perjury and sent to prison.

As much as I liked John Ben and the job at the AG's office, I wanted to travel and see the world during the summer of 1954. My efforts to secure a job in Europe or even on a fishing boat in Alaska failed, so I settled for selling bibles door-to-door in Ohio. I was conscripted for the job by a fellow debater named Irven DeVore. Irven was a coordinator as well as salesman—what we called "the straw boss." He signed up several other college students for this sales adventure to the Midwest, including Baylor student Max Sherman, who sold the Good Book in an adjoining county while living in Wapakoneta, Ohio.

Before we were turned loose on the unsuspecting public, we went through a training program at the historic old Maxwell House Hotel in Nashville, Tennessee. A fire later destroyed the Maxwell House, but not the coffee named for it or my memories of Nashville. After one of the training sessions, Irven and I attended the Grand Ole Opry in the Ryman auditorium. We saw Minnie Pearl, Roy Acuff, and Grandpa Jones before Nashville was as big in the country music business as it is now.

From Nashville, we drove to Lima, Ohio, where we rented a room. We divided Allen County in half for our respective sales territories. I took the south half, and Irven took the north. I knocked on nearly every rural door in the southern half of Allen County, peddling a large family bible and several other books for those not disposed to buy yet another bible for the house that already had several.

I soon realized that door-to-door sales was not my cup of tea; yet hitch-hiking home after a day of failed sales efforts was even worse. I solved the transportation problem by purchasing a 1942 Chevrolet for $65. With a $20 tune-up, the "new" Chevy—compared to the '37 model—helped me complete the summer sales experience and get back to Texas. Although I learned that sales and theology were not to be part of my long-range plan, I recognized that aspects of sales relate to the practice of law and political campaigning. I also made two friends who were to be important in my life: Irven DeVore and Max Sherman.

Irven was the son of a Methodist minister and had been a child preacher of the gospel. By the time we were in Lima, he had become agnostic and was more interested in anthropology than selling bibles. We had long discussions about religion and anthropology. When combined with my experience of talking to hundreds of people about the bible, my Baptist views about religion were somewhat liberalized. Irven and I remained friends, despite running against each other for UT student body president in the spring of 1955. (I won.) Irven went on to become a distinguished anthropologist at Harvard. I last saw him at the University of Chicago in 1958, where he was doing graduate work.

Unusually successful at selling bibles, Max returned to the Midwest for several summers as a coordinator and top salesman. He was elected student president at Baylor and was an advocate for its membership in the United States National Student Association (USNSA or NSA). We later served together in the State Senate and nearly ran against each other for Texas Attorney General in 1984. Max did run for AG but lost. He served as President of West Texas State University (now Texas A&M at Canyon) and later as Dean of the LBJ School at UT. We remain good friends.

One of the high points of my summer in Ohio involved a couple of visits to Chicago. Judy Crawford, a young woman I met three years earlier at the Y meeting in Cleveland, invited me to visit and stay at her family's home near the University of Chicago. Judy introduced me to Chicago,

Judy Crawford, Chicago, 1953

and I have had a love affair with the city ever since. We walked along Lake Michigan, visited museums, saw plays, and attended concerts. The family took me to Grant Park and Soldiers Field for the first time. About 45 years later I would attend many board meetings in an office building overlooking the park, the field, and the new Millennium Park.

Despite my lack of enthusiasm for sales, Chicago distractions, and time spent in philosophical discussions with Irven, I was moderately successful as a bible salesman. Unlike several who became discouraged and returned home, I stuck it out and actually saved a few hundred dollars. During the latter part of August 1954, I finished my sales, delivered the books, and headed home for Texas in my 1942 Chevy.

I stopped on the way to attend the Seventh National Student Congress at Iowa State University in Ames. This was my first experience with USNSA (the largest national college student organization in the United States during the 1950's and '60's), but it wouldn't be the last. I made many new friends from all over the United States. This meeting set me on a path that would significantly affect my life.

In my junior year at UT (1954–1955), I held down three part-time jobs. I waited tables at the Phi Gamma Delta fraternity house for my room and board. The U.S. Air Force ROTC program paid me $65 per month for my last two years in the program prior to receiving my commission. I also returned to the Capitol to work for state representative Vernon Stewart from Wichita Falls during the 54th Regular Legislative Session—my first job with the Texas Legislature.

EXTRACURRICULAR ACTIVITIES

Involvement in extracurricular activities at UT greatly enriched my college experience. Some of the activities were like old friends and made me feel at home: the Y, church, speech, debate, and discussion groups. Other involvements outside the classroom were new: fraternity; student government; concerts; political organizations; foreign films; intercollegiate athletic events; and cultural programs.

I started my college education with three days at the Y Freshman Camp, sponsored by the University YMCA/YWCA (the Y). We learned about all aspects of UT student life from upperclassmen; it was an excellent way

The University YMCA/YWCA, 1953

to begin the freshman year. UT had no freshman orientation at the time, though it now requires all incoming students to participate in a program similar to the Y camp. The Freshman Camp introduced me to the University Y, where I made many friends, some for life. For years the University Y was a significant venue for students to discuss current issues, meet student leaders, and learn of progressive campus initiatives. I was an active member of the Y throughout my UT undergraduate years and served on the Y cabinet and as chairman of its upper class council. *The Politics of Authenticity* by Doug Rossinow discusses the importance of the Y in the 1950's and 1960's.

A modern building owned by the Church of Scientology, with fast-food restaurants, Scientology programs, and dorm rooms, now stands where the Y was located on Guadalupe and 22nd streets. The demolition of the wonderful historic Y building, and failure of a well-intentioned effort in the 1960's to replace it with a modern facility that would be "self-supporting" is too sad to recount. As a loyal Y alumnus, I pledged $1000 to help secure construction financing for the new building. When the project failed, I lost a thousand bucks and the Y lost its building.

The University Baptist Church and the Baptist Student Union (BSU) were also important religious organizations for me. I dropped out of the BSU in my second year but remained active in the Y, where I discovered the Christian Faith and Life Community (CF&L). The CF&L was an organization where students lived in a communal setting and devoted time each day to lectures, theological and philosophical discussion, and chapel worship. Joe Mathews was the charismatic and dynamic director who, along with Reverend Jack Lewis, created the curriculum with works of theologians like Paul Tillich, Martin Buber, and Reinhold Niebuhr to supplement the teaching of the Old and New Testaments. Though I never lived at the CF&L, I attended some of its lectures and discussions, and that limited exposure had an important influence on me.

My interest in speech and debate continued. I joined the Lutcher Stark Debate Club and participated in several speech contests during my freshman year and won or placed as a finalist in several of them. I traveled to Mary Washington University in Fredericksburg, Virginia, where I participated in a national collegiate debate tournament. Although I was only a freshman, my debate partner for the Virginia tournament was a law student named Newton Schwartz. On the long train ride back to Texas, Newton confided in me that he would either be a millionaire by the time he was 30 or incarcerated in Ft. Leavenworth. Fortunately, Newton made his million, though some people would say he narrowly missed Leavenworth.

In the spring of 1953 I was elected to membership in the Silver Spurs, a men's student service organization, and in 1960 to the Friar Society, the oldest and most prestigious honor society at UT Austin. I was elected abbot (president) of the Friars shortly afterwards. It was limited to male student leaders at that time but is now coeducational. I was named as a Distinguished Alumnus of the Friar Society in the fall of 1991.

FRATERNITY AND NEW FRIENDS

During the summer of 1952, Larry Robinson and I attended a Phi Gamma Delta (Phi Gam, sometimes referred to as "Fijis") rush party at the lake home of a Wichita Falls alumnus. We had a good time, and I was invited to a party at the Phi Gam House during rush week. Since I was going to a Y freshman orientation camp scheduled three days earlier, I signed up to visit the rush parties of several fraternities, including Phi Gamma Delta, while looking for a part-time job. I did not anticipate receiving an invitation to join a fraternity, and if I did, I knew I couldn't afford it. Nevertheless, it was an opportunity to meet some new friends, see a few old ones, and get a free meal.

The Phi Gams had a strong group of alumni in Wichita Falls, as well as two undergraduate active members from there. After attending a couple of rush parties at the Phi Gam house, I was invited to pledge the fraternity. I graciously declined and explained that I could not afford the initiation fee, monthly dues, and other expenses related to fraternity membership. The next day the same members came to my dorm and informed me that several alums from Wichita Falls had offered a membership scholarship that would pay for my initiation fee, monthly dues, and six dinners each week. After brief consideration, I accepted. Ironically, the Phi Gam scholarship was much larger than the one I received from UT for tuition and books. I shall always be grateful to L. H. (Shino) Cullum and Ray Arnhold, Sr., the Wichita Falls men who funded most of my Phi Gam scholarship.

Fraternity membership consumed much more time than I anticipated. Pledge training, social events, work details, Sing-Song practice, and participation in intramural competitions were expected. Long treks to and from work and dorm to the Phi Gam house for dinner and meetings also cut into time for homework and class preparation. Between these treks and pledge training "walks" on some weekends with my pledge brothers (when we were taken blindfolded into the countryside and expected to find our way home), I chalked up more miles afoot than I ever did in Wichita Falls with paper routes and Boy Scout hikes.

The Phi Gamma Delta House, circa 1953

Phi Gam was one of the largest and strongest fraternities at UT during the 1950's, with approximately 120 members, including 35 pledges. The fraternity produced some able student leaders for the campus. My pledge class was composed of young men from all parts of Texas—big cities and small towns. Brad Fowler from Austin was president of the pledge class, and Jack Ratliff from Sonora later became president of the fraternity.

In addition to a recently renovated fraternity house, the Phi Gams owned a piece of prime Lake Austin party property known as the Fiji Lake House. Parties occurred nearly every weekend, either at the Fiji Lake

Fiji Island Party with Lee Davis, 1954

House or the fraternity house. Pledges were expected to get a date and attend. Since I didn't have a car, I double-dated with either a member or pledge brother who did. I dated and danced with more girls in my freshman year than all three years of high school. Beer was always flowing on Friday nights and at parties, and practically everyone drank, except me. Remembering admonishments from my mother and the Baptist Church, I did not imbibe any alcoholic beverages during my first three years of college, with a few exceptions. To their credit, my fraternity brothers never pressured me or anyone to drink. One party, when I did fall from grace, stands out and is captured on film. A heavily spiked punch at a Fiji Island Party at the Lake House is responsible for a picture of me in costume, carrying my date, Lee Davis, on my back.

Because members and pledges were encouraged to make their grades, study halls and tutoring by members were available. Not making adequate grades meant scholastic probation and no advancement to full membership in the fraternity. Despite my busy academic and work schedule, I made my grades with a solid B average. After substantial physical exercise and the final right of passage called "hell week," I became a full-fledged member of Phi Gamma Delta.

Intramural sports were important to the Phi Gams, and they succeeded in many competitive activities with other fraternities and campus organizations. I played handball and won my share of matches but never carried away a trophy for athletic participation.

UT Intramural Speech trophy, 1953

I also represented the fraternity in intramural speech contests during 1952–1953 and won all of them, for which we received trophies. At the end of the year, Phi Gamma Delta won first place and was presented with a huge trophy, so large that it would not fit into the house trophy case. In fact, it was larger than some awarded for Southwest Conference football championships. The fact that the trophies were purchased from the brother-in-law of the chairman of the intramural speech program may have had something to do with the disproportionate size, but we accepted them anyhow. When I visited the Phi Gam house for an alumni luncheon in 2004, I was amazed to see that the fraternity had enlarged its trophy case and still had the "monster" trophy from 1953.

During my junior year I lived at the Phi Gam House and waited tables in its dining room each day. Savannah Jackson, an ample African American woman, was chief cook, assisted by Daisy, who seldom spoke. She didn't need to because Savannah spoke so often, and with such authority, that we all knew who was boss of the kitchen. Savannah was a good cook, and no meal was complete without Cheez Whiz. Savannah's cooking, minus long walks to and from work at the Capitol and UT Dorm B, put some pounds on my skinny frame. Living at the house, I also became better acquainted with our house mother, Mary Pryor, a wise, patient, and trusted surrogate mother to me and many other fraternity members.

Fraternity membership and the friends I made through that association contributed greatly to my social development, college experience, and success in other extracurricular activities, particularly my election as student body president in 1955.

STUDENT GOVERNMENT AND POLITICS AT UT

On October 21, 1952, I was elected president of the Freshman Student Council. As pledge brother Jack Ratliff and I walked from the fraternity house to the meeting where the election was to occur, we discussed which of us should run for the presidency. Jack, formerly an outstanding student leader at Sonora High School, suggested that I should be the candidate because of my Hi-Y experience as Youth Governor. Without too much argument, I deferred to his "good judgment." Eleven candidates for president were each allowed two minutes to speak. With the support of Jack, my other pledge brothers, and Y friends, I won, and my experiences in student politics and government at UT began.

Freshman Council president with secretary, Teddy Moody, Daily Texan, *October 1952*

As a result of the freshman presidency, I met other student leaders and was appointed to several campus committees. The Silver Spurs, a campus service organization, elected me to its membership in the spring of 1953. I was also chosen by the *Cactus* (the UT yearbook) as a "Goodfellow" in 1953 and an "Outstanding Student" in 1954.

The Texas Intercollegiate Student Association (TISA) was a confederation of student governments from most of the private and public colleges and universities in Texas, and I was a delegate to its spring meeting in 1954. At the time, I was sharing a small apartment on Wichita Street with Lewis Stephens, a UT law student and former president of TISA while at Hardin Simmons in Abilene. I met student leaders from all parts of the state at the TISA meeting and became interested in the opportunities for intercollegiate exchange of ideas and information. Because of this interest, I was named as a delegate to attend the NSA Congress at Iowa State University in August 1954.

In September 1954, the UT Student Association agreed to undertake a project to be known as the TISA Central Agency. Its purpose was to strengthen college student governments in Texas through exchange and dissemination of information. I was named as the first director of the TISA Central Agency—not to be confused with the Central Intelligence Agency, which is involved in another story told in Chapter Five. A small space was made available on the fourth floor of the Student Union Building, and for the first time in my life, I had an office.

The *Daily Texan* (the UT student newspaper) named me "Boy of the Week" and recounted some of the information about my selection of UT for my college education, part-time work, and student activities in its February 27, 1955, issue.

Irven DeVore and I filed as candidates for presidency of the UT student body in April 1955. I was nominated by the Representative Party, which was heavily supported by fraternity and sorority members. Irven ran as an independent. A brief but vigorous campaign ensued with speeches, forums, signs, considerable handshaking and requests for the students' votes. Candidates running for election to various student offices joined in the campaigning, including Willie Morris, a candidate for editor of the *Daily Texan*. On Wednesday April 27, 1955, I was elected President of the Student Association by what the *Daily Texan* called a landslide.

Shortly after the victory parties, a petition was filed in the Student Court

WILLIE MORRIS AND RAY FARABEE
. . . after hot campaigning, cool relaxation   Photo by Collins

Soaking my feet with Willie Morris after our election on April 27, 1955, Daily Texan *photo*

complaining of illegal campaign material. James Dickson, a candidate for head cheerleader, and his fraternity had printed 2,300 handbills that requested students to vote for the candidates of the Representative Party. According to student campaign regulations, campaign materials were to be stamped or identified as printed by Hemphill's Bookstore #3, and all of mine were. Dickson's handbills had not been stamped, but I knew nothing about the handbills until late in the morning on the day of the election and was unaware of any irregularity. Dickson, the "campaign culprit," lost to Harley Clark in the runoff election and never served as head cheerleader.

The Student Court handed down a favorable ruling for me and the Representative Party winners, but the contestants appealed to a three-judge court including Dean Page Keaton and Gus Hodges at the law school. This court reversed the Student Court's ruling. The matter was then appealed to the Board of Regents, which affirmed the appellate court opinion setting aside the May election, and confirmed reinstatement of the Representative candidates who won, including me, until a new election could be conducted in the fall of 1955.

The court fight and resulting appeals made good news copy, at least for the *Daily Texan* and complainants. For the first time in my life, I was the subject of political cartoons and negative editorials.

Despite distractions of the election contest, I served as Student Body President for about half the summer of 1955 and intended to return in the fall and run in the special election. I made appointments to various student committees and boards. Logan Wilson, the President of UT, proposed a freshman automobile ban that I strongly protested. Unfortunately, I developed mononucleosis in mid-summer and temporarily dropped out of school, but I was able to go to the University of Minnesota as chair of the UT student delegation to the 8th USNSA National Student Congress. While there, I would make decisions that would change my life and role in student government, launching me into another new world of discovery and possibilities.

DeVore, Farabee File For Student President

IRVEN DeVORE is an indepen- | RAY FARABEE is Representa-

*Election day, April 27—Irven
and I take time out for barbecue*

ELECTION EXTRA

THE DAILY TEXAN

'The First College Daily in the South'

Weather:
Wednesday: Partly cloudy skies, scattered shows and rainfall with moderate easterly winds, low of 56, high of 78 expected.

Literary Special
May 1

VOL. 54   Price Five Cents   AUSTIN, TEXAS, WEDNESDAY, APRIL 27, 1955   Four Pages Today   NO. 159

UT Voters Put Farabee, Morris, Siegel, Holder, Richards In; Yell Leader Run-off

EXTRA Edition, April 27, 1955—3,659 votes to 1,729

*May 10, 1955, sworn in
by Jerry Wilson*

After the Storm . . . A Storm—

This cartoon by Neil Caldwell captures the circumstance—no fun for the guy at the helm.

Issue in Court Challenge: Cheerleader Candidate failed to have campaign literature stamped at "Hemphill's #3"

Appellate Court reverses Student Court rules and sets aside election of Representative Party Candidates, June 28, 1955.

As recommended by the appellate court, Dean Arno Nowotny reinstated the winners of the April election and ordered a fall election in October 1955. The Board of Regents affirmed the opinion of the appellate court and appointment of the officers to serve until a fall election.

National Student Association
Years: 1955–1956 and 1957–1958

*A world where there are differences without hate; where men
become brothers in the sight of God and in the human heart; . . .
This is the world we desire . . . so . . . we pledge ourselves to stand
with freedom loving students throughout the world . . . that one
day we may live together as brothers in peace and harmony.*
—Excerpt from the Student Creed, USNSA Report, 1957

T HE ABOVE QUOTE was and is idealistic—some would say naive, particularly during the 1950's. Our country was in the middle of a cold
war with the Soviet Union. The United States was deeply divided about
racial segregation, discrimination, and fear of the "communist menace."
College students at the time were referred to as the "silent generation." The
United States National Student Association (USNSA, NSA, or National
Student Association) was idealistic, and so was I. NSA and its leaders were
not silent about the most important issues of that era.

The two years I spent with the National Student Association as a full-
time officer and employee were some of the most important of my life.
Traveling throughout the United States, visiting more than 200 colleges
and universities, and working with Congressional leaders, college administrators, and student officers provided leadership experiences far beyond
what I could have gained by staying in Texas. As a national student leader,
I was confronted with challenging issues and ideas. On a personal level,
the two years with NSA led to my marriage to Helen Rehbein. Had I not
made the unlikely decision to drop out of UT in 1955, I would not have met
Helen, and had I not postponed my Air Force active duty for an additional
year with NSA, I would not have married her.

It all started in August 1955 when I was elected Student Government
Vice President (SGVP) of USNSA for the academic year of 1955–1956.

After that year, I returned to UT and completed my undergraduate degree, which included my first year of law school. I also received a commission as a Second Lieutenant in the U.S. Air Force, with orders to report for six months of active duty in October 1957.

I attended the USNSA Tenth National Student Congress at the University of Michigan in Ann Arbor in August 1957 for the purpose of seeing old friends, without thought of spending another year with NSA. However, my friend and former NSA president, Allard Lowenstein, persuaded me to run for the presidency of NSA, and I was elected for the 1957–1958 academic year. My tour of active duty in the Air Force was postponed until January 1959.

Pictures of the NSA officers for 1955–1956 and 1957–1958 with some background information may be found at the end of this chapter.

WHAT WAS THE USNSA?

The National Student Association was a confederation of college student bodies represented through their student governments. National student organizations existed prior to World War II in the United States and other countries, and were sometimes known as "national student unions." Edward R. Murrow was president of the National Student Federation of America (NSFA) during the early 1930's before becoming the most celebrated foreign correspondent of World War II. At the start of the war the NSFA ceased functioning. The NSA was organized in September 1947 on the campus of the University of Wisconsin at Madison. In 1977 it merged with the National Student Lobby to become the United States Student Association (USSA).

In 1953 the NSA Liaison Committee of the National Association of Deans of Women, National Association of Student Personnel Administrators, and American College Personnel Association found USNSA to be the most representative national student organization in the United States. This fact was recognized by national leaders and student organizations throughout the world during the USNSA's thirty years of existence.

USNSA had approximately 300 member schools representing about 600,000 students through their respective student governments when I became vice president in 1955. At the time I completed my term as president of NSA in 1958, membership had grown to 372 schools with over a million students. The size of member colleges varied from the very small, with 200 to 400 students, to large state universities with thousands of students. Numerous small Catholic men's and women's colleges participated. NSA member schools were more concentrated on the East and West Coasts and throughout the Midwest.

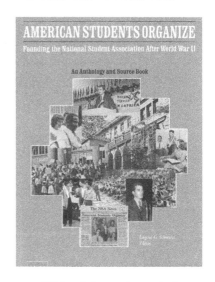

NSA anthology and source book

A comprehensive anthology and source book about USNSA entitled *American Students Organize, Founding the National Student Association After World Ward II*, edited by Eugene G. Schwartz, was published by the American Council on Education in 2006. For more information see www.AmericanStudentsOrganize.org.

A BIG DECISION, SECOND THOUGHTS, AND FACING THE MUSIC

When I went to the National Student Congress at the University of Minnesota in August 1955, I had no thought of becoming an officer of the organization. My plan was to return to UT and run again for the student presidency in the October special election. However, I was appointed to chair a congress committee on desegregation, which was the hot topic of the student conference. According to the *Daily Texan*, I "succeeded in welding together sharply divergent opinions from both northern and southern delegates into a report that was adopted by the combined NSA Assembly with only two or three dissenting votes."

With the successful negotiation of a comprehensive statement on college desegregation, a number of delegates approached me about running for Student Government Vice President (SGVP). After my initial negative response, the pressure increased, and the challenge of taking on the newly established full-time office of SGVP was too tempting. I allowed my name to be put forward and was elected with little opposition. After the usual excitement that comes with winning an election, I began to have second thoughts. As my fellow Texas delegates left to return to college, I asked myself, "What have I done?" I experienced a sharp pain in my side (apparently psychosomatic) and visited the Student Health Center at the University of Minnesota. A medical doctor examined me, found no appendicitis, and sent me on my way—not home to Texas, but to a place I had never been: Philadelphia, Pennsylvania.

Before departing for Philadelphia, we had our first staff meeting of the new full-time officers: Stan Glass, president and former SBP from the University of Illinois; Gene Preston, UCLA, National Affairs Vice President; Clive Gray, University of Chicago, International Affairs Vice President; and myself. The two other elected officers were Joel Sterns, Northwestern University, Vice President for Educational Affairs, and Jim Turner, University of North Carolina, Vice President for Student Affairs; they remained in college, joining us in Philadelphia in the summer of 1957.

From Minneapolis we went to a camp in northern Wisconsin where we spent four days recuperating from the congress and getting to know each other. Stan, Gene, and I then traveled on to Philadelphia, stopping briefly at Oberlin College in Ohio to attend the United States Assembly of Youth.

Philadelphia wasn't the most logical place for national headquarters, but NSA received donated space on the 12th floor of the Gimbel Building, adjoining Gimbel's department store. My office was sparse—a desk and typewriter surrounded by filing cabinets; however, I was on the road traveling most of the time. My first trip was to Austin to move out of my apartment, resign as student body president, and "face the music."

The "music" that greeted me upon arrival in Austin was the *Daily Texan* headline "Farabee Vacates UT to Take NSA Post." Editor Willie Morris criticized my decision to resign and drop out of the university in an editorial entitled "Farabee's Decision—Was It Justified?" He concluded that it was not. The September 25, 1955, Sunday edition of the *Daily Texan*, included my picture with those of Juan Perón and Dwight D. Eisenhower. In "News

This Week In Headlines

● Sunday:
FARABEE VACATES UT
TO TAKE NSA POST
—The Daily Texan

Faces" for the week, Argentine President Perón was a "deposed president," President Eisenhower was a "stricken president" with a heart attack, and I was a "resigned president." If the University of Minnesota Student Health Center had diagnosed me as having appendicitis, I could have been deposed, resigned, and stricken, but not all in one week.

Managing Editor J. C. Goulden was kinder in his "University Town" column, outlining various charges about my resignation and brief student presidency. J. C. set out his rebuttal to each of the charges asserted against me by my detractors with the headline: "The Farabee Story: The Defense Rests." Although J. C. (now known as Joseph C. Goulden) did not go to law school, he became a successful and well-known author. One of his many books is *The Superlawyers*, published in 1971. Based on his defense of my controversial record as student president at UT in 1955, J. C. was my "Superlawyer."

TRAVELS WITH NSA

In 1960 John Steinbeck traveled across the United States and wrote his best seller *Travels with Charley—In Search of America*. During the school years of 1955–1956 and 1957–1958, I traveled back and forth across the United States several times, visiting many colleges and universities, meeting diverse student leaders, and making lifelong friends—including a future wife. I learned a lot about myself and my country, and realized that my decision to resign the student presidency, drop out of UT, and spend the year with NSA was the opportunity of a lifetime.

NSA operated on a tight budget. I traveled by plane, train, bus, and automobile when available. Expense accounts were limited; and the monthly salary of each full-time officer was $250. Overnight accommodations were dorm rooms, the YMCA, and homes of fellow student leaders. Stan Glass owned a car, which I used on occasion. Student leaders with an automobile frequently gave me a ride to the next college in the area.

I never hitchhiked, but Bob Kiley, the SGVP when I was president, did hitch a ride on occasion. Once he caught a ride with a man who made a sexual advance toward him. Kiley jumped from the moving vehicle, with briefcase in hand. Kiley made it out safely, but the briefcase didn't, except for the handle, which Bob took with him as he hit the ground. This NSA experience may have contributed to Kiley's later commitment to public transportation. After serving as Executive Assistant to Mayor Kevin White in Boston, Bob became Chairman of the New York's Metropolitan Transportation Authority and is credited with greatly improving the subway system in New York. For a comprehensive article about Bob Kiley and his work to restore the London subway, see "Underground Man" by William Finnegan, pages 52–63 of the February 9, 2004, issue of the *New Yorker*. Bob succeeded me as President of NSA for 1958–59.

My NSA travels began in the South as I visited Baylor and SMU in September 1955 and then went on to Oklahoma University and colleges and universities in Arkansas, Louisiana, Mississippi, Alabama, and Georgia. From Atlanta I took the train back to Philadelphia and immediately left for Penn State.

The trip to Penn State was interrupted by news of a tragic event. One of my closest friends at UT, Mary Dannenbaum, was struck by an automobile when crossing 24th Street in Austin in October. She never regained consciousness and died a week later. I returned to Austin for a memorial service and then traveled on to Houston with her family for the funeral. Also, when I was President of NSA my father died in October 1957. His death occurred the night before I was to depart for Europe on my

Mary Dannenbaum, 1935–1955

first trip abroad to visit several student unions in Europe and participate in the International Student Travel Conference in Rome. I canceled the trip and returned to Wichita Falls.

After each of these funerals, I redirected my travel back to Philadelphia through the southern states. On one trip I visited the University of Louisville, Transylvania University, University of Kentucky, Berea, Maryville, University of Tennessee, Knoxville College, Fisk, Tennessee State, Vanderbilt, Peabody, and Memphis State. My diaries reveal a thirst for experiencing and becoming acquainted with each new place. In a memorable visit to Knoxville I wrote about a Saturday afternoon in November describing "Street corner evangelists, blind singers, massive country crowds, beggars, & pandemonium."

Many of the schools I visited were Roman Catholic, including larger ones like Notre Dame, Fordham, and St. Louis University, but most were small women's colleges like Webster, Maryville, St. Theresa, Rosary, and Dominican. The college with the longest history of NSA membership in Texas was Our Lady of the Lake in San Antonio. Food at Catholic colleges was more spartan than most. At a men's Catholic school in Kansas, the priests hired several Spanish nuns to cook and help with domestic chores. Not familiar with cooking liver, they boiled it, turning it into a white mass—no pun intended. Though a Baptist, I learned to say "Hail Marys," attend mass, and be thankful for such a loyal Catholic NSA constituency.

My tour of the Midwest included St. Louis and colleges in Missouri and Kansas, where I stopped in Great Bend, Kansas, to celebrate my 23rd birthday with my brother Jimmy, his wife Jo, and nieces Varonia and Lynan. Two years later Jimmy and his family moved to Norman, Oklahoma. When I made a speech as NSA President to the Oklahoma University Student Council, I took Varonia with me.

The winter of 1955 found me in the northeast visiting a series of colleges including Fordham, Hunter, City College of New York (CCNY), Cornell, Rochester, Syracuse, and Albany. For Monday, December 12, 1955, my diary describes a good day:

> Ahhh! There are days and then there are good days! This was a good day. 8:00 Conf. with U. of R [University of Rochester] NSA people; 10:00 Conf. with U. of R. SBP, Mary Boat; 11:00 Conf with Freshman ldrs-Ann Funkhouse & Bobbie ____; 12:00 Lunch at U. of R. Nursing School & long talk with Lee Octavel—tour through hosp. & discussion of religion, NSA & govt; 5:00 Rochester Institute of Tech. speech & group affiliated; 6:00 Dinner at Ruth Ann Williams' home. Wonderful meal; 8:30 Meeting with all colleges in City [Rochester]; 10:00 Mtg with Tom Forbes, Jr. Pres., & ideas for Program.

That, indeed, was my idea of a good day; selling schools about the benefits of NSA membership was better than selling bibles.

The major mid-year meeting of NSA, the National Executive Committee (NEC), was always scheduled for the last week in December at the University of Chicago. Stan Glass, Gene Preston, and I drove to Stan's home in southern Illinois near St. Louis. We spent my first Hanukkah/Christmas with the Glass family in Collinsville. My diary reflects that Stan, though Jewish, gave Gene and me presents in the presence of a traditional Christmas tree. We had dinner at one of the country clubs in St. Louis. At the home of one of Stan's relatives I discovered gefilte fish, which I didn't find as tasty as the turkey and dressing. Then we went to see the Harlem Globetrotters. It was another good day—one of the best Christmases (and Hanukkahs) I can remember.

From Collinsville, we drove back to Chicago for the NEC, which met in the Frank Lloyd Wright Roby House just off the campus of the University of Chicago. Reports on policy, budget, and personnel matters were presented, discussed, and acted upon as necessary. One of the actions taken at the meeting was to hire a new Executive Secretary. I recommended Jim Dalton, a good friend with whom I shared an apartment at UT during the summer of 1955. Jim was hired and joined our team in Philadelphia. While with NSA, he met Tel Friedman. They were later married and now live in Austin. We remain good friends.

When we returned to Philadelphia from Chicago, I planned my itinerary for January–May 1956. The first trip was to the Boston area, where I visited the NSA International Office off of Harvard Square, Harvard, Radcliff, Framingham State Teachers College (now part of the University of Massachusetts), Wellesley, and Pine Manor Junior College. While in Boston, I stayed in Adams House at Harvard and was very impressed with its "house system" of dorms. I attended the Harvard Chapel for Sunday services. On January 15, I wrote friend Lee Hite: "Bishop Angus Dunn...preached ... they have a very impressive schedule of guest [ministers] including Neibuhr, Tillich, and Van Dusen for the coming two months. Buttrick is the regular pastor..."—a long way from the First Baptist in Wichita Falls.

Despite my chaotic travel schedule, I dated a few girls along the way. In Boston I had several dates with a student leader at Newton College of the Sacred Heart. I wrote Lee: "Must tell you later of the very delightful . . . girl I dated

Mary Lacy Kelly, circa 1956

when in that area, Mary Lacey Kelly." In a later diary entry: "Dinner at Durgan Park in Boston with Bob & Ann Timmons & Jack Pew [Phi Gams from UT doing academic work at Harvard] & Mary Lacey. Ran into Dan Squibb of Austin in DP. [Durgan Park] Went dancing with Mary Lacey afterwards."

The trip home was not as enjoyable as the week in Boston. My diary tells the story:

Off to New York. Short on Cash. Sore throat. Flat [tire]. No money & big harangle (sic) over check. Picked up hitchhikers for toll money. Upon arrival in N.Y. found out about Tom Mitchell's [former NSA officer] death. Train to Philly. Got wrong street car. Long Walk Home.

Later in January 1956, the diary relates another bad travel experience after a busy day:

Train back into NYC. To Travel Office [NSA had an office in New York City for its student travel services] & change of clothes. Lunch with Ralph Della Cava. Mtg with Sophia Rush of Nat'l Self-Govt Com. Mtg with Dave Davis & Simonson [at] Travel Office. Dinner with John Hendricks [Travel Director] & wife in Carnegie Hall Restaurant. Tour through Ephron Gallery. Show—"Tiger at the Gates." Picked up by Hi-way patrol on trip home—speeding. Stan fined. Woke everyone up trying to get $ to bail him out. Got to bed at 5:00 AM after bailing Stan out.

If I had been as philosophical as my entry on December 12, I might have said "Ahhh, there are days—good days, and some bad days [or nights]," but I didn't, because there were so many good days and nights. In fact, I totally forgot about the flat tire on the way back from Boston and the "bail out" on the way to Philadelphia until I read about them in my diary.

My longest trip for NSA began on February 19, 1956. I traveled more than 6,000 miles from the East Coast across the northern United States to Seattle, down the West Coast to Los Angeles and back to Texas, across the South to Atlanta, and home to Philadelphia on May 15. At one point, I had worn out my shoes and had them repaired in California, while wearing a borrowed pair that didn't fit. After three months on the road, my white Dacron drip-dry shirt had turned yellow. I visited more than 65 colleges and universities, saw the western part of the country for the first time, and made many new friends, including Helen Rehbein, the woman I would marry in December 1958.

While serving as president of NSA, my travel was more limited—mostly on the East Coast, particularly Washington, D.C., the Student Travel office in New York City, and the International Affairs office in Cambridge, Massachusetts. When traveling to other NSA offices or meetings, I frequently visited member colleges in the area; however, the job of president required more fund-raising and administrative work.

MEMORABLE MEETINGS

In the fall of 1955, President Dwight D. Eisenhower called a White House Conference on Education in the United States, the first of its kind. NSA was one of the few student organizations invited to participate. Stan Glass and I attended the meeting in Washington, D.C., and I wrote a report about the conference that was published in the January 1956 Student Government Bulletin.

Texas had a large delegation attending the White House Conference, including Governor Allan Shivers and my old friend and mentor, Dr. Read Granberry. One of the major issues of the conference concerned federal aid

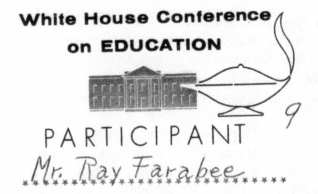

Conference logo used with article I wrote for Student Government Bulletin, *Jan. 5, 1956*

to education. Although federal aid for public schools is now universally accepted, it was highly controversial at the time.

Granberry wrote me a cordial letter after the conference expressing the "Texas Position" in opposition to federal aid to education. Another Texas Governor, George W. Bush, would later become president and advocate massive federal aid and federal controls of public education, all under the banner of "No Child Left Behind."

As president of NSA, I testified in 1958 before the U.S. Senate Labor and Public Welfare Committee in favor of federal loans to college students. The ultra-conservative author M. Stanton Evans cites my testimony in his 1961 book, *Revolt on the Campus*, and castigates me and NSA for our "efforts on behalf of federal intervention in education" (p.149). Federal aid for college student loans, scholarships, and grants now amounts to billions of dollars, and neither Democratic nor Republican leadership—including President Bush—would think of revoking these popular programs.

When I testified before the U.S. Senate Committee, I met Senator Ralph Yarborough, who was a member of the Labor and Public Welfare Committee. His Administrative Assistant was Jim Boren from Wichita Falls, the son of the president of Midwestern State University and brother of my high school debate partner Marilyn Boren. Senator Yarborough questioned me about the need for federal scholarships and whether grants would be better than loans. I acknowledged that scholarship aid should be considered but focused more on enacting a broad-based federal loan program for college students. In fact, a federal loan program was first enacted by Congress and later expanded to federal scholarship programs.

Lyndon B. Johnson was the senior U.S. Senator from Texas and Majority Leader of the Senate. His Administrative Assistant was Walter Jenkins, also from Wichita Falls. On March 7, 1958, Jenkins arranged a meeting for me with Johnson to discuss the student loan program. Johnson was receptive, but preferred to discuss other youth programs related to his early experience as Southwest Director for the National Youth Administration (NYA) during the New Deal. He asked me about the possibility of initiating similar programs. I had no specific ideas for him at the time, but several youth programs emerged in the Kennedy-Johnson years, such as the Peace Corps, Youth Corps, and Head Start. I feel that these were very appealing to Johnson because of his NYA experiences. Shortly after my visit with LBJ, I received a warm letter of interest from him.

𝔘𝔫𝔦𝔱𝔢𝔡 𝔖𝔱𝔞𝔱𝔢𝔰 𝔖𝔢𝔫𝔞𝔱𝔢
𝔒𝔣𝔣𝔦𝔠𝔢 𝔬𝔣 𝔱𝔥𝔢 𝔇𝔢𝔪𝔬𝔠𝔯𝔞𝔱𝔦𝔠 𝔏𝔢𝔞𝔡𝔢𝔯
𝔚𝔞𝔰𝔥𝔦𝔫𝔤𝔱𝔬𝔫, 𝔇. 𝔆.
March 18, 1958

MAR 20 Rec'd

Dear Ray:

Thank you so much for your kind letter and enclosure of March 7. I was delighted that I had the opportunity to meet you at the Texas delegation luncheon. It is a distinct honor for you, and for Texas, that you are president of the National Student Association.

As you know, Senator Hill and the members of his Committee are now studying the many educational proposals which have been introduced in the Senate. Let me assure you that I shall give very thorough consideration to any of these measures that are presented to the Senate Floor for action.

I shall, of course, be most happy to have your observations and suggestions at any time.

With warmest regards, I am

Sincerely,

Lyndon B. Johnson

Mr. Ray Farabee
President
United States National Student Association
1234 Gimbel Building

LBJ response to March 7, 1958, meeting

I briefly met Richard Nixon and his wife Pat at the White House Conference on Education in 1955. Two years later I had a more substantive meeting with Nixon, facilitated by his Administrative Assistant Charles McWhorter. The vice president was exceptionally cordial. We talked about national and international student issues. Several weeks later, I received a photograph of us that was personally inscribed, "To Ray Farabee with appreciation for his dedicated public service and with every good wish for

To Ray Farabee with appreciation for his dedicated public service and with every good wish for the years ahead from Dick Nixon

Meeting with Vice President Nixon, 1958

the years ahead . . . from Dick Nixon." I suspect McWhorter may have written the inscription, but the picture was helpful to offset some of the red-baiting about NSA at the time and to show that the organization was a national player.

My mother loved the Nixon picture and proudly displayed it in the living room of the 2313 Ninth Street house until her death. The Wichita Falls Y used it for an annual meeting after I returned to practice law there.

One of the more unusual meetings was my speech to the annual convention of the National Automobile Dealer's Association at the Eden Rock Hotel in Miami Beach, Florida, in the spring of 1958. The association was a large group with deep pockets, so all my expenses were paid. The subject of my speech was "What Cars Will the Next Generation Buy"—not my usual talk about student government, higher education, or the international student movement. I arrived in Miami with a sore throat and a bad cough from the freezing Philadelphia weather; however, my training served me well; I made a good speech, saying that college students would like to see smaller and more fuel-efficient cars. I suspect the message was not universally popular among the "big fin" car dealers of that era. My prognostications were amazingly accurate. Within the next ten years, U.S. auto manufacturers and dealers did a better job meeting consumer demand for smaller automobiles. For the first time, I received a fruit basket, bottle of whiskey, and an honorarium for a speech. I enjoyed the fruit, fellow officers and staff enjoyed the Scotch, and the honorarium helped balance the NSA budget.

The National Student Congress culminated each NSA year and was preceded by the National Student Body Presidents Conference. As SGVP, I was chairman and responsible for the 1956–1957 SBP Conference, which provided an opportunity to see many of the student leaders I met on the road, including Helen Rehbein. She was still engaged, but we became better acquainted.

Eleanor Roosevelt was the most memorable of the national leaders I met while an NSA officer. She served on the NSA National Advisory Council and addressed the Eleventh National Student Congress at Ohio Wesleyan in August 1958. Although Mrs. Roosevelt was the oldest member of our Advisory Council, she expressed youthful and progressive ideas. I last saw her at Chatham College in Pittsburgh when Allard (Al) Lowenstein and I were on our way from New York to Appleton, Wisconsin, in 1958.

Of all the past NSA officers I met, Al Lowenstein was the most unforgettable. He was assassinated in his New York law office in March 1980 by a deranged former friend. No past NSA president has had as much impact or public attention as Al. Books have been written by and about him. Two such books are *Lowenstein: Acts of Courage and Belief,* edited by Gregory Stone and Douglas Lowenstein (Al's nephew) and *Never Stop Running,* by William H. Chafe.

Presentation to Mrs. Roosevelt at American Assn. for United Nations, Nov. 20, 1957

DESEGREGATION AND THE SOUTH

Just as desegregation led to my election as an NSA officer, much of my time, both as SGVP and president, was devoted to this cause. NSA membership was sparse in the South, but I traveled and spent more time in the South than any other region. Two unforeseen deaths (Mary Dannenbaum in 1955 and my father in 1957) took me back to Texas and led to additional trips through Texas and various Southern states on my return to Philadelphia.

From a current perspective, it is difficult to visualize how segregated the South was 50 years ago. Education, transportation, restaurants, movie theaters, drinking fountains, restrooms, and lodging accommodations were segregated. Contrary to the enunciations of the time about "separate but equal," public services and facilities available to people of color were grossly unequal and discriminatory. To the overwhelming majority of white southerners at the time, it was "just the way it always had been"—and to some, "the way God intended it." Whatever theological beliefs prevailed, southern political leaders from the courthouse to the state house were hell-bent on maintaining the status quo of segregation.

NSA's policies from its founding in 1946 were clear and unequivocal in opposition to segregation and discrimination based on race. These policies were a factor in the sparse membership of Southern schools, but more representative of the rest of the country.

As I traveled the South, I found southern black and white student leaders generally receptive and courteous. In fact, the only time black and white students were likely to meet together to discuss such issues was through student organizations like NSA, TISA, the Y, and some church groups. Unfortunately, few opportunities like this existed in the Deep South. As desegregation and protests for and against it progressed, interracial communication declined during the 1950's and 60's.

Two major events in Alabama illustrate the imminent crisis in race relations while I was traveling with NSA. One was the admission of Autherine Lucy to the University of Alabama on February 7, 1956, and the other was the Montgomery bus strike, triggered by the refusal of Rosa Parks to give up her seat and move to the back of the bus, where no

Autherine Lucy addressing NSA Congress, 1956

seats were available. My diary entries for February 9 and 10, 1956, reflect the importance of the Lucy case to NSA:

Wed. 2/9/56: Work today, primarily centered around a statement for USNSA on the riots at U. of Alabama over 1st Negro under-graduate. Called Tuscaloosa & talked to Walt Flowers [SBP at U. of Alabama]and called Stan in Wash. [DC] & Clive [International Affairs VP] in Cambridge, Mass. Waiting to receive statement from Flowers.

Thur. 2/10/56: Again our work centered around Lucy Case at Alabama; did not receive Walt's statement; had to call him in Ala. for it. Wrote press release for AP, UP & INS. I took release to [Philadelphia] Bulletin. Wrote letters for Stan to Ala.

Desegregation of Central High School in Little Rock, Arkansas, took place shortly after I was elected president of NSA for the 1957–1958 school year. By comparison, the Little Rock riots, National Guard involvement, and national and international press coverage greatly exceeded that of Autherine Lucy. I wrote to President Eisenhower, Governor Orville Faubus, and other elected officials expressing NSA policy positions for integration. Working with the International Office in Cambridge, we advised student unions around the world of NSA's opposition to segregation and support for the nine black students at Central High School.

NSA held an International Student Relations Seminar (ISRS) each summer before the National Congress. I thought a similar Southern Student Human Relations Seminar (SSHRS) could be worthwhile and set out to secure funding for it. After sending proposals to several foundations, NSA received a $6,000 grant from the Field Foundation in New York. I was the director for the first two seminars in 1958 and 1959. The Field Foundation funded an expanded program known as the Southern Project in 1960, which was directed by my friend Connie Currie. I consider the establishment of SSHRS as one of the most important accomplishments of my two years working as an NSA officer.

National Guard at Central High School, Little Rock, Arkansas, 1957

A TALE OF TWO UNIVERSITIES

As in Dickens's *Tale of Two Cities*, "It was the best of times. It was the worst of times," during the last half of the 1950's. Although NSA membership increased, I experienced two big disappointments in my home state: one at Baylor University and the other at Southern Methodist University. Both were related to race, federal aid to education, and the "Red Scare."

The student governments at Baylor and SMU expressed interest in NSA membership in 1955. I visited each school and corresponded frequently with their student leaders.

In April 1956 I visited Baylor and had a conference with the Baptist Student Union (BSU) chaplain, the provost, and one of the academic deans. It became apparent that the problem was not with the student government, but with the administration, which disagreed with NSA on the issues of desegregation and federal aid to education. On several occasions the chaplain stated that Baylor was a "conservative" university but did not "have moss on its back." He went on to tell me the story of Philemon and his slave, Onesimus, seemingly as a rationalization for segregation within the Christian context of love and forgiveness. The Provost used the term "nigger" and "nigra" while discussing desegregation and race relations.

The three administrators told me the trustees were likely to veto any action of the students to affiliate with NSA, which would in their opinion be the "worst thing that could happen to the students, Baylor, or NSA." When the *Houston Chronicle* ran an editorial entitled "Baylor Student Controversy Shows Trend of the Times" and noted the charge of "some student leaders that [NSA] is a left-wing organization," we realized our efforts at Baylor had no chance of succeeding.

The administration at SMU was not opposed to NSA. In fact, I was an overnight guest in the home of the president of SMU, Dr. Willis Tate, for my spring visit to the campus in 1956. Although Dr. Tate and most student government leaders favored joining NSA, an active group of conservative students led a vigorous campaign against NSA in a campus-wide referendum. I will never forget attending the student forum the night before the referendum about NSA membership. It turned into a rally against NSA. My report to the Philadelphia office captured the spirit of what happened:

Crowd was overwhelmingly opposed to NSA and every time a candidate spoke against it [NSA], there was much shouting, whistling & applause. Joe Scott, Editor of the *Campus* [student newspaper], wore one of the anti-NSA "Vote No" cards; as he was recognized, he pointed to the card & then put his thumbs down, and there was even more shouting & applause.

A majority of the undergraduate students at SMU were members of fraternities and sororities, and their national organizations became involved because of NSA's opposition to discriminatory clauses excluding students on the basis of race or religious faith. National fraternity and sorority offices wrote letters to student members urging them to vote as a block against NSA. Hammers and sickles were painted on doors, and a sign over the Kappa Sig house read "Vote No NSA." Some of the student comments were more dramatic and mean-spirited such as these examples quoted from my notes:

Example from anti-NSA campaign at SMU

"I don't want my children to be taught by communists & that's why I'm voting against NSA." "You're for NSA, you must have Negro sex appeal"—a statement by one girl to the chair of the Student Union who was for NSA.

Two girls who wrote an article in favor of the NAACP received a box with 2 red roses [with a note] which stated "Two red roses, for two pink ladies, who are too liberal for this campus."

Advertisements in the student newspaper included those for and against NSA. Ads against NSA were more effective. One of the ads for NSA had a banner headline "NSA IS NOT COMMUNISTIC." As I wrote the National Office, "the innuendos here were not the best." One thousand students voted against the NSA and 500 voted for affiliation.

Two memorable comments are worth mentioning from the Baylor/SMU experience. One was from a Baylor student leader, Ruth Parker, who said, "They told us there would be pie in the sky by and by; but we found there was a fly in the pie by and by." The other was the very good advice that Dr. Willis Tate of SMU gave me as we walked home on the spring evening after the horrific NSA forum/rally. He said, "Ray, just remember the Latin phrase *'Illigitimus Non Corborundum'* which interprets to 'Don't let the bastards beat you down.'" The observations of each have served me well on various occasions for more than fifty years.

As documented on the current websites of both Baylor and SMU, each university now seeks and accepts federal money and promotes federal scholarships and loans for their incoming students. More important, each university is now desegregated and has respectable numbers of African American students enrolled in undergraduate and graduate programs—to me a fact having greater Christian implication than the story of Philemon's slave.

NSA staff postcard, 1956

As for the red-baiting issues raised at SMU, my "comrades" back in Philadelphia found it more humorous than I did and presented me with a comic postcard with a Texas-looking kind of guy asking, "Me, a Red?" Lest anyone think I'm picking on SMU and Baylor, it is worth noting that UT had a similar referendum in 1948 when affiliation with NSA was rejected 2,533 to 1,847. It did affiliate in 1953; otherwise, I would not have been elected an NSA officer.

NSA INTERNATIONAL PROGRAMS

Students have been important historically in bringing about change in many countries, not the least of which is our own. Examples may be found in Prague, Hungary, France, Mexico, Chile, and all over the world. Some student protests were crushed, at no small cost to the students, as in Tiananmen Square of Beijing; but lasting impacts frequently remain. Protests often begin with students from various universities through a student union or national student organization (NSO).

NSA had a strong interest in the international student movement throughout its history. Twenty-five students from various U.S. colleges and universities attended the 1946 Prague World Student Congress. Practically all of the delegates to that Congress were associated with NSO's from their respective countries. However, the United States had no unified singular organization that could say it represented the college students of the United States. After the Prague Congress concluded, the 25 American students returned and initiated an organizational committee that led to the organization of NSA. It is worth noting that the chairman of the committee, Jim Smith, was another UT student president who dropped out of college to lead the effort.

The International Union of Students (IUS) was the principal world student organization at the time NSA was organized. However, the IUS was increasingly dominated by the Soviet bloc, and NSA never affiliated with it. In fact, NSA was one of the principal leaders in organizing the International Student Conference (ISC), which provided an alternative for NSO's that wished to participate in world affairs without domination by the Soviet Union. The business of the ISC was managed by the Coordinating Secretariat (COSEC) in Leiden, the Netherlands. More information can be found about the importance and role of NSO's in foreign countries and the role of NSA on the international scene in American Students Organize.

Three areas of NSA international activities during my year as president are described in this chapter: The NSA educational travel program; the U.S./Russian student editor exchange of 1958; and the covert funding of NSA international programs by the CIA.

Thousands of American students traveled abroad in the 1950's, 60's, and 70's through the USNSA educational travel program, operated by its non-profit subsidiary Educational Travel, Inc. (ETI). Offices for ETI were in New York near Times Square. It offered student travel packages ranging from the modest Hobo Tour to deluxe Red Carpet Tours. In addition, ETI published a series of low-cost student travel books and guides. It also sponsored an International Student Identity Card that qualified students for price discounts and other services in 30 countries.

As president of NSA, I was also ETI president and chairman of its board of directors. Paradoxically, I never traveled to Europe on a tour while an

NSA officer. I did spend more time in New York, learning about the travel business and management, which was helpful in later years.

USNSA educational travel—1958

NSA student travel brochure from the 1950's

One of the more interesting international programs involved a groundbreaking foreign exchange program with the Soviet Union. During the Cold War, all exchange programs with Soviet Bloc countries were prohibited. In 1958, the Department of State asked NSA to organize and administer a short-term exchange of United States and Russian student editors. Six American students were selected from 55 applicants across the country. Young editors from student papers like the *Daily Tar Heel* at Chapel Hill visited Soviet universities, collective farms, and young pioneer facilities in Moscow, Baku, Tashkent, and Kiev, during May 1958.

In June 1958 I met the Russian student editors who arrived in New York very early in the morning. They were not students; their ages ranged from 28 to 38. The USSR delegation was associated primarily with nationally distributed student and youth publications controlled by the Communist Party. None of them spoke English, so we communicated through their interpreter.

When we arrived at their hotel rooms, the delegation chairman proposed a toast with Russian vodka they had brought with them. Although I had strayed from my Baptist upbringing and had a drink now and then, I had never tasted vodka or consumed any alcoholic beverage at 8 a.m. in the morning. However, I did my patriotic duty, consumed "the breakfast of champions," and proposed a toast to our guests and the new "student" exchange program.

We took the Russian editors to see *My Fair Lady*, which was playing on Broadway at the time. The next day the editors departed for Boston, Chicago, Los Angeles, Salt Lake City, North Carolina, and Washington, D.C., where they met with Vice President Richard Nixon. I left the editors in New York but rejoined them in Washington for their last few days in the United States.

THE CIA CONNECTION

Ramparts magazine, on February 14, 1967, ran a full-page editorial announcement in the *New York Times* (NYT) disclosing that NSA had received large sums of money from the Central Intelligence Agency (CIA). A front-page NYT news article confirmed receipt of the CIA funds covertly through several foundations since the early 1950's until 1966. This time period covered the two years I was an officer of NSA. I was not aware of the secret funding while I was SGVP, but learned about it when I was president of NSA in 1957.

During the several months after the NYT/Ramparts disclosure, NSA received more news coverage than in its 30 years of prior existence. Every major daily newspaper in the United States and much of the world carried the story with follow-up articles and editorials. Even the *Wichita Falls Times*, where I was raising a family and practicing law, carried an Associated Press (AP) article on its front page, headlined "Student Group Tells Secret Ties to CIA." In one day I went from being considered a dupe of the communists by some to being a dupe of the CIA by others.

News coverage about the NSA/CIA connection did not quickly fade;

Late breaking news in Ramparts *magazine and* New York Times, *1967*

it accelerated. On February 24, 1967, *Time* magazine ran a comprehensive cover-page feature about "The CIA and the Students." The cartoon on page 14 of the *Time* article is one of the better comments on the paradox of being called a communist by some, only to later learn of the CIA funding and NSA activities to offset the communist influence on students around the world. According to a *Dallas Times Herald* article on February 16, 1967, the SMU student government decided to affiliate with NSA—the CIA did what I couldn't.

Numerous editorials throughout the country discussed the pros and cons of the NSA/CIA connection. The *Dallas Times Herald* was more critical with its comment headlined "Spies From the Campus." James Reston wrote thoughtful editorial comments in the February 17, 1967, *New York Times*. Senator J. William Fulbright wrote an extensive article in the NYT *Sunday Magazine* of April 1967 that expresses how I felt, and still feel, about my own involvement as a president of NSA:

> The fair evaluation of any human act requires that due account be taken of the time and circumstances in which the act took place. I believe that if I had been a student leader in the late nineteen forties or early fifties, and if an apparent important Government official had approached me confidentially and told me I had a unique opportunity to perform a patriotic duty by accepting funds from a secret Government source in order to have done what I thought needed to be done anyway, I would have found it difficult indeed to turn such a proposal down.
>
> I would have found it difficult because in those early days of the cold war, when Russia was still ruled by Stalin, Communism seemed clearly to be an extremely menacing aggressive force, one which used student meetings as one of many instruments in a centrally directed design for conquest.

They did, and I did. That is, I was invited to dinner by a prior NSA president in October 1957 in Washington, D.C. After signing a non-disclosure agreement, I joined several others in a nearby room and was advised of the CIA funding for several NSA international programs through foundations, primarily the Foundation for Youth and Student Affairs.

For the reasons listed, i.e., the death of my father, cancellation of my trip to Europe, and refocus on desegregation, my involvement with CIA was less than it might have otherwise been. I had some communication with persons, either hired by the CIA or connected with it; but they never controlled or influenced national policy. As to international policy, we were on the same page; we were seeking to counterbalance the IUS and to present truths about such events as the Hungarian Student Revolt and suppression of academic freedom for students and faculty, whether in the Soviet Bloc, South Africa, Cuba, Algeria, or elsewhere.

Based on what I read from the media after the disclosure of the NSA/CIA connection, the amount of covert financial support to NSA increased in the years after my return to private life in Texas. Contrary to the statements in Ramparts, I doubt that the CIA or its funding had any significant impact on national or international policy because of the very diverse and democratic nature of the National Student Congresses and NSA student leadership.

I joined eleven other past presidents of NSA on February 25, 1967, in a statement responding to suggestions by Ramparts that NSA had been controlled, trapped or misled by the CIA funding. I was invited to speak about the CIA-NSA controversy in Wichita Falls and the surrounding area.

Contrary to some expectations, disclosure of the NSA/CIA connection and related publicity did not destroy NSA. The loss of CIA funds, end of the cold war with USSR, and finally the breakup of the Soviet Bloc spelled the end of the NSA international program, ISC, and COSEC. The number of member schools remained about the same and the students represented by those schools actually increased. The Vietnam War, rise of student activism, and polarization of students into various interest groups altered the nature of NSA and its programs. In 1978 NSA merged with the National Student Lobby to form the United States Student Association (USSA). USSA traces its origins to the beginning of NSA at the University of Wisconsin 1946.

Cartoonist's "View of how things do change," Time *magazine, February 24, 1967*

USNSA OFFICERS 1955–1956

Clive S. Gray	Gene R. Preston	Joel H. Sterns	Stanford L. Glass
International Affairs	National Affairs	Educational Affairs	President
Vice President	Vice President	Vice President	Univ. of Illinois
Univ. of Chicago	UCLA	Northwestern Univ.	

Not pictured: Ray Farabee, Student Govt. VP and Jim Turner, Student Affairs VP, Univ. NC

officers 1957-58

RAY FARABEE

President Ray Farabee, 24, served as student body president at the University of Texas in 1955, a position he resigned upon election as USNSA's student government vice-president in 1955-56. A pre-law student, he served as chairman of the board of directors, Texas Student Union, directed the central agency of the Texas Intercollegiate Student Association, was president of his Freshman Class, and a member of Phi Gamma Delta. Other positions he held on campus were YMCA program chairman and chairman of the Board of Publications.

DONALD CLIFFORD

Executive Vice-President Donald Clifford, 22, was student body president at Catholic University of America, Washington, D. C. and chairman of USNSA's Mason-Dixon Region in 1956-57. A graduate magna cum laude in political science, he was an editorial consultant to the campus yearbook, editorial board member of the student newspaper, president of the University Debating Society, and a member of Phi Kappa. He attended the 1955 International Student Relations Seminar at Cambridge.

BRUCE D. LARKIN

International Affairs Vice-President Bruce D. Larkin, 21, received his AB with general honors at the University of Chicago, where he continued as a graduate student in international relations. President of the Student Union and party leader of the Independent Student League at Chicago, and a member of Alpha Delta Phi, he has served USNSA as Illinois-Wisconsin Region chairman 1954-55, National Executive Committee chairman 1954-55, and international affairs vice-president, 1956-57.

WILLARD JOHNSON

Educational Affairs Vice-President Willard Johnson, 21, served as student body president at the University of California, Los Angeles in 1956-57 and participated in the International Student Relations Seminar at Cambridge this year. A senior honors student in political science, he received the Pasadena and John Muir Junior College Order of Distinguished Service in 1955. He also founded the Pasadena Youth Council, served as its first president, and initiated UCLA's "Project Africa."

ROBERT KILEY

Student Government Vice-President Robert Kiley, 22, graduated magna cum laude from the University of Notre Dame School of Commerce. He served as Commerce Senator in student government and as USNSA's Ohio-Indiana Region chairman in 1956-57. Active in the Young Christian Students, he received the dean's award for academic achievement and service in his college, was selected the outstanding member of the Student Senate, and outstanding senior at Notre Dame in 1957.

REGINALD GREEN

Student Affairs Vice President Reginald Green, 22, graduated summa cum laude at Whitman College in 1955, where he was editor of The Pioneer, student newspaper, a member of Tau Kappa Epsilon, and an Executive Council member in student government. A Woodrow Wilson National Fellow, he received his MA in economics at Harvard, where he served on the Graduate Student Council. A 1955 member of the International Student Relations Seminar, he has served on USNSA's National Executive Committee and the National Interim Committee.

1958–1961: Love and Marriage; USAF and Law School

*The very brief, but full visit with you in Des Moines was much
better than I can express on paper. I hope it shall not be too long
before I see you again. It is good when there is so much to talk about
and that we touched upon so many things which are yet unfinished.*
—April 29, 1958, Ray Farabee letter to Helen Rehbein

THE ABOVE EXCERPT is from the first of 44 love letters from me to
Helen prior to our marriage on December 6, 1958, in Appleton, Wisconsin. Looking back, our letters to and from one another tell of a cross-country courtship and describe the last of the 1950's for us and those times.

After the wedding and a brief honeymoon in the frozen north, we
headed for Wichita Falls and Dallas where I served as a second lieutenant
in the U.S. Air Force for six months. From Dallas we moved to Austin to
finish my last two years of law school. Helen had interesting jobs in Dallas
as a newspaper reporter and in Austin as an assistant dean of women; she
became pregnant with our first child during our last year in Austin before
we moved to Wichita Falls to commence law practice and start a family.

FIRST MEETING AND VISITS

I first met Helen when I was Student Government Vice President (SGVP)
of USNSA and was visiting the University of Wisconsin at Madison. We
met on the afternoon of Friday, March 9, 1956, in the Student Union building. I made various diary entries for the day, and then wrote, "talked with
Helen Rehbein, SBP [student body president] to be, for 3 or 4 hours." Based

on the time spent with Helen that day and during the rest of her life, it was the most important meeting of the day, year, and my life.

At the time we met, Helen had received nominations for student president from both of the major student political parties. She was very knowledgeable about student government. I was impressed and invited her to participate in the Student Body Presidents Conference (SBPC) in August at the University of Chicago. I corresponded with Helen on several occasions after our meeting in Madison and requested her to assume leadership responsibilities for the national conference. We met again in Chicago and came to know each other better.

Helen was one of the most impressive student leaders I encountered during my 1955–1956 tour of duty with NSA, and I found her attractive and interesting to talk with. But there was one problem—she was engaged to Hap Hornbostel. Although I had only honorable intentions, I couldn't help but notice the very large diamond engagement ring on her left hand when I saw her in Madison and Chicago. As attractive and interesting as I found Helen, I assumed that she would marry the chap (I didn't know his name at the time) at the end of her senior year and become a wealthy housewife in Beloit, Appleton, or elsewhere in Wisconsin.

Helen Rehbein, 1956

Not being one to give up hope, I wrote Helen on June 8, 1957, nearly one year after I last saw her. Following a chatty discussion about law school, the Texas heat as compared to Wisconsin, and my heavier non-legal reading of Arthur Schlesinger, Sarte, and J. D. Salinger, I popped the question—not whether she would marry me, but whether she was still engaged or married to someone else, asking:

> And what about Miss Rehbein? Hoping it's still "Miss Rehbein," are you engaged, pinned, married, etc? If so, congratulations; if not, congratulations. And not to be too inquisitive, but what are your plans for [the]

coming year as to employment, residence, etc. After it's over, what were your comments on the year in perspective? Will you be at the NSA Congress [at the University of Michigan]?

Not surprisingly, Helen didn't answer this bumptious letter (though she retained it), and didn't attend the NSA Congress in Michigan. I continued assuming she was still engaged or married. When I was president of NSA during 1957–1958, I learned she was working for *Better Homes and Gardens* magazine (BH&G) in Des Moines, Iowa, and still a "Miss," which brings me to my next letter and an important dinner date in Des Moines.

I wrote Helen in Des Moines on April 17, 1958, that I would be traveling in Iowa during the last week of that month and suggested dinner on Sunday night, April 27. After spending a day in Ames at Iowa State, I traveled to Des Moines where I visited Helen at the duplex apartment she shared with two other *Better Homes* employees. I then took her to dinner where we had a wonderful visit. My feeling about our visit is captured in the introductory quote from the letter of April 29, written as I flew back to Philadelphia.

My next letter was from the Eden Roc Hotel in Miami, Florida, where I was addressing the National Automobile Dealers Association about student priorities for the next generation of autos. The news at that time was about Fidel Castro and the overthrow of the Batista government in Cuba. Since that was the closest I had been to Cuba, I joshed about Castro and signed the letter "R. Farabee (Simon Bolivar of Wichita Falls, Texas)"—an embellishment for a former bible salesman and itinerant student leader.

LOVE LETTERS AND THE COURTSHIP

As busy as we were, we wrote long letters about everything from current events to daily activities, mine with NSA travels and Helen's challenges of work. It took no more than a few letters, and we were planning our next meeting for the weekend of June 7, 1958, in Washington, D.C. The Russian student editors were in Washington that weekend. Despite the distractions of official business, the capital city worked perfectly for our second date. We heard the Marine Band play at the Lincoln Memorial, had dinner with the Soviet "students," and found time for long talks into the night.

One of the subjects of our conversation was the problem of "time and distance." That sounds like a physics problem, but it referred to the future of our relationship. In her letter of June 16, 1958, Helen wrote:

> You know, I was thinking about this time and distance business the other day and, although they certainly are important factors, if something or someone is important enough to you, even time and distance can be overcome. There certainly isn't any doubt about the important place you have assumed in such a short time—unless I admit how I felt two years ago now—and since I do feel as strongly as I do, I wouldn't miss any opportunity to be with you for any period of time—no matter how short—and a short time is so much better than no time at all.

Between the U.S. mail and several relatively short visits during the summer of 1958, we overcame the problems of the short time we had known each other and the distances between Des Moines and Philadelphia. We seldom talked on the telephone. Cell phones didn't exist; long distance rates were expensive; and both of us were on the move, particularly me with NSA travels to Miami, Boston, New York, Cleveland, and other places.

Our next visit was in Chicago over the Fourth of July weekend. Helen and her roommate Jo Harris drove from Des Moines on the Fourth and stayed on the near North Side of Chicago with a friend named Grace Kaminkowitz. I flew in from Philadelphia and stayed with Jim and Tel Dalton at the University of Chicago on the South Side. In a letter dated July 1, I wrote, "I'm ready for the shores of Lake Michigan and the coolest woman I know, Helen Rehbein!" We walked the Lake shores, watched people flying kites, visited with each other for hours over coffee in the Loop, and ate dinners at Jack Diamond's Steak House and a Greek restaurant where men folk-danced in a circle. The two days, without the distraction of Russian editors or NSA business, were very important in the growth of our love and understanding of each other.

Shortly after our Chicago visit, we both wrote similar letters about how much those few days meant to us. Helen's articulation was the best and provided insight into her feelings, when she wrote:

> It was wonderful to see you and know you better and it is a strange and good feeling to know that for once I am in a situation where "protec-

tions" don't seem important or as necessary as usual. Unafraid of being hurt or disappointed and certain of the uncertainties, i.e., certain that in many ways I love you very much, but uncertain about the future of that love or the definition of it, if it can be defined—and with the uncertainty that should breed insecurity, for the first time there seems to be a form of security—security that comes with the knowledge or feeling (whatever it is) that this is fine and good and the goodness of it gives one little room to question or doubt as has always been the case in the past. (Letter of July 8, 1958)

On August 1, I drove a 1953 Volkswagen Beetle from Philadelphia to Columbus, Ohio, to direct the first NSA Southern Student Human Relations Seminar (SSHRS). The borrowed blue VW was important because it not only carried me to Columbus but later to Chicago, where I proposed to Helen, and then on to Appleton, Wisconsin, to meet her family. UT Law classmate Bill Foster loaned me the old, but sporty, VW while he and his wife visited family and friends in Europe for six weeks. In my letter to Helen of August 3, I reported that the VW burned more oil than gasoline, and we—the VW and I— laid down a significant trail of blue smoke along the Pennsylvania Turnpike. A new head gasket and tune-up restored the VW, which carried me across the Midwest and back to meet the Fosters upon their return.

The cross-country '53 VW Beetle

Before leaving Philadelphia, I invited Helen to join me in Columbus for the weekend of August 9–10. She did, and despite the distractions of NSA business, we had another good weekend. In my letter to Helen on August 11, I wrote:

I don't find words to explain how much the weekend with you meant—
it seems inadequate to describe the two days as merely good, wonderful,
or something else—and I think this becomes more of a problem as we
love and understand each other more fully. So much is simply a matter
of experience or feeling, and these aspects of our love seem to grow and
be more real.

Except for a final report, I finished my part of the SSHRS on August 15
and moved from Columbus to Ohio Wesleyan for the Eleventh National
Student Congress in Delaware, Ohio. Although this was the busiest part
of my year, I wrote Helen several letters during the Congress describing
speeches, meeting Mrs. Roosevelt, and the politics for the election of new
NSA officers. Helen's letters had a hard time keeping up with me, but we
confirmed important travel plans.

After the Congress, I drove to Chicago in the VW and met Helen, who
arrived by train from Des Moines. We had lunch in a German restaurant
in the Loop. Somewhere between the sauerbraten and potato pancakes, I
asked Helen to marry me. She did not immediately accept my proposal, but
we visited about marriage and its meaning for several weeks. We drove to
Appleton that afternoon where I met Helen's parents, Wilmer and Myra
Rehbein, and her brother George. I stayed for a couple of days. Helen and
I drove out to Lake Winneconne, where her parents had a summer home;

*The Rehbein Family September, 1958: Myra, Wim,
Helen with Blackie the Cat, and George*

the next day we ventured to a sports car race in Elkhart, Wisconsin. I didn't enter the blue VW in the race, but we had a wonderful time as fall began to move into Wisconsin.

Helen had talked to her parents about me, letting them know that we were "serious" about each other. Since she had not yet accepted my proposal to marry, I didn't have to ask Wilmer for his daughter's "hand in marriage." It was probably a good thing, considering that I was an unemployed skinny Texan, in an older, borrowed Volkswagen, not even finished with college, and a potential replacement for Hap Hornbostel of Beloit. It may have taken some persuasion by Helen, but her parents were gracious hosts. By the end of my two days in Appleton, the Rehbeins seemed to like me, and I was off to return the borrowed VW.

After delivering the VW to the Fosters in New York City, I returned to Philadelphia to close out my office in the Gimbel Building and help move the NSA staff to new office space near the University of Pennsylvania. I traveled to New York, Princeton, N.J., Washington, D.C., Chapel Hill, and Greensboro, North Carolina, communicating with Helen along the way. I made my best case for marriage in a letter dated September 27, 1958:

> To reiterate what I said in prior letter & last night (by phone), I want very much to marry you and for you to be my wife because I love you— respect you—have tremendous confidence in you—and for many, many reasons, which I know or don't know, but merely feel, and these feelings will grow ...

Apparently it worked, because in my next letter the issue was not *whether* we would get married, but *when* we would tie the knot. I wrote, "I find it hard to think in any terms other than getting married in December." In the second week of October, I flew from Philadelphia to Chicago where Helen was at a meeting for BH&G. We spent a day in Chicago and two days in Appleton to break the news to her parents and discuss a wedding; then we drove back to Des Moines. In the process, we decided to get married on December 6, 1957, in Appleton, before I entered the Air Force.

I returned to Wichita Falls on October 15 and immediately wrote to Helen about how great the five days were. My mother was in better health than usual and happy about my plans for marriage. I wrote in jest about one problem with mother:

The greatest shock and disappointment came with her criticism of the Democratic Party and continued support for Eisenhower. Woe is me!!

This effort at humor may have had a double purpose, since Helen was still a card-carrying Republican. With marriage, many changes would occur for both of us, one of which was Helen's political affiliation.

THE WEDDING AND RELATED TRAVELS

With the wedding fewer than two months away, we had many things to do. The first priority was to get some transportation, that is, a car. Neither Helen nor I had an automobile or the money to buy a new one. I hawked the used car lots of Wichita Falls and found a green 1954 Ford for $500. Perhaps the most distinctive thing about this "new" used car was the sound it made. It had pipes, rather than the usual muffler, and it would roar when accelerating and go "Pop! Pop! Pop!" when decelerating. I drew Helen a picture of the car in my letter of October 16, 1958. With a few bumps and grinds along the way, the "green monster of the road" lasted for the first five years of our marriage.

Another priority was Helen's teeth. Shortly before our decision to get married, her Des Moines dentist told her she had very soft teeth that were subject to cavities and would wear away in a few years—hopefully not because of grinding her teeth about me; it was a preexisting condition. The estimated cost of removing the outer portions of her teeth and replacing

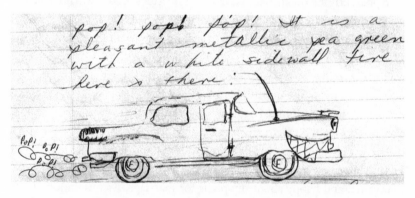

Author's drawing of the green 1954 Ford, Oct. 16, 1958, letter to Helen Rehbein

them with porcelain caps was several thousand dollars. I loved Helen, with or without good teeth. Fortunately, her parents paid for the extensive dental work prior to our marriage as their wedding gift for us. This meant several weeks of painful dental work in Des Moines during her last month and a half with BH&G; however, she had no significant dental problems thereafter.

Helen visited Wichita Falls November 8–9. The trip provided a number of "firsts," including her first trip to Wichita Falls (where we would live for the greater part of our marriage) and introduction to my mother, some family, and friends (none of whom could attend the wedding in Appleton). Although her dental work was in mid-stage, with a mouth full of temporary caps, it was a very successful trip. We bought our wedding rings in Wichita Falls and had them engraved.

The month in Wichita Falls was more productive than anticipated. I wrote many letters to Helen and made important plans for our married life. Considering how much I had been away from home, it was a good to spend some time with mother, rake leaves, help with home repairs, play racquetball and tennis with old friends, and read. Some of the books included *Look Homeward Angel* and *You Can't Go Home Again* by Thomas Wolfe, *Citizen Tom Payne* by Howard Fast, *Black Boy* by Richard Wright, and a book of plays by Paddy Chayevsky.

On November 19, I headed for Iowa in the green Ford, spending the night in Norman, Oklahoma, with my brother Jim and his family. With the help of Helen's roommates, we loaded the car in Des Moines and drove to Appleton, where I spent my 26th birthday on November 22 with Helen and her parents. We completed plans for the wedding that was to occur in two weeks. I then flew to North Carolina to chair a seminar for which I had raised money from the Ford Foundation while president of NSA. The subject of the meeting was "Student Responsibility," but my mind was turning to marital responsibility.

From North Carolina I flew to New York where I joined Allard Lowenstein, the best man for our wedding. I selected Al because he persuaded me to run for president of NSA. But for that additional year that took me to Des Moines, I would not have renewed my acquaintance with Helen. After spending the night at Al's parent's apartment in Manhattan, we started our 25-hour drive to Appleton. We drove straight through, stopping only for coffee, meals, and a visit with Eleanor Roosevelt at Chatham College in Pittsburgh.

Chatham is a women's college, and Mrs. Roosevelt was a guest lecturer in residence at the time. She was staying in one of the women's dormitories. It was dark by the time we arrived in Pittsburgh, and men could not enter the dormitory. Al sent word to Mrs. Roosevelt that we were there. She came out to Al's car and visited with us through the car window. Al was a longtime friend of Mrs. Roosevelt, and she was very cordial. I met her at Ohio Wesleyan, when she spoke to the NSA Congress, and another time when I presented

Allard Lowenstein with Mrs. Roosevelt at the NSA Congress, 1958

a certificate of appreciation for her work with NSA. She smoked a cigarette while we visited. I guess it was a habit she developed while married to FDR, though I don't recall ever seeing her smoke except on that occasion. After a 20-minute visit, we said good-by and drove off into the night toward Chicago and Appleton.

Although Al was Jewish, he learned all of the old Southern Baptist hymns while an undergraduate at the University of North Carolina at Chapel Hill. To stay awake, we sang "Shall We Gather at the River," "Just as I Am," "Jesus Loves Me," "Amazing Grace," and others. With the help of the Lord, Mrs. Roosevelt, and a lot of coffee, we made it to Appleton on December 3. This was the Rehbeins first opportunity to meet my best man. I don't know what their first impressions might have been, but like so many of us, they never forgot him.

Helen and I decided that the men in the wedding would wear dark blue suits, rather than tuxedos. Everyone had a dark blue suit but Al; he had a blue blazer, which he had outgrown. We went to one of the local men's clothing stores, and he purchased a new dark blue suit that fit considerably better than the blazer. Since Al went on to marry and was later elected to Congress, I presume he got some additional use of the Appleton dark blue suit.

One more Lowenstein story: Al always had several things going on at the same time. This constant activity led to the title of William H. Chafe's 1993 biography of Allard, *Never Stop Running*. At the time of our wedding, Al was preparing for a trip to South-West Africa (now Namibia), which was theoretically a protectorate of the United Nations but under the harsh control of South Africa. He was interested in recruiting a person with significant technical ability to assure safer travel in the undeveloped country. Helen's brother and possibly other persons suggested the name of Hap Hornbostel, the man formerly engaged to Helen. Hap was known for his excellent technical skills. Al was ready to drive to Beloit and find Hap one or two days before the wedding. Neither Helen nor I thought this was a good idea, first because of the possible conflict since she had been previously engaged to Hap, and second because we weren't sure that Al would get back in time for the wedding. We strongly discouraged his plan to recruit Hap on the eve of our wedding. Thankfully, he concurred with our wishes and got himself (and me) to the church on time.

The wedding was in the Appleton First Presbyterian Church, then located on the edge of downtown, adjoining the Lawrence University campus. The maid of honor was Jo Murray (now Harris) who worked with Helen at BH&G and became her best friend while in Des Moines. The bridesmaids were Sally Wilkinson Adams (Helen's best friend from Appleton School days) and Sally Benzies Bock (Helen's best friend while at the University of Wisconsin).

No member of my family could be present for the wedding. Jim Dalton,

December 6, 1958: The Wedding, First Presbyterian Church, Appleton, Wisconsin (left to right) Sally Adams, Sally Bock, Jo Murray, Helen & Ray, Al Lowenstein, George Rehbein, Jim Dalton, Bill Parsons, Don Hoffman

the only Texan attending, came from Chicago with his wife Tel. Jim and George Rehbein (Helen's brother) were my groomsmen. Don Hoffman (a former SBP at Madison and later an NSA president) and Bill Parsons were our ushers. I became acquainted with Don and Bill through NSA. Helen was a beautiful bride; the wedding and related parties went smoothly.

After the wedding, the Rehbeins had a reception for friends and relatives at the Conway Hotel. We made a quick getaway to avoid tin cans and horns as we fled Appleton for our first night as a married couple. After a brief chase by well-meaning friends, we drove north about 45 miles to a wonderful old lodge for our honeymoon. Although we had planned to spend two nights at the lodge, the Ford was overcome by the six-degree weather and wouldn't start. Also, Helen was not feeling well. Fortunately, she had a AAA membership that dispatched someone to start the car. We drove back to Appleton and commenced packing for the trip to the warmer climates of Texas.

The green Ford was loaded to the brim, and we were driving at night when a loud swooshing sound emerged from the car engine. I stopped the car, raised the hood, and tried to see what was wrong. Stupidly, I touched that part of the engine block making the noise. This dramatic gesture did not stop the swoosh, and I made a louder noise after blistering my finger. We soon swooshed down the highway to the next service station and asked them to check the engine. Although I feared the worst, the problem was minor. A loose spark plug had come out, and this accounted for the "swoosh" and my burnt finger. The mechanic put the plug back in, tightened three others, and we traveled on into the night.

After a good visit with my brother Jimmy and his family in Norman, Oklahoma, we drove to Wichita Falls before checking out housing in Dallas.

HONEYMOON IN DALLAS WITH
THE U.S. AIR FORCE

The U.S. Air Force ordered me to report to Hensley Field, Dallas, Texas, on December 26, 1958, for a six-month tour of active duty. Hensley was in Grand Prairie, across from the Dallas Naval Air Station. I anticipated my tour of active duty beginning earlier in December, so the twenty days between our wedding and reporting date gave us time to go to Dallas and lease an apartment, and return to Wichita Falls for Christmas.

We located an apartment on Marsalis Street in the Oak Cliff section of Dallas. The apartment was on the Grand Prairie side of Dallas and relatively close to downtown. As a bonus, it was within walking distance of the Dallas Zoo, and best of all, the rent fit the tight budget of a second lieutenant's monthly salary of $355.68. Since we had no furniture, we rented a furnished apartment. After moving into our "new home," exploring the byways to Hensley Field, and checking employment ads for Helen, we made it to Wichita Falls for the holidays.

This was Helen's first Christmas away from home, where the Rehbeins celebrated the holiday in a big way, with a large tree, many gifts, and lots of family and friends. Upon our arrival at 2313 9th in Wichita Falls, Helen found the opposite—no tree, no gifts, and very little family. Helen cried herself to sleep that night, but we were up in the morning, searching for a tree, buying gifts, and locating food for Christmas dinner. The trees were picked over by that time, but we found a scraggly one at the nearby A&P food store. With the old decorations from Christmases past and some newly purchased ones, the tree was presentable for Christmas Eve. Helen turned our Cratchit-like prospect into a very nice Christmas, and the size of the trees and number of gifts grew substantially in the years to follow.

After a good Christmas dinner, we drove back to Dallas to commence my tour of active duty and Helen's quest for employment. When I showed up at Hensley on December 26 in my blue uniform, bedecked with second lieutenant gold bars, only a few people were there to greet me, but I returned the salute of the enlisted men on duty and signed in. Although I was classified as an intelligence officer, no intelligence function existed at the base. As a result, I served as a training officer, when the need arose, and otherwise cooled my heels.

When it came to jobs, Helen had a more meaningful opportunity. She applied for an opening in the Women's News and Entertainment section of the *Dallas Times Herald*, emphasizing her experience at *Better Homes and Gardens,* her home economics degree, and her leadership skills at the University of Wisconsin. Vivian Castleberry, editor of the women's section, hired Helen, and the Farabee family was fully employed. Having only one car presented some logistical problems, but with the Dallas Public Transit buses and my pick-up services, it all worked out.

The six-month stay in Dallas was our real honeymoon—a good way to start married life. It was one of the few times in our lives without the pressure of academics, activities and family duties, or the stresses that came with law practice, politics, and leadership responsibilities. Movies, symphonies, and opera provided entertainment. We attended evening lectures at SMU, read books, and visited friends and my relatives in Dallas. Best of all, we had time to get to know each other in all the ways that letters and weekend visits did not provide.

Although she had limited journalism experience, Helen quickly learned the basics of daily newspaper writing, and it was not long until we saw her bylines in the *Dallas Times Herald*. One of the benefits of her job was free tickets to entertainment and cultural events, though Helen sometimes had to write reviews about them.

Despite the boredom of my Air Force work, or the lack thereof, the six months flew by quickly, and we were soon turning our thoughts to the summer and return to law school in September. Helen left the *Times Herald* with a strong letter of recommendation for potential employment in Austin. I left the USAF with new skills on how to operate a movie projector and teach driver's safety courses, together with orders to complete two weeks of active duty each year and attend monthly reserve meetings.

After leaving our winter clothes and other worldly possessions in Wichita Falls, we drove to the cooler climate of Wisconsin and spent an enjoyable three weeks in Appleton and at Lake Winneconne. We fished, and I learned, in a limited way, how to operate a motorboat. Helen made inquiries about employment in Austin, and we received word of an opening at UT for an assistant Dean of Women. Helen applied by mail, with a strong recommendation of the Dean of Women at the University of Wisconsin, and was hired, sight unseen, before we departed for Texas.

On our way back to Texas, we stopped in Ashton, Illinois, and visited with Helen's maternal grandmother, Ada Griffith. "Mother Griffith," as she was fondly known to her

*With Mother Griffith in Ashton,
Illinois, summer of 1959*

many grandchildren, was a wonderful, kind, and gentle person. She was unable to attend the wedding, and this trip was my first time to meet her. We got along well.

A NEW LIFE AT UT

We returned to Austin in August 1959 and searched for a place to live, locating a solid old duplex at 2828 San Gabriel where we lived the next two years. Short of furniture, we bought a new bed, converted Helen's twin bed from Des Moines to a couch, purchased some used items, and built bookshelves galore with cinder blocks and boards.

September 28, 1959, the Dallas Times Herald *headline*

Helen's new employment made head-lines in the Living section of the *Dallas Times Herald*, proclaiming, "Helen, Ray Farabee Begin New Life at UT," and we did. Helen was making enough money for us to get by, but I didn't feel right about her working and providing the total support. I considered applying for a job in the Austin offices of either Lyndon Johnson, then–U.S.

Working part-time for Senator Yarborough

Senate Majority Leader, or with Senator Ralph Yarborough. I knew both of the administrative assistants to the senators, and thought I could secure a job at either office.

It was my impression that Helen and I would come closer to having a life of our own, with opportunity to study law, if I worked for Yarborough. I did get a part-time job working for him that accommodated my law school class schedule. I read Texas newspapers every day, including weeklies like the *Tulia Herald* and *Kountz News,* and sent the senator several reports each week, with my analysis of the Texas news. I worked with other staff members when they were in town and handled constituent visits and office calls. On occasion, I drove the senator to various Texas cities and enjoyed visits with him.

Helen and I met the senator's wife, Opal Yarborough, who was a lovely person. She gave us some monkey grass that we planted in our yard on San Gabriel Street. Another person I met while working for Ralph Yarborough was William Wayne Justice, then a state district attorney in Athens, Texas. Justice was later appointed U.S. District Judge for the Eastern District of Texas and handed down monumental court decisions concerning Texas mental health, prisons, and desegregation. I came to know him better when I was General Counsel at the UT System. The details of his life and major court decisions are reported in *William Wayne Justice: A Judicial Biography* by Frank R. Kemerer, published by the University of Texas Press in 1991.

Helen enjoyed her work with the Dean of Women's office. Dorothy Gebauer was the Dean of Women, assisted by Margaret Peck and Helen Flynn. The building where Helen and the other deans worked was later named for Dean Gebauer. In addition to counseling students, Helen worked with sororities, the Panhellenic Council, and other women's activities. As in everything, she was very effective and popular. Carol Keeton Strayhorn, the former State Comptroller of Texas, recently told me that Helen was a role model for her as a student, mayor of Austin and state comptroller.

*Helen (second from left) with Deans Margaret Peck,
Dorothy Gebauer, and Helen Flynn, fall of 1960*

I introduced Helen to old friends, including Willie and Celia Morris, Bill and Mary Arnold, Bud and Joyce Mims, Jane Upton Howell, Harley Clark, the Osborns, and the Cookseys. We made new friends during the two years in Austin. George Rehbein, Helen's brother, did his tour of active duty with the Wisconsin Air National Guard in Texas and visited us. I came to know members of the UT Student Life staff better as Helen's husband than I did as a student leader during my undergraduate years.

Mark Howell, Jane Upton's husband, became one of my better friends during our last two years of law school. I did not know Mark before 1959. We spent more time with the Howells than any other couple, while in Austin for law school. Mark was from a distinguished El Paso family, a graduate of Stamford, my moot court partner, and a Republican. Over the course of our two years in law school and many political discussions, Mark became one of the more committed and ardent Democrats I have known. Mark and Jane returned to El Paso where he practiced law until his death in 1999.

The last two years of law school were more enjoyable than my first year, and my grades reflected it. Jim Cowles and I took the Bar examination during the last semester of our senior year. We compared our responses to the exam at the end

Hamburgers with Mark and Jane Howell at Married Student Housing, 1960

of each day, and many of Jim's answers differed from mine. I was convinced I had failed the exam, but we both passed with the same grade. I suppose it was our superior Wichita Falls reasoning that carried the day, rather than any specific answers. Remarkably, Cowles and I started public school together, played in a country western band, were college roommates, and graduated from law school at the same time in 1961. We remain close friends today.

The winter of 1960–1961 was an exciting time. Helen became pregnant with our first child. After considering several places, I decided to return to Wichita Falls when I graduated from law school in May 1961.

Helen's doctor recommended she avoid the strains of moving, and she traveled to Wichita Falls by airplane. I rented a trailer and Bill Arnold helped me load it with our limited earthly belongings. The 1954 green Ford and I pulled the U-Haul to Wichita Falls in early June 1961 to begin a new family life and law practice.

Return to Wichita Falls;
A New Family and New Life:
1961–1973

MOST PEOPLE GRADUATING from my high school in the 1950's did not return to their hometown of Wichita Falls after going away to college or working elsewhere for more than two years. I did, and it worked well for me, Helen, and our family. It is true that "you can't go home again" to the place of your past because nothing ever stays the same. Wichita Falls had changed while I was away. It was larger and more diverse, and major changes would occur during the 27 years we lived there.

From a personal point of view, I had also changed during the nine years I lived in Austin, Philadelphia, and Dallas. I had seen most of the United States, been involved with numerous work experiences, and received a good education from UT. At age 28, I was more mature, confident, and knowledgeable than when I left Wichita Falls for college in 1952. I was also married, about to become a father, and had my first job as a lawyer.

In this chapter I share some memories of family, friends, and community activities while living in Wichita Falls. Although I make references to my law practice, I devote the next chapter to recollections about that practice, some memorable cases, clients, and related Bar activities.

GETTING SETTLED AND STARTING A FAMILY

With Helen in her sixth month of pregnancy, finding a suitable place to live was important. We located a nice bungalow at 1935 Pawhuska in Wichita

Falls (off the Old Seymour Road in Indian Heights) and promptly rented it. It was close enough—but not too close—to my mother's home. Best of all, it was air conditioned, which helped Helen endure the heat of the Wichita summer and her last months of pregnancy.

Prior to starting my new job, I completed two weeks of active duty with the air force at Sheppard Air Force Base in Wichita Falls. This gave us access to the Base Exchange, where we bought dozens of diapers, a baby bed, and other things to begin our new life as parents.

Wichita Falls was a good place for a young attorney to begin the practice of law in 1961. I started with one of the best firms in the city: Jones, Parish, Fillmore, Rob-

Pregnant Helen at Pawhuska,
August 1961

inson & Lambert. The three senior partners were Harold Jones, a former mayor of Wichita Falls, Clyde Fillmore, a former district attorney and survivor of the Bataan Death March in World War II, and Elmer Parish, an outstanding civil defense lawyer and Democratic Party leader. Larry Robinson was a friend since Boy Scout days, and Larry Lambert was active in the community and the Methodist Church. All were able trial lawyers (primarily on the insurance defense side of the docket) and good mentors for a beginning attorney.

The most important focus of our life was the anticipated arrival of our first child in September. The baby arrived one or two weeks late, and it was a long hot summer for Helen. We went to classes at the Wichita General Hospital to learn how to hold the baby, change diapers, bathe him, and perform other necessary tasks. We bought books on the subject, including possible names for boys and girls, as we had no idea whether it would be a boy or girl. Helen knew it was an active critter, kicking her here and there, anxious to break out of the womb in the last several months of pregnancy. On the advice of the books, our pediatrician, and classes, we took long walks in the neighborhood. A few dogs were bothersome, and I was fearful that the child would have a phobia about dogs (which was not the case).

Helen began to experience labor pains around 2 or 3 a.m. on September 17, 1961. We made a classic rush to the hospital in the green Ford, with visions of having to deliver the baby on the way. Our anxieties were for naught; the baby didn't arrive until 10 or 11 a.m. I had ample time to do all of the expected preliminary activities, including advising grandparents of the imminent arrival, checking in briefly at the law office, buying cigars, and pacing the floor after Helen was taken into the delivery room. (Fathers weren't allowed in the delivery room at that time.)

After what seemed like hours of extended labor, for both me and Helen, the baby arrived. It was a boy! We had settled on the name of Steven Ross for a boy. "Ross" was the name of someone in Helen's maternal lineage that went back to colonial days (but not Betsy Ross!), and "Steven" just sounded good.

Helen's mother, Myra Rehbein, came from Appleton to help for the first week or two. Annie Lee gave plenty of advice. After a few days in the hospital, which was then customary, baby Steven and mother Helen came home to 1935 Pawhuska. Edna and Jack Rice lived next door on Pawhuska. Edna had several children, and her help was probably the most relevant as we adjusted to the rigors of early child care. Although the advice of family and friends was helpful, there is nothing like "on the job training," and we got plenty of it—24 hours a day, seven days a week for the first months.

What an interesting time to start a family. Helen, like most mothers, did not work outside the home during early childhood development. The availability of child care services was limited. Diapers were cloth, not the disposable paper products, which interestingly were being developed by Kimberly Clark near Appleton and would soon replace the cloth ones. A diaper service came every two days, picking up a can of dirty diapers and returning clean ones. The milkman delivered the milk every day or two in glass bottles, gathering the empty ones for recycle, before we knew the meaning of the word. Steve drank

Helen and Baby Steve, April 1962

his share of milk and used lots of diapers, and I changed my share of his diapers when I was home from work.

FIRST HOUSE AND SECOND CHILD

After practicing law and living in our rented house on Pawhuska for about a year, we started thinking about purchasing a home. Though the law firm gave me a raise after the first year, our income was still limited. Credit cards, as we know them now, had not been invented—no Visa or MasterCard. We did have a revolving Sears credit card that paid for the bountiful German Christmases, children's clothing, and appliances. Other stores sold on credit, and the banks handled short-term loans for consumer items such as furniture and cars, but the Farabee family lived conservatively. We owed little and devoted only a small part of our budget to interest payments.

We looked at homes for sale in various parts of the city. Some were too expensive, others not big enough or near a school that we thought best for our children (though we had only one child at the time). We finally found a house that we could afford and met our expectations. It was an older frame house located on Hayes Street. But there was a problem; we didn't have the money for the required down payment. My senior partner Harold Jones helped by pledging a savings account to secure our obligation for the 20% down payment, and we purchased our first home.

1413 Hayes was a typical American bungalow house, similar to many throughout the Floral Heights and Southland additions in Wichita Falls. In some ways it was like 2313 Ninth, where I was born and raised, but larger,

First House—1413 Hayes, Wichita Falls

located on a tree-lined red brick street, and not as busy as 9th Street. The house was originally built in 1927. A former owner named Jim Allison built a two-story addition on the back of the house, which provided a second bathroom, a family room, and an office/bedroom upstairs. Like many houses in the area, 1413 Hayes had some history. Jim Allison, an early publisher of the *Record News,* was a longtime owner. Allison sold the *Record News* to the Howard family, which owned the *Wichita Falls Daily Times.* The merged papers are now the *Wichita Falls Times Record News,* owned by the Scripps Syndicate.

Similar to 2313 9th, the house on Hayes had a large front porch and double garage with an attached small apartment that once served as a "servants' quarters" for the main house. As Helen became more active in the community, we rented the apartment for little or no money, with the understanding that the tenant, usually a college student, would be available for babysitting services. Shortly after we moved into 1413 Hayes, Helen became pregnant with our second child, and we needed more babysitting services.

During the five years we lived on Hayes, we entertained new friends we met through law practice, community activities, and Sheppard Air Force Base. Helen and I repainted much of the interior, and I scraped and repainted the outside of the house. Though a lawyer, I became a pretty good house painter, gardener, and repairman.

On February 5, 1964, our second child, David Lee Farabee, was born at Wichita General Hospital. Helen's pregnancy and delivery were less dramatic than the first time around. No barking dogs, except our own (Mimi), and David arrived right on schedule. No need for another parents' training course. I was highly experienced at changing dirty diapers. In our discussion

Steven and his new little brother, David Lee, June 1964

of possible names for the second child, I suggested the name "Chandra" if it was a girl. Helen vetoed that idea, but it was a non-issue since we followed the Jack and Annie Lee tradition of spawning only male children.

David was a good baby. He had red hair as a child, which perhaps explains an ill-temper toward his older brother during the early years! A better explanation could be found in sibling rivalry and having to wear Steve's hand-me-down clothes. After ten or fifteen years they got along much better and are now best friends.

SUMMER VACATIONS AND
CHRISTMASES IN WISCONSIN

We were fortunate to spend at least two weeks each summer in the cooler climates of Wisconsin with Helen's family. As the children grew older, Helen and the kids drove up for the whole month of August, and I would join them for the last two weeks. With this pattern, Steven and David came to know their Wisconsin grandparents much better, and the Rehbeins became better acquainted with their Farabee grandchildren.

In the early years, we drove 20 hours from Wichita Falls to Appleton, stopping only for gasoline, meals, and restrooms. This was before the interstate highway system, so getting around St. Louis, Chicago, and Milwaukee was torturous, particularly without air-conditioning.

Helen would purchase a sack full of puzzles and games at Gibson's Discount Store, which would occupy the boys until Lawton (about 50 miles) or Oklahoma City (100 miles). From then on, except for sleep time, it was mediation of numerous disputes between Steve and Dave. Sometimes Helen would invent clever games like who could identify the most out-of-state license tags or counting billboards and farm animals. When all else failed, we separated the kids—one in the front seat and the other in back. However, this usually led to arguments as to who would sit in the front and who would sit in the back, which then fostered the doctrine of periodic rotation.

When we finally arrived in Appleton, the trauma and stress of the 1200-mile trip with the "Katzenjammer Kids" (comic strip characters from the 1930's) and their sibling rivalries proved worth it. It was cool, both in temperature and lack of hometown stress. We quickly embraced the good-

Supper with the Rehbeins at Lake Winneconne, August 1966

natured way of the Badger State and its people. Appleton was a model small Midwestern city. Its economy seldom fluctuated, the crime rate was low, and Lawrence University provided intellectual stimulation. Prange's, W. A. Close, and Treasure Island were our favorite shopping places, and you couldn't beat George's Piano Bar or the Yacht Club on the Fox River for dinner and drinks.

More important than Appleton—at least for us—was the fun, solitude, and good times the family had at the Rehbein cottage on Lake Winneconne. The kids learned to fish and water ski. Corn on the cob, fresh out of the Wisconsin fields, and homegrown tomatoes with fried perch freshly caught out of the lake was standard fare.

The Rehbeins had two aluminum boats, both powered by outboard motors. I bought the first of several boats for my kids—a green canoe. The boys enjoyed water skiing, and the next boats were a progression to bigger and better ski boats for the lakes around Wichita Falls and finally for Austin's nearby lakes. Steve became an expert water skier and captain of the UT Water Ski Club. He was nationally ranked among collegiate water skiers while at UT, and it all began at Lake Winneconne.

As the boys grew older, the 1200-mile trip became easier: no arguments between the kids, the highways and bypasses had been greatly improved, our cars were air-conditioned, and had good sound systems. We were also more likely to stop along the way to visit friends or see the sights, making the trip more pleasant. We spent some of our Christmases in Appleton. White Christmases are few and far between in Wichita Falls, but Wisconsin nearly always has snow and frozen lakes. There was always a big tree, lots of gifts, and a fire in the fireplace. Uncle George Rehbein had a snowmobile. With the lake frozen over, Winneconne is a different place in the winter, and the boys and I learned to snowmobile across the lake and along forest trails. Although I now have some doubts about the environmental and aesthetic impact of snowmobiles, it was good family fun at the time.

1512 BUCHANAN: THE MARTIN-FARABEE HOUSE

On February 25, 1968, Helen and I purchased the house on two Wichita Falls lots known as 1512 Buchanan, which I will sometimes refer to as "1512." We wanted a larger home with a bigger yard in the same neighborhood and grade school area as 1413 Hayes. Fifteen-twelve fit the bill and our budget.

A wonderful old house, 1512 Buchanan was built in 1924 by Wichita Falls attorney Bernard Martin and his wife Ada Belle. They lived in the house until Bernard died in June 1967. Helen and I lived there until April 1988 when we moved to Austin; my son David, his wife Terri, and their family have lived there since then. David and Terri have restored much of 1512 to its original condition. Since only Martins and Farabees have lived there during its 80-year history, 1512 is known as the Martin-Farabee Home.

A lot of Wichita Falls and Texas history is associated with the Martin-Farabee house. Some of the more notable persons who have been guests at 1512 include: Texas Governors Dan Moody, James V. Allred, Mark White, and Ann Richards; U.S. Senators Lyndon B. Johnson when he was Majority Leader of the U.S. Senate (before he became president), and Ralph Yarborough; many judges including U.S. District Judges Fritz Lanham and Barefoot Sanders; authors J. Frank Dobie, Walter Prescott Webb, and James Hoggard; Lt. Governor Bill Hobby; more than 50 years' of state senators representing the district that includes Wichita Falls (Ben G. O'Neal [Martin's law partner], George "Cotton" Moffett, Jack Hightower, and myself); and actress-dancer-singer Mary Martin, Bernard Martin's first cousin. On several occasions, Mary Martin danced on the terrazzo front porch.

The Martins did little to 1512 during the last 20 years of their lives.

Though in good structural condition, it needed paint and some modernization. The Martins never burned coal, but 1512 has a coal shoot and had a cast iron coal furnace that was converted for use of natural gas. A good duct system existed for the heat, but there was no central air-conditioning. Our first investment was the installation of a modern central air and heating system. When the contractor observed the antiquated gas heating system, he declared that he would not spend a single night there—though the Martins had survived fine for more than 40 years. We didn't take any chances and said good-by to the coal furnace, though 1512 may have been the only house in Wichita Falls with a coal shoot.

The interior of the house, with its thick plaster on lath walls, king cornices, and 10-foot ceilings, had not been painted for 20 years. Before moving in, Helen, the kids, and I would go to 1512 after work; for several weeks we repainted most of the walls and ceilings. Ada Belle Martin had put very expensive sculptured wool rose carpet throughout most of the house. The rose-colored wall-to-wall carpet covered a wonderful oak hardwood floor. Although the carpet was still in good condition after 30 years, Helen didn't like it but concluded that it would never wear out. Over the first year or two, we replaced the Martin's carpet. To their credit, David and Terri have restored the hardwood floors. The kitchen was by far the most antiquated part of the house, and we modernized it, with Helen painting the old cabinets in an attractive antique blue; her painting was the subject of an article in the local paper.

The Martin-Farabee House at 1512 Buchanan, Wichita Falls

In 1958 I observed a home library that belonged to a Princeton professor. Since then I had dreamed of having such a library in my own home. The room adjoining our master bedroom on the second floor was the perfect space for an office/library, with a fireplace and a door to an outdoor porch, which we later converted to a greenhouse. A cabinetmaker lined two walls with bookshelves, cabinets, and desk spaces. I stained and varnished the new cabinetry, quickly filling the bookshelves and realizing my dream. I have maintained the dream with multiple bookshelves in my Austin home.

The garage apartment for 1512 Buchanan was larger than the one on Hayes Street. Like so many of the houses in West Floral Heights, it was once a true servants quarters. There were bells connected to the main house, including one on the floor under the dining room table, which would bring help from the servants quarters when needed. Different people who lived in the garage apartment during our tenure would help with our children and the house. Ruth Pearson occupied the quarters for the longest amount of time and was very helpful with the children as Helen became more active in state and national mental health advocacy. When Steve was old enough, he moved into the apartment and occupied it until he went to college.

David and Terri lived in the apartment during the first year of their marriage, while finishing their degrees at Midwestern. Abe Lemmons lived in the garage apartment before our time while a student at Hardin College (now Midwestern State University); he went on to become head basketball coach at Pan American University, UT Austin, and then Oklahoma City University.

Our children quickly developed friends in the neighborhood, and 1512 was the gathering place for boys to think up all kinds of creative ideas and mischief. Once, Steve, Dave, and Kyle Brown from across the street dug a cave in the Burlisons' shrubbery, which was not wholly appreciated by the Burlisons or their shrubs. Numerous football and

Steve flying through the air with the greatest of ease, 1973

baseball games occurred on the Brown's vacant lot across the street. At times Steve devised ramps for flying through the air on his bicycle; he later perforated our new fence with homemade Chinese throwing stars (four-pointed pieces of sheet metal). Fortunately, he did not perforate his brother or any neighborhood children. At one point the boys laid out a putting course on the new green carpet in our spacious living room for their neighborhood friends to improve their golfing skills. Steve and Dave learned to ride their first bicycles on Buchanan and purchased their first automobiles while living there.

After Helen's death, I gifted the Martin-Farabee Home to my sons. David later purchased Steve's interest. David and Terri's three children have grown up at 1512, just as Steve and Dave did. Although rare these days, it is special to have my children and grandchildren attend the same schools I attended, that is, Zundelowitz Junior High and Wichita Falls High School. Some of my happier moments have been walking the neighborhood with my grandchildren and telling them about my paper routes and boyhood experiences.

WICHITA FALLS FRIENDS

During my lifetime, I have had a number of closer friends that come within the poetic definition of Guy Clark's song *Old Friends*. They "shine like diamonds . . . you can always call [them] . . . Lord you can't buy 'em." Some I have mentioned in earlier chapters and others will be discussed later. The several friends I write about here are those who come to mind who were in Wichita Falls during part or all of our 1961–1988 years. They were often guests in our home, and we also visited in theirs. Some were clients, lawyers, doctors, educators, or just "old friends"—but always persons with whom we could have substantive conversations, share thoughts, and always count on. Some are deceased, and most have moved elsewhere. Nevertheless, I still communicate with those who are alive.

Larry and Lynn Robinson come to mind first. They were the first couple to invite us for dinner in Wichita Falls, even before we were married. We frequently visited in their home after our return. Larry was my law partner and mentor, and I am the godfather to their son Edward. One memorable experience was when Larry introduced me to Willie Nelson and his music. Willie was not at the height of his fame when he played the Cavalier Club in Wichita Falls, but Larry was quick to recognize genius in both trial lawyers and country western singers. Unfortunately, Larry was killed in a small plane crash in Hot Springs, Arkansas, on October 7, 1968, with three of his clients. I was a pallbearer at his funeral and co-trustee, with Larry Lambert, of a trust for Lynn and Edward.

Skipper Truly, one of the Westerners, was another old friend who returned to Wichita Falls about the same time we did. He and his wife Janelle rented the house next door to us on Hayes Street. Skipper went to work for the local school district teaching English at Reagan Jr. High.

Skipper Truly, 1934–1972

He loved teaching and wanted to be a writer. We spent many hours visiting with the Trulys, talking into the night about authors and novels we were reading at the time. Skip served as Santa Claus for the neighborhood, and thrilled our children before they became more skeptical about Santa's existence.

When Skipper was in his third year of teaching, he began experiencing blackouts. The medical diagnosis was a mild form of epilepsy. The school district terminated his contract because of his condition. It would have been an easy disability to accommodate, but no Americans with Disabilities Act existed then. Another good teacher was lost. Skipper had difficulty getting a job because of his disability, and finally worked as a tutor and television repairman. In the early 70's, Skipper died of a massive brain hemorrhage at the Truly ranch, where he and his family then lived. The Westerners reassembled and served as pallbearers. Skipper is buried on the ranch in Clay County.

Don and Mary Morgan became good friends during our early years in Wichita Falls. Both were from Austin, and Don's first lawyer job was with a prominent plaintiff's firm in Wichita Falls. The Morgans' children were about the same age as ours, and our families spent many hours together. Don and I regularly drank coffee and discussed a multitude of issues on

Sunday mornings in the kitchen of the Hayes Street house while our wives took the children to Sunday school. The Sunday coffee klatches seemed to meet our spiritual needs at the time. Don and Mary moved to Galveston County to practice law. He was later elected as a District Judge there. Don administered my oath of office for Governor of Texas in 1985 while I was President Pro Tem of the Texas Senate. By sheer coincidence Don and Mary lived only two blocks from us in Austin. Don passed away in 2007.

John and Olivia Reusing became good friends in 1962. John was in the Air Force at Sheppard when I first met him through a political campaign by Judge Graham Purcell for the U.S. congressional seat for our district. John was a bright, articulate, and outspoken Pennsylvania native. Fellow campaign workers did not know what to make of John, but he was a dedicated Democrat and a hard-working volunteer. The very things that worried some people, appealed to me. As I think about it, this was frequently the case with some of our new friendships in Wichita Falls. John finished his degree at Midwestern University and took a job as the tennis coach and government teacher at a local high school. He was an excellent tennis coach and teacher, but his outspoken nature led to the non-renewal of his teaching contract. He and his wife Olivia moved to Washington, D.C., where he became a successful lobbyist, but true to the pattern, he offended some and moved back home to Reading, Pennsylvania. We remained good friends until his death from cancer in 2000.

Because of Helen's involvement with the local mental health association, we met several psychiatrists at Sheppard Air Force Base (SAFB), which had one of the major psychiatric units for that branch of the service. Two of them and their families became closer friends. Richard and Ellen Marks were from New York. Richard and I played tennis, and we came to know them well before they completed their tour of active duty and returned to Manhattan. They invited us to visit them at Martha's Vineyard, and we were their guests when we took our children to New York City.

Paul Cantalupo was the other SAFB psychiatrist who became a good friend. On the Christmas Eve that Paul became engaged to wife Ellen, we were the first to know and share the good news. We stayed with the Catalupos at their home in Bellaire, California, on several occasions, including Helen's choice of Los Angeles and the Cantalupos for the celebration of her 50th birthday.

Dr. Blair Coleman and his wife Jane became closer friends after our return to Wichita Falls. We spent many of our New Years Eve's at parties in the Coleman's home. Blair, an excellent cardiologist and internist, was my first family physician. He has a great appreciation for opera, and between Helen and Blair, I learned to appreciate opera. Blair is now retired, but I still visit with him and his present wife Ann when in Wichita Falls.

Three other couples who became good friends during the Wichita Falls years were Jerry and Dolores Fox, Herb and Randy Apple, and Don and Ceil Waldrip. Jerry Fox was the City Manager for Wichita Falls during most of the years we were there. Herb was president of Industrial Development Incorporated (IDI), successor to the chamber of commerce, and responsible for many of the new businesses that located in Wichita Falls during the time we were there. Don Waldrip was Superintendent of the Wichita Falls Independent School District (WFISD). I did legal work for IDI and the WFISD.

Jerry Estes and Ray Clymer, two other clients, became good friends. Jerry was president of North Texas Federal Savings and Loan Association (NTFS&L). Jerry died in 2006, and I spoke about our friendship and his meaningful life at a memorial gathering in Bastrop, where he and his wife Claudia moved after retirement, and another service in Wichita Falls. Ray Clymer was president of Dennison Poultry and Egg Company, d/b/a Golden Distributing Company. I write more about Jerry and Ray in the next two chapters concerning my law practice and the State Senate.

ANNIE LEE, JIMMY, AND EDWIN DURING THE WICHITA FALLS YEARS

My brother Edwin lived at 2313 9th with my mother much of the time between 1961 and his death in 1972. Jimmy and his family lived in Norman, Oklahoma; they visited on holidays and other occasions. When problems occurred with Mother or Edwin, the responsibility to help fell to Helen and me, as it should. The last ten or twelve years of their lives presented some difficult times, as well as good memories.

As mother grew older, her tuberculosis became inactive, but she continued to experience respiratory problems. Despite poor health, she thrived on taking care of Edwin and showering her new grandchildren with love.

Mother's driving did not improve with age. We would take the children to her home, or she would come by for visits with them. She was not deterred from driving until she backed from her driveway into another car on 9th Street. No one was hurt, and it didn't cause much damage to either car; however, she didn't have liability insurance. Although this was unfortunate for the person she backed into, it resolved a problem we were dreading. She had no resources to repair her car or that of the other driver. The law took her driver's license and solved a problem that confronts many as their parents get older.

Edwin had a serious drinking problem. This condition contributed to the divorce with his second wife, Louise, and difficulty in holding jobs. The most traumatic experiences for me, and Edwin, were the two occasions on which I had to commit him to the Wichita Falls State Hospital Alcoholism Treatment Unit. The unit was crowded and had the stigma of mental illness, though his commitment was for an addiction problem. The Sheriff's Office would send a couple of deputies to take him before the court and on to the State Hospital. It was humiliating to him and extremely painful for me, but four weeks at the State Hospital would dry him out. He was angry for several months after each release, but the anger passed and our friendship grew.

*Edwin and daughter
Suzanne, 1960*

Later on, Edwin went on a "toot" to Mexico in his old Studebaker, a popular car in the 1940's and 50's. He made it to Mexico, tanked up on tequila, ran his car in a ditch on the way back, and broke his neck. With better luck than Leroy had and Jimmy would later have, Edwin recovered, except for a loss of feeling in his left little finger. He spent several weeks in a South Texas jail for DWI, after being released from the hospital in a neck brace.

Edwin's trials and tribulations should not detract from his better qualities. He was a good dental technician and machinist. I have no doubt that the environmental hazards of each of those jobs, together with a pack of cigarettes a day, caused his emphysema and demise. I came to know Edwin much better during the last several years of his life. He came to the

Buchanan Street house often, and we had long visits. He was a reader, and we shared thoughts about books we were reading and national events.

In August 1969 Brother Jimmy was returning to Norman from Kansas, where he had been working. It was late at night, and he either fell asleep at the wheel, or a steering problem occurred. The pickup truck ran into a ditch and Jimmy received a serious blow to his head. Someone found him the next morning and took him to a small hospital in rural Kansas. After additional hospitalization in Norman, he returned home but continued to experience intensive headaches. A month after the accident he became unconscious and was rushed to St. Anthony Hospital in Oklahoma City, where his condition was diagnosed as an acute subdural hematoma. He underwent neurosurgery to his head and was unconscious for nearly a month.

Annie Lee and Jimmy, circa 1964

Each week we traveled to Oklahoma City with Mother to visit Jimmy in the intensive care unit and discuss his condition with his wife, Jo Dell. As Jimmy slowly regained consciousness, it became apparent that he had sustained serious brain damage from the hematoma. After several months of hospitalization in Norman and rehabilitation therapy in Denver, Jimmy returned home to Norman. He had no short-term memory capability. Jimmy's wife could not take care of him because she had to work to support their family. He was placed in the Veteran's Hospital in Norman where he stayed until his death in 1986.

We periodically visited Jimmy at the veteran's hospital. He could recognize Mother, me, his wife, and his older daughter, but not his youngest child or Helen. The conversations were limited because he could not remember anything said for more than 20 or 30 seconds. Our visits were important, even though Jimmy would never remember them; his condition took its toll on Mother, but she found solace in continuing to care for Edwin.

On October 24, 1972, prompted by a downturn in Edwin's condition, Mother asked me to come and persuade him to enter the hospital. I responded immediately, but he refused to go. He was embarrassed that he was unable to pay his last hospital bill for the broken neck. I assured him something could be worked out, but to no avail. Then I suggested that our Cousin Billie Redd, the registered nurse who helped deliver me, take a look at him and determine whether he needed hospitalization. He agreed, and asked me to prop him up and light his cigarette. I did so, but it was his last. By the time I returned with Billie, he was deceased. He had died from lung failure.

After the funeral, Annie Lee was at home alone. Although we visited and checked on her frequently, Mother became more depressed, and her physical condition deteriorated. Within a month she quit eating and complained that everything she ate nauseated her. In another month she was in the hospital, though the doctor could not find anything wrong other than the conditions that had plagued her life for so many years. By January 1973 she was so weak that her doctor recommended placing her in a skilled care nursing home, which we did. Helen or I visited her in the nursing home nearly every day. We both witnessed the steady decline, not only in her health but also her consciousness. Fed with tubes, she could barely speak or recognize us by the end of February.

While in Austin with Helen at a school law conference, I received a call from Dr. Ben Huckaby advising that my mother's condition had worsened and she would not likely recover. As a good physician should, Ben asked whether I wanted him to take additional measures, although death appeared inevitable. I inquired what might be done, and he explained a procedure for draining her lungs. I said, "Do whatever you can and we'll be home immediately." Mother survived, but three weeks later the same circumstance arose, and I rushed to the nursing home. Mother was unconscious, her life maintained by a series of tubes and artificial feeding. Death was imminent. I made the decision that further heroic efforts were no longer appropriate, and Annie Lee Farabee passed away on March 30, 1973.

As I review the clippings, pictures, and recollections about Edwin, Jimmy, and Mother, it strikes me, and probably anyone reading this, that there was a lot of sadness involved. Some may ask why I write about it. The best answer I can give is to recount the many good memories and to recognize the importance of knowing the truth and facts about illness—whether physical or mental—or self-destructive addictions. I don't think we can know as much about life—its failures and successes—unless we experience and know something about family problems and death. It's all a part of life.

COMMUNITY INVOLVEMENT AND ACTIVITIES

We became involved in the community more quickly than most young people who had either returned or who never left the city. This was true even though we never belonged to the country club, dance clubs, or some of the more traditional organizations.

One of the first groups I joined was the Southwest Rotary Club. Not as large or prestigious as the Downtown Rotary Club, the Southwest Club was comprised of good men, including an old friend and professor, A. F. Edwards, who taught my Texas government and history courses at Midwestern during the summer of 1953. I admired Rotary and its international programs. My father-in-law, a member of the Appleton Rotary, generously paid my dues for the club during the first two years of my membership. I was elected president of the club for 1965–1966 and maintained a long period of perfect attendance before the commitments of the State Senate made it impractical to continue membership.

Helen and I participated in a Great Issues study group, which met one evening each week at the Kemp Public Library. It was similar to the Great Books discussion groups but focused on reading and discussion of contemporary issues of politics, economics, and social values.

Both Helen and I attended concerts sponsored by the North Texas Civic Music Association and the Wichita Falls Symphony Orchestra. I was elected to the Board of the Civic Music in 1963 and later served as a Board member and Vice President of the Wichita Falls Symphony. Helen was an officer of the Symphony Women's League. We purchased season tickets to the Symphony soon after our return to Wichita Falls and attended most of the concerts throughout the time we lived in Wichita Falls. I still contribute to the Wichita Falls Symphony annual fund drive.

I quickly re-involved myself with the local YMCA, playing handball and joining its service organization, the Y's Men's Club. It was the first organization of which I was elected president after returning to Wichita Falls. All of its members were younger, as compared to those of Rotary. I knew some

Wayne Alison, myself, and Glynn Purtle Y's Men Presidents, 1963–1965

of the members when I joined, met others, and conscripted a few new ones, including fellow attorney Tom Huckaby.

Our club was invited to attend the 1964 annual YMCA meeting, and being members of the Y, we had a vote. Two YMCA buildings existed in Wichita Falls: the Central YMCA for white members and its branch on the East Side for African Americans. Men from various old families and businesses comprised the Board of the Y. These men were all white, except for perhaps one black member. I don't remember any persons of color attending the annual meeting. After the usual program and reports on the Y for the past year, the chairman of its board asked if there was other business to come before the meeting. Tom Huckaby stood and made a motion that the Wichita Falls YMCA, Central and East Side, desegregate and eliminate all discrimination based on race. The room became very quiet; the chairman then asked if there was a second to the unexpected motion. Again, a moment of silence. It appeared that Tom's motion would die for the lack of a second. I stood and seconded the motion, telling of my high school experiences at integrated Y meetings and the unequivocal position of the National and International YMCA against discrimination based on race. With little or no discussion, someone moved to postpone consideration of the motion, which passed on a voice vote.

The Y Board quietly eliminated all discrimination based on race about two months later. I would like to think it was because of the Y's Man's motion, but the U.S. Air Force policy against discrimination, as articulated by the Commanding General at Sheppard Air Force Base, was probably more determinative. SAFB was a major contributor to the United Way, which helped fund the Y. However, the Y's Men, particularly Tom Huckaby, got the ball rolling. I only regret that I did not make the motion myself, and I would be ashamed of myself to this day had I not seconded it.

Helen became increasingly active in the community as the children were out of the cradle, and we had available child care. Because of her counseling experience as Assistant Dean of Women at UT, Helen selected the local mental health association as her principle volunteer effort. She was barely involved before they elected her as vice president of the Wichita County Mental Health Association. Shortly afterward, the president of the local Association moved to Houston and Helen became president. As president of the local Association, she instituted new programs serving the community and the Wichita Falls State Hospital (now the North Texas Mental Hospital: Wichita Falls Campus). Helen then became active in the statewide Texas Mental Health Association and served as its president on two different occasions for a total of four years prior to her death. She was also vice president of the National Mental Health Association.

Both Helen and I were frequently asked to speak to various community groups and participate on panels at Midwestern State University. In May 1964 I delivered the commencement address to graduating seniors at Wichita Falls Senior High, the school where I graduated 14 years earlier. My topic was "Commitments for Commencement." The speech seemed to be well received.

Helen's name was suggested for membership in the local Junior League, but she was not selected, reportedly because several members thought she was "too liberal." This was ironic because she later delivered programs to the group and served on its advisory board.

I became active in politics after my return to Wichita Falls—not by running for political office, but by working in campaigns and the local Democratic Party. My law firm asked me to help Judge Graham Purcell in his runoff race for Congress in January 1961. I worked half-days and weekends for a month, and Purcell won. Later I was the county campaign coordinator for several statewide candidates including Franklin Spears (a friend and former Student Body President at UT then running for Attorney General), Barefoot Sanders (another former SBP at UT, running against John Tower for U.S. Senate), U.S. Senator Ralph Yarborough, and Bill Hobby, who was running for Lieutenant Governor. Spears and Sanders lost, though they carried Wichita County. Spears was later elected to the Texas Supreme Court, and Sanders appointed United States District Judge for the Northern District of Texas. Yarborough and Hobby won Wichita County and their statewide races.

My political work for Yarborough in his campaign for reelection to the U.S. Senate was not popular in some segments of the community. His opponent was George Herbert Walker Bush, then a former Republican Texas congressman. I didn't know that Bush would later become Vice President and the 41st President of the United States. Even if I had known, I still

Farabee Family for Franklin Spears (r), 1968

would have helped Senator Yarborough, as a matter of loyalty and respect for him. I will write more about politics, elections, and Bill Hobby in the chapters about my own campaign and service in the State Senate.

The first and only elective office I held, prior to the State Senate, was in my Wichita Falls neighborhood. At the request of County Democratic Chair Prof Edwards, I ran for Democratic Chairman of Precinct 22 in 1970. Contrary to what Prof predicted, there was another candidate. Francis Harvey, a friend and neighbor, was nominated. I won by one or two votes and served in the position for the next two years. Helen helped me run the Democratic Primary elections. At that time, everyone from the courthouse to the state house, except Wichitan U.S. Senator John Tower, was a Democrat, and nearly everyone voted in the Democratic Primaries, rather than the Republican ones.

Precinct 22 (now 40) in Wichita County has an interesting history. As reported in Robert Ripley's *Believe It or Not,* the four persons receiving the most votes in the 1934 Texas primaries and general election lived in Precinct 22: James V. Allred, Tom Hunter, and Charles C. McDonald (Democrats) and Grover Bullington (Republican). Allred won in a runoff election with Tom Hunter and beat Bullington (John Tower's father-in-law) in the general election.

Governor Allred's widow, Jo Betsy, lived two blocks from us on Hayes Street, and she voted, with her aged mother Daisy Miller, in our precinct elections. Helen related the following story while running the precinct elections for me: Daisy was nearly blind and deaf. Jo Betsy was allowed to help her mother vote. Mrs. Allred loudly explained the ballot to her mother and all could hear. An incumbent candidate for reelection that year was Warren G. Harding (not kin to the former President). When Jo Betsy got to the state comptroller candidates, she read their names loudly, and Daisy said in an equally loud voice, "I remember Warren G. Harding; I think he was President. Cast my ballot for Harding!"

When David Farabee was born, Mrs. Allred gave us a check for $3 as a gift for the new baby. We were so proud to have a check signed by the former Texas First Lady that we never cashed it. Her bank account may have been out of balance for the remainder of her life. She was a good neighbor and wonderful lady. I later served with her son David Allred in the Legislature, and my son David currently serves in the same State Representative position.

Despite my Democratic ways, I was appointed to the board of directors of Texas Bank & Trust in Wichita Falls in June 1971. Netum Steed was appointed to the bank board at the same time. Netum, very successful in the oil and gas business, had served as the Republican County Chair. We became good friends while on the board, and he supported me in my campaign for election to the State Senate.

In January 1977 I was elected to the Board of Directors of North Texas Federal Savings and Loan Association (NTFS&L). I had performed legal services for NTFS&L for several years prior to my appointment to the board. I served on the bank and savings and loan association boards until we moved to Austin in 1988.

The volunteer activity of which I am proudest is my work in founding Wichita Falls Education Translator (WFET), a nonprofit corporation that owned and operated KIDZ-TV. Wichita Falls had no public broadcast station prior to KIDZ-TV. During a spirited campaign by the local television stations to keep cable television out of our city, KAUZ-TV started broadcasting *Sesame Street*. When the TV stations won, KAUZ dropped the popular children's program. I did legal work for KAUZ-TV, and Bill Hobbs, the KAUZ station manager, suggested bringing Dallas KERA-TV by translator for re-broadcast in Wichita Falls.

I contacted KERA-TV in Dallas, and it agreed to furnish its signal to Wichita Falls, without cost. However there were several problems—KERA had no funds for purchasing a transmitter, hiring an engineer, or providing building and tower space needed for retransmitting the KERA signal.

We organized WFET as a Texas nonprofit corporation and elected officers and a board of directors. I was elected president and Tuck Harvey secretary. I did the legal work to qualify WFET as a 501(c)(3) with the Internal Revenue and secure an FCC license. We raised the necessary funds to equip and pay operating costs. KAUZ-TV donated tower space and land for the transmitter and equipment. My client W P Howle Brick Contractor and the bricklayers union donated the materials and labor for the building. We were up and running within a year, and *Sesame Street* was available again, together with a world of other good programming. It could not have been accomplished without the generous support of KAUZ-TV, engineer Leon Hoeffner, Tuck, and many other volunteers and contributors.

Wichita Falls Law Practice: 1961–1988

[The law] is a jealous mistress, and
requires a long and constant courtship.
—Joseph Story, 1829

MY FORTY YEARS of law practice from 1961 to 2001 was a long and constant courtship of the law: 1961–1988 in private practice; 1975–1988 making laws in the State Senate while in private practice; and 1988–2000 as General Counsel for the University of Texas System. I always had a great love for the law, and that devotion to the legal profession and our system of jurisprudence continues in my retirement.

The practice of law has been very rewarding to me—not only in material benefits, but also as the most interesting work I can imagine.

As with most "affairs," not all can be told in deference to attorney-client privilege, secrets of the dead, failing memory, and sheer lack of space. Nonetheless, my goal with the following recollections is to capture some of the facts, history, and feelings about lawyers, partners, clients, cases, transactions, and professional activities of my time at the bar.

Helen was supportive in getting me through the last two years of law school and understanding that my practice required long hours and some time away from home. It was the only mistress she would allow.

WICHITA FALLS LAW PARTNERS:
THE PASSAGE FROM PUP TO PARTNER

Law schools teach history, principles, and subject matter of the law, but they don't impart much about practical aspects of how to succeed as a law-

Wichita Falls Times

Wichita Falls, Texas, Friday Evening, September 8, 1961   Page 13

Wichitan Joins Law Firm

The Wichita Falls law firm of Jones, Parish, Fillmore, Robinson & Lambert has announced the association of Ray Farabee, 28-year-old native Wichitan, with the firm.

Farabee, son of the late Jack W. Farabee and Mrs. Farabee, 2313 Ninth, was an honor graduate of Wichita Falls High School and holds a bachelor's degree in business administration and a law degree from the University of Texas.

During his seven years at the

Force Reserve, Farabee was president of the student body at the University of Texas in 1955, president of his freshman class and abbott of the Friars Society.

He is former president of the United States National Student Association and chairman of the board of Educational Travel Inc., a non-profit organization for American students traveling in Europe.

Farabee and his wife reside at 1935 Pawhuska. Mrs. Farabee

1961 newspaper article about return to Wichita Falls

yer. That learning process occurs through mentoring and hands-on experience. If a new lawyer lands in the right place, at the right time, works hard, and is lucky, he or she usually does well in the legal profession. I was fortunate to begin practice at the right time and place; I worked hard, and with some luck, did well.

In August 1961 I commenced my law practice as an associate with Jones, Parish, Fillmore, Robinson & Lambert (the Firm). It provided a good balance of mentoring from partners, working with attorneys, and "gofering" activities ranging from errands to minor court appearances. However, it was not long before I was handling my own files and cases.

Changes within the Firm accelerated my opportunity to learn more and do more. Elmer Parish left the Firm in 1963, and I became a partner in 1965. Harold Jones departed in 1967 to become president of the City National Bank (now Bank of America), and the Firm name was changed to Fillmore, Robinson, Lambert & Farabee. Then came more changes. Glynn Purtle was hired as an associate in 1965 and became a partner in 1969. Larry Robinson died in a plane crash in 1968; David Smith was hired away from another insurance defense firm as an associate, and was partner for a short time before returning to his hometown of Victoria, Texas. Roger Lee joined us as an associate in 1970 and became a partner in 1974. Tom Bacus, Michael Spurgers, and Jay Cantrell were also associates in the 1970's.

In May 1979 I left the Firm to become a partner in the law firm of Sherrill and Pace (S&P). Leaving the Firm was a difficult decision. I had been happy and doing well as a partner with Fillmore, Lambert, Farabee & Purtle; but S&P was larger and offered the prospect of more assistance during the times I was required to be in Austin with the State Senate. Because of its size and specialties, S&P provided some additional economic benefits. S&P did less trial work and more oil and gas, wills, estates, and corporate practice than the Firm did. Except for my general practice, the attorneys in S&P were specialists, each focusing on specific areas of law.

Joe Sherrill, Bob Pace, Caven Crosnoe, Lonnie Morrison, and Bob Goff were partners when I joined the S&P firm. Ken Hines, Rick Bowersock, and Roy Sparkman later became partners while I was there. Lonnie Morrison left S&P in 1982 and established his own firm with Steve Shelton, specializing in litigation matters. Lonnie was president of the State Bar of Texas in 1993–1994.

In March 1988 I left my law practice with S&P and the State Senate to become a Vice Chancellor and the General Counsel of the University of Texas System. The Firm dissolved in 2002 with the retirement of Clyde Fillmore and Glynn Purtle. Ironically, the Firm's phone number, 723-0981, is now that of Mikal Lambert, son of my former law partner Larry Lambert.

Although I have fond recollections about all of the partners and many associates with whom I worked, four senior partners: Harold Jones, Clyde Fillmore, Elmer Parish, and Larry Robinson, helped most in making my passage from a pup lawyer to partnership. My progress occurred, in part, because of two unfortunate or tragic circumstances.

HAROLD JONES was a major community and business leader of Wichita Falls, and to the extent that we had one, he was the managing partner. Harold made most of my early assignments, always had time to

Harold Jones, circa 1962

visit, and pointed me in the right direction in everything from trials to land titles. Harold was like a father to me and the other young attorneys in the Firm. Two examples of this include the unsolicited loan of $100 for our vacation trip to Wisconsin and the pledge of his savings account to secure the down payment for purchase of our first home in Wichita Falls.

The first large case I brought to the Firm was a divorce that potentially involved a substantial family estate and trust. My client and I had dated in high school. After graduation from college, she married a ne'er-do-well, and they came to live in Wichita Falls. The errant husband was represented by a seasoned local attorney, known among other things, for hardball tactics. Texas law then required proof of grounds for divorce before the marriage could be dissolved. Grounds for divorce were not a problem in this case: there were no children and practically all property was the separate estate of my client. The seasoned attorney who represented the husband remarked, "We need to talk." I went into his office, where he advised me that his client would testify to being involved in an unspeakable act with my client's mother. True or not, that information should have no bearing on my client's right to a divorce, except one more of many grounds for divorce. However, should the testimony occur, it would cause stress and embarrassment to my client and her family. I was in a dither and sought Harold's advice. He listened to my story, leaned back in his chair, chuckled, and said, "Ray, it's like they say, 'If you haven't tried it, don't knock it!'" Harold had never tried "it," but he had tried many cases and knew the reputation of the other attorney for such shenanigans. My fears were quieted and I marched forward to secure the divorce and preserve the family fortune and reputation.

Harold served as Mayor of Wichita Falls and had a great interest in the improvement of the city's public parks. Long after he was mayor, one of his wealthier clients asked his advice about disposing of a large tract of land within the city limits along the Wichita River. Harold suggested the option of gifting it to the city, taking a substantial tax deduction, and assuring the memory of the client's mother forever. She liked the idea, and Lucy Park was created. Because of his many public contributions and remarkable vision, the Wichita Falls City Council renamed an older park at 9th and Broad Streets the Harold Jones Park.

When Harold left the Firm to become President of City National Bank, I inherited many of his clients. My Austin neighbor Judge Don Morgan, who commenced law practice in Wichita Falls about the same time I did, observed, "Harold Jones was the greatest gentleman at the bar I have ever known." I agree.

CLYDE FILLMORE: Although Clyde wasn't always the most polished gentleman, he was one of the best trial lawyers I ever witnessed. Shortly after commencing work at the Firm, Clyde took me to Gainesville, where I observed my first civil jury trial. Supposedly, I was to participate, but Clyde needed little help from me. The plaintiff was a cowboy who claimed to be permanently disabled because of a defective horse his employer furnished him for rounding up the dogies. Lawyers quickly selected a jury, and the plaintiff's attorney put his client on the stand to tell his

Clyde Fillmore, circa 1965

story, which he did . . . and more. Clyde demolished the cowboy plaintiff on cross-examination for telling too many "stories" that were untrue. The plaintiff's attorney requested a brief recess, wood-shedded his client, and moved for a non-suit. After the short trial, we had a good time driving home, as Clyde related stories about some of his memorable trials, both as District Attorney for Wichita County and as an insurance defense lawyer.

The City of Wichita Falls hired Clyde to defend them in a negligence suit involving a young man who was severely injured when his motorcycle slid down because of some loose gravel from the unpaved shoulder of the street. The injuries and loose gravel were not in doubt; however, Clyde captured the minds of the jury by demonstrating the power a person feels while on a motorcycle. Straddling his old briefcase in front of the jury, Clyde revved up the engine of his imaginary motorcycle and hit the gravel covered turn at what the jury must have perceived as 80-miles per hour. Clyde poured the plaintiff out, saving the taxpayers thousands of dollars. It is worth noting that shortly after the trial, the city paved the shoulders on the "S" curve of Grant Street. When I was elected to the State Senate, Clyde gave me his old briefcase. I never rode it to Austin, but I carried it for years back and forth from Wichita Falls to the Capitol.

Clyde was not only an outstanding lawyer; he was a remarkable human being. With only one year of college education, he completed his law studies through a correspondence course in eight months, passed the Bar exam, and received his law license in 1929 before his 21st birthday. Dedicated to public service, he served on the Wichita Falls school board, as well as innumerable civic and religious boards and committees. He wrote a book about his experiences as a prisoner of war and survivor of Japanese imprisonment during World War II, as well as two books of poetry. I was pleased to serve as master of ceremonies when the Wichita County Bar honored Clyde on his 90th birthday with a banquet and creation of an endowed scholarship in his name. Clyde continued to practice law until he was 92 and died on October 10, 2004, at the age of 95.

ELMER PARISH: In contrast to Harold and Clyde, Elmer was the more complex and inscrutable of the senior partners. Tall, quiet, and reserved, I first had the impression that he didn't like me, but I was wrong. Shortly after my trial experience with Clyde in Gainesville, Elmer invited me to go with him to the U.S. District Court for the Northern District of Texas in Wichita Falls, where he was defending the Fort Worth and Denver Rail Road against a claim by one of its employees. Elmer demonstrated his photographic memory during the jury selection. After a quick review of the jury list, he proceeded to call each potential juror by name without referring to the list—a feat few lawyers can or could perform.

Elmer was more politically active than the other senior partners. Like Clyde, he had been District Attorney for the 30th Texas Judicial District. He managed several U.S. Senate campaigns for Lyndon B. Johnson in the Wichita Falls, and served as parliamentarian for County Democratic conventions. Elmer had good reason to think he would be appointed to the Federal Bench when Johnson was elected Vice President. He was an outstanding lawyer and on the short list for the appointment. Reportedly, the FBI did its customary background check, only to find that Elmer was prone to drink, not just a bit, but quite a bit. He failed to get the appointment he so greatly coveted, and Sarah T. Hughes was appointed to the position. But for the drinking problem, Elmer might have been the judge to swear in Lyndon Johnson as President after the assassination of John F. Kennedy in 1963.

When Elmer left the Firm in 1963, he asked me to consider leaving Jones, Parish, Robinson and Lambert and go into practice with him, assuring me I would have more cases and make more money. I respectfully declined and learned later that his drinking and related business errors resulted in his separation from the Firm. Elmer retained the railroad account and a number of clients for whom he did personal work. We remained friends. He continued a productive solo law practice and died of a heart attack in the 1980's.

Larry Robinson, circa 1964

LARRY ROBINSON was an outstanding lawyer. He was my coach and mentor as I developed my own trial docket and individual clients. Bright, quick, and articulate, Larry could negotiate and drink all night with the plaintiff's lawyers. Insurance company adjusters were amazed with his trial preparation, settlements, and jury results in those cases that went to a verdict. Larry also developed his own group of business clients, particularly subcontractors in the construction business.

In 1967, Larry Robinson, Larry Lambert, and Glynn Purtle bought a single-engine, four-passenger Cessna 172 airplane. Although Lambert and Purtle were licensed to fly the Cessna when it was purchased, Robinson never took flying lessons. On October 6, 1968, Larry and Frank Stewart, a pilot and CPA, departed Wichita Falls with their construction contractor clients Don Harris and George Cox in the Cessna 172 for a business/fishing trip to Arkansas. As they were flying into Hot Springs, Arkansas, on Monday October 7, the Cessna hit a power line, the plane crashed, and all four were killed in the accident.

A memorial service was held for Larry in the 30th District Courtroom. More than 100 local attorneys attended and many spoke of their respect, friendship, and admiration for him. Although I was president of the Bar Association at that time, I chose not to preside, but made the following statement at the end of the service:

> Whatever I am today I owe in large measure to Larry Robinson. What Mr. [Ewing] Clagett said about this untimely death, the sadness that we all feel and have expressed here is so very true. By the same token, all of Larry's life was lived so fully and completely; he sensed and he knew the vitality of life and lived it to the full measure, not just for himself,

but for all the people around him. When I met Larry Robinson, I had never heard about debate, extemporaneous speech, or things like that. He motivated me, and opened opportunities that I would not have had. I wouldn't be a lawyer today or hardly know what a lawyer is if it weren't for Larry Robinson. Because he lived life to the fullest and had a concern for the people around him, a deep concern, we are a better Bar and community and we shall deeply miss him.

The term "legal secretary" is now out of vogue, and the preferred titles are paralegal, legal assistant, and/or administrative assistant. Regardless of the title, I have great appreciation of those assistant/legal secretaries who helped me through 27 years of private practice and 13 years of public practice with the UT System. A good skilled legal secretary, in many ways, is more important than a law partner, as the partner takes care of his or her own business. On the other hand, the lawyer's secretary is taking care of his or her boss's business—getting out correspondence and pleadings, taking calls, billings, scheduling, meeting deadlines, supervised drafting of documents, and many other tasks that kept my legal ship afloat and on course.

Hired in August 1962, Beverly Smith (now Beverly Sloan) worked for me nearly one-half of my forty years of law practice until February 1980. Beverly had no legal experience when I first hired her, but she was (and is)

1973 Boss of Year picture with Beverly Marshall and my legal secretary Beverly Smith

bright, highly motivated, honest, and hardworking. Bev first served as my secretary and the Firm receptionist. While together, we learned the nuts and bolts of law practice. Despite the distractions of egotistical lawyers, bumptious clients, and a few bums who wandered in off of 7th Street, she mastered the skills and nomenclature of the law. I could not have managed my law practice, run for office, and served in the State Senate without Beverly.

In forty years of practice, I had only five legal secretaries: Beverly Smith at the Firm; Debbie Frazier and Jean Ann Chasteen at S&P; Shirley Schnieder and Beverly Page at the UT System. In 1973 and 1983 I was selected as "Boss of the Year" by the Wichita County Association of Legal Secretaries, two meaningful recognitions during my law practice.

MEMORABLE LAWYERS

As with almost everything, many changes have occurred within the legal profession since the early 1960's when I began the practice of law. Some of the differences then, as compared to now, were: greater civility among competing lawyers; less specialization; few attorneys set fees on the basis of billable hours; shorter pleadings and discovery; no support technology, except for land-based telephones, typewriters, and elemental copy machines. Many changes have been positive, such as improved ethical compliance, required continuing legal education, improved systems of legal aid for those who cannot afford a lawyer, and better tech support.

Courthouses were open on Saturday mornings in the early 1960's, and all lawyers in our Firm showed up for at least a half-day of work, though at a slower pace and without coats and ties. Many of us took an extended coffee break on Saturday morning in the old Kemp Hotel before it was demolished in 1963 and replaced by a shiny new Holiday Inn. The coffee was never as good at the Holiday Inn, but the conversation remained the same—tales about past and present lawyers, trials, and the latest courthouse gossip. Typically reticent, I listened intently and became good friends with many fellow lawyers of that day.

Some of the lawyers, other than my partners, who stand out in my memory are:

PHIL KOURI: Not viewed as the most outstanding or upstanding member of the Wichita County Bar, Phil was certainly one of the most colorful and humorous. Short in stature, of Lebanese descent, very bright, and quick as a cat, Phil had a wonderfully deep voice; some might call it, with justification, a "whiskey voice." Phil would take just about any case that came through his office door. He could tell humorous stories on himself and others. Many started out as a partner or associate with Phil (including Larry Robinson), but no one stayed very long. To say that Phil "drank a bit" would be an understatement, but he had a drive and resilience that usually got him up in the morning to turn another case or two, sometimes for too little, and other times for more than it was worth. Phil liked to joke about the difference between him and a whore. Though I suspect he knew something about them, I will forego his characterization of prostitutes, but he called himself a "cunning little runt"—and he was, but a lot more. Phil died in the late 1970's.

BOB L. WILSON: Bob easily falls into the category of one of the smartest and brightest attorneys I have ever known. Selective in the matters he accepted, Bob specialized in worker's compensation cases before the law was changed to make such cases less remunerative for attorneys. By the time of the plaintiffs' depositions, Bob's clients were thoroughly prepared, had not worked since the alleged on-the-job injury, and had seen the "right" doctors, who would likely testify that, in their expert opinion, the plaintiff was not able to perform the ordinary tasks of a worker, which would result

Bob L. Wilson, circa 1965

in a decision of total and permanent disability and 30% of the recovery for Bob. He seldom tried a case, settled nearly all of them for good money, and became wealthy in the process. A great talker, Bob swapped stories well into the night, accompanied by substantial amounts of whiskey or cognac, preferably Corvoissier. For those of us on the opposing side of Bob's cases, this was hard work, but somebody had to do it, usually Larry Robinson and sometimes me. Customarily, Bob would pack up several briefcases full of files, take them to Dallas where most of the insurance companies had their regional offices, and settle his cases before suit was ever filed.

Bob loved politics and was (and is) an ardent Democrat. When I ran for the State Senate, he was very supportive, advising and making his private plane available on several occasions. While I served in the Senate, my tort and worker's compensation reform legislation stressed our friendship, and his political support waned. However, when we met representing our respective clients, we did business, because turning cases was his business, and he came to do business. A highly competitive, effective, and helluva lawyer, Bob is now retired and lives in Wichita Falls with his wife Billie. He travels, checks the market each day, counts his money, and goes to the American Legion Club one evening each week—now the only time he consumes alcoholic beverage.

JACK BANNER: In 1990 Clyde Fillmore wrote a poem in honor of Jack Banner. The first two verses read as follows:

> Jack Banner can't play the piano, or the flute,
> But he can play havoc in a lawsuit!
> He's quite a sport,
> Everywhere except in court;
> There, it's no holds barred;
> That's why I'm so bruised and scarred!

Jack and I found ourselves on opposing sides in several large trials. He won some, and I won some; however, I always came away "bruised and scarred." Jack was one of the most able trial lawyers in North Texas until his retirement. Jack was a fierce competitor and exuded confidence. During one trial, Judge Sarah T. Hughes asked him in open court why he kept smiling at the jury. I guess he thought he was going to win. Actually he got a favorable jury verdict, but the judge set it aside and I won at the U.S. District Court level. Unfortunately for my client, Jack won on appeal at the Fifth Circuit. Outside of the courtroom he was a good friend and lots of fun. Jack served as President of the Texas Trial Lawyers Association while I was in the State Senate. We disagreed on several legislative matters, but it never affected our friendship. Jack was a multitalented trial lawyer and did not hesitate to venture outside the personal injury field to tackle a big divorce case or complicated business litigation matter. Jack died in 2005.

HOWARD MARTIN: Howard was the leading criminal defense and divorce lawyer in Wichita Falls. Although he could have restricted his practice

Howard Martin

to white people who could pay substantial fees, Howard, like his father Bernard before him, represented African Americans as well. Howard served his time as District Attorney and knew criminal law forward and backwards. He was tough, tedious at times, and always tenacious, which irritated some attorneys; but he was one of the best, particularly in nasty divorce proceedings. The thought of him being on the other side was a deterrent to either getting a divorce or representing someone who was. Howard loved to tell stories about actual cases. One often repeated story was about an African American woman who came to him complaining about the Gem Theater, where Negroes were relegated to the balconies with no restrooms available for the "Colored." The client had found a seat in the dark balcony and sat down, whereupon she immediately smelled something which turned out to be human excrement. Her complaint to the theater management fell on deaf ears. To his credit, Howard took the case and sued the Gem Theater for damages, but he recovered little or nothing and charged no fee for his services.

Although some called Howard a "nigger divorce lawyer" and a "pain in the ass," I call him a "gem" of the Wichita County Bar. I am also very proud to have owned the Martin-Farabee House, where he was raised before he went to college at Stanford University. Howard died in 1988.

BAR ASSOCIATION ACTIVITIES

The term "bar" has several different meanings in the English language, but as used in this discussion of lawyers, it refers to bar associations and other groups of attorneys. When I think of some attorneys I have known, I wonder whether references to local pubs and taverns became known as bars because of the legal profession, but the term, as used with reference to lawyers, is derived from the early English common law and court system.

I was an active member of the Wichita County Bar Association during the 27 years of my private law practice in Wichita Falls. I made many good friends through bar activities and seldom missed a meeting of the local association or the annual State Bar Convention. With over 100 members, our local bar association was larger than many in Texas, but not nearly as big as those in Houston, Dallas, San Antonio, Ft. Worth, or Austin.

In 1963 I was elected to the Board of Directors of the Junior Bar of Texas. The Junior Bar, now the Texas Young Lawyers Association, is an organization within the State Bar of Texas for attorneys 35 years of age and younger. Helen and I attended its board meetings in various Texas cities and made many friends through the young lawyers' group. I was elected secretary-treasurer of the Junior Bar in 1965 and vice president in 1966 in statewide elections. I was asked to run for president of the organization in 1967, but declined.

I was elected president of the Wichita County Bar Association in 1968. In addition to presiding at monthly and called meetings, I was instrumental in accomplishing three important projects.

The first was the completion of the Lawyers Lounge on the third floor of the Wichita County Courthouse. The Lounge was a convenient place to have a cup of coffee and visit with fellow attorneys; it was also a worthwhile space for settlement negotiations and making business calls before cell phones were available.

*Pictured with Presiding Judge Louis T. Holland, Jack Banner, and Appellate Judges
from Ft.. Worth, while President of the Wichita County Bar Assn., March 22, 1968*

The second and third initiatives involved improved access to legal services. We established the first lawyer referral system for Wichita County, whereby a person in need of legal assistance and without an attorney would have access to an organized system for selecting a qualified lawyer. At that time, advertising by attorneys was prohibited, and persons without a lawyer were left to find an appropriate attorney by word of mouth, solicitation (which was and is still illegal), or wandering from law office to law office.

Wichita County had no organized legal aid program or office for persons unable to afford a lawyer in civil law matters. In 1968–1969 federal and state-funded legal aid programs did not exist in Texas. Some of the larger Texas cities had legal aid offices. With the very substantial help of Al Nice, we established the county's first lawyer referral and legal aid office. Al was head of the Sheppard Air Force Base judge advocate group and had retired in Wichita Falls. He staffed the county bar's first organized legal aid effort as a volunteer, doing initial interviews of persons in need of assistance.

Where appropriate, Al referred qualifying persons to various members of our local bar who volunteered for one or two pro bono referrals each year. In 1978 West Texas Legal Services Inc., a nonprofit corporation funded primarily through federal grants, opened a branch office in Wichita Falls to provide civil legal services to low-income persons, and local attorneys continue to provide pro bono legal assistance through the West Texas Private Attorney Involvement Program (PAI). Because of my interest in legal aid for low-income families, I served on the State Bar Committee for Legal Services for the Disadvantaged in 1970–1971. In 2003 I was appointed by the Texas Supreme Court to the board of directors for the Texas Equal Access to Justice Foundation (TEAJF) and reappointed in 2006 for another three-year term. TEAJF distributes more than 15 million dollars each year for legal aid services.

After practicing law for several years, clients and friends approached me about drafting their wills and probating the wills of deceased relatives. With the help of my partners, I developed experience in this area of practice, but I felt the need of more knowledge of estate planning. In cooperation with Don Williamson, a trust officer at the City National Bank, we organized the North Texas Estate Planning Council for attorneys, trust officers, and accountants interested in estate planning. I was elected as the first president of the organization in 1967.

MEMORABLE CLIENTS, CASES,
AND TRANSACTIONS

The foundation of any private law practice is its clients. The Firm had a good client base, and it was not long before I developed my own group of people and businesses that looked to me as their lawyer. Clients, like lawyers and their firms, were constantly changing, but there were some long-term clients in my Wichita Falls practice.

They included the following: Ray Clymer and his business, Denison Poultry & Egg Company; Jerry K. Estes and North Texas Federal Savings and Loan Association; the Wichita Falls Independent School District (WFISD); Don Waldrip, who was Superintendent of the WFISD; Industrial Development, Inc. (IDI) that became the Wichita Falls Board of Commerce and Industry (BCI); Texas Bank & Trust; KAUZ-TV; Guarantee Abstract and Title Co.; Dub Dennis; W. P. Howle; Liberty Mutual Insurance Company; Burlison Packing Company; Gus Buder and his company Arcadia Refining Co; Buddy Henderson and his family company Henderson 66 Sales; Cochran News Agency; Shem and Phillips Cunningham and their family business Scott Manufacturing, which made Scott's Level Best overalls; Dr. C. E. and Gwen Jackson, black educators and community leaders; Paul Scheurer; Tommy Alexander; the Hargrave Ranch; Washex Machinery Corp; CertainTeed; Texas Electric Service Co. (now TXU); and many other businesses and individuals that I helped with lawsuits, adoptions, estate plans, probates, divorces, real estate transactions, debt collections, bankruptcies, oil and gas matters, incorporations, and partnerships.

FIRST TRIAL: My first trial was a contract dispute in the Justice of Peace (JP) court. After extensive research, I determined I was entitled to a summary judgment. I took law books with me to persuade the JP, who was neither a lawyer nor interested in what the law said. The judge overruled me in favor of an old friend of his. I learned several lessons from that experience, one of which was that you don't always win even though the law (as you see it) is on your side, particularly in JP court. Another was the old saying that if you don't win, try, try, and try again; and I did, with better luck.

RAY CLYMER: My next case in JP court occurred two years later and was significantly more important. Harold Jones asked me to defend a new client in town by the name of Ray Clymer who owned the Denison Poultry and Egg Company (DP&E), which was about to be evicted by a landlord who wanted his refrigerated warehouse back in time for the Thanksgiving and Christmas seasons. Ray had made timely rental payments and substantial improvements to the leased premises, and said he had a year-to-year lease. The landlord claimed it was a month-to-month lease, subject to cancellation on one month's notice. Unfortunately, the lease agreement was verbal, and we had a swearing match, with thousands of DP&E frozen turkeys and chickens about to be evicted to the warm streets of Wichita Falls—not a happy prospect for the holiday season of 1964.

This time I did not take any law books with me, but I had an articulate client with an appealing case. Just visualize thousands of homeless frozen turkeys and chickens; however it was another case of "blind justice" in the JP court. The judge chose to believe the landlord and his attorney Gene Ritchie. We appealed to District Court and asked for a jury. Gene was ill and his partner Howard Martin assumed representation of the landlord. After a spirited trial, justice was done! The jury found that there was a year-to-year lease, and DP&E poultry was served up for Thanksgiving and Christmas dinners.

Ray Clymer, circa 1970

I hasten to add that I had tried other cases in District Court and won them by the time we went to trial in the DP&E case. Otherwise, I would have joined the turkeys, and Clymer would have had a malpractice case if I lost. As it turned out, I won more than the case; I won the best client of my private law practice.

Ray Clymer became an important business leader in Wichita Falls in the late 1960's. To the surprise of many, he secured the Coors distributorship for a large area of North Texas, including Wichita, Grayson, Denton, and Collin counties. With Erle White, he became the owner of KAUZ-TV. More important for the community, Ray was one of the most effective leaders for industrial development in the history of Wichita Falls as president of Industrial Development, Inc., and its successor, the Board of Commerce and Industry. Some of the new industries and employers Ray helped bring to Wichita Falls included Sprague Electric Company, the PPG float glass plant, the CertainTeed spun glass plant, Washex Manufacturing, Cryovac, James V. Allred Prison Unit, Howmet Turbine, and AC Sparkplug Division of General Motors. More than any Wichitan in recent history, Ray Clymer has been a major statewide political and governmental leader. He has served on the boards of the Texas Parks and Wildlife Agency, Texas Industrial Commission, and the Texas Coordinating Board for Higher Education.

FIRST CRIMINAL CASE: My first District Court case was as a court-appointed attorney to defend an African American man accused of breaking and entering a woman's home in the middle of the night. Since he was identified by the woman, arrested at or near her house, and could not remember anything about where he was at the time of the crime because of his inebriated condition, my defense of the defendant was somewhat limited. On cross-examination of the woman, I established that my client didn't steal anything, threaten, or touch her, and she didn't scream. I did the best I could with this evidence, and to my amazement and that of the judge, the jury took a long time returning its verdict of guilty. The foreman of the jury was an oil man originally from St. Louis named Gustavus Adolphus Buder III, better known as "Gus." As a result of my performance in this first criminal case, Gus became one of my better clients.

BUDER CUSTODY CASE: After doing some work for the Buder family oil company, Gus asked me to sue his ex-wife for custody of their four children. I explained the difficulties for a father to secure custody of young children from their mother and asked what his grounds might be. He didn't have any specific answer other than the children did not like their strict German stepfather, their mother frequently fed them peanut butter sandwiches, and the kids preferred to be with Gus and his new wife. This did not appear to be a strong case for changing custody, and the children were not of an age where their preferences would count for much, if they could testify at all. I advised Gus of these realities, but he insisted we file the suit right away before his ex-wife took the children to Colorado.

With full disclosure to my client that his chances of winning were slim to none, I filed the suit and requested the court to appoint a social worker to evaluate the living conditions of the children and recommend what would be in their best interest—to be with their father or their mother. After pretrial discovery and completion of the social worker's report, we went to trial before Judge Arthur Tipps without a jury. The attorney for the ex-wife was as sure that he would win the case as I was doubtful we would win. The social worker confirmed that the ex-wife appeared to be a good mother and that no dramatic grounds for changing custody existed; however, it was her opinion that it would be in the best interest of the children, based on their preferences and negative attitudes toward their stepfather, for Gus to have custody. Judge Tipps granted custody of the children to Gus, with reasonable visitation rights for the mother. The mother appealed, but the Court of Appeals in Fort Worth sustained the District Court's ruling. Gus later moved back to the St. Louis area with the kids, where they grew up, and Justice was done—but I have been suspicious about peanut butter sandwiches ever since. The appellate court opinion discussing this custody case may be found at 434 SW 2nd 177.

CALIFORNIA WALK-IN CASE: One day early in my practice, a tall man from California named Doyle Wooley walked into our law office and requested a lawyer. As the youngest and most available, I drew what turned out to be the lucky card. Doyle told me an interesting, but unlikely, story that he was the heir to more than 300 acres near a community in Wilbarger County known as "Bug Scuffle." Doyle, it seems, was the product of a short-term marriage that was annulled when he was a baby. His mother moved to California, remarried, and changed Doyle's last name to that of her new husband. After some research, I determined the story was not unlikely, but true. I filed suit against the estate of the natural father Tom Kelly and secured the acreage for my client. The case was on a contingent fee basis and produced considerable remuneration for the firm. Although I was not a partner, Harold Jones insisted that I receive a bonus, which helped pay the delivery expenses for my second son, David. Later, Doyle moved to Electra, not far from Elliot, aka Bug Scuffle. I organized a corporation for him, and continued as his lawyer until 1988 when I left private practice.

PORTWOOD CASE: Not all family feud cases turned out as well as the Wooley one. Harold Jones asked me to help with a dispute between an old family named Portwood from Baylor and Archer Counties. The Portwoods, including our clients Jessie Lee Portwood Hargrave and Sam Portwood, inherited thousands of acres and related mineral rights from their father W. H. Portwood. Family disputes between the Portwood heirs were not uncommon, some resulting in litigation and a few with more dramatic expressions of anger. A TV miniseries could be written about the Portwoods, right up there with *Deadwood* and *Dallas*. As the case moved forward, I became the principle attorney for our clients.

Mrs. Hargrave and daughter Dannie Shawver were two of the nicest persons I have had the privilege of representing, and Sam Portwood was a gentleman. I cannot say the same for the two family members they sued— Dannie Portwood Fancher and Harry Portwood. Dannie was tougher than a boot, and Harry was meaner than a junkyard dog. The lawsuit took years to research and get to trial. It involved huge overriding oil and gas royalties taken by Danny Fancher and Harry Portwood, allegedly for "damages" to their surface estate. The minerals were owned by all of the family, including our clients, but the surface owners had the leasing rights. Briefly stated, the law requires a person with the right to lease other co-owner's oil and gas rights to do so with "utmost fairness." After one of the longer trials in the history of Wichita County, the jury found that the defendants did not act with "utmost fairness," but held that my clients had knowledge of the transactions (which they denied) and failed to bring suit within the time required by law. Another law firm represented the children of a deceased brother, and they prevailed because limitations do not run against minors until they turn 21 and have knowledge of the breach of fi-

Danny Shawver and Jessie Lee Portwood Hargrave

duciary duty. Judgment on the verdict was appealed, but it was sustained by the Court of Appeals in Fort Worth. See 251 SW 2nd 904 (1975).

The Firm handled the Portwood case on a contingent fee basis and did not recover the large sums for which I hoped. Mrs. Hargrave and Sam Port-wood reimbursed us for our expenses, which were substantial, and voluntarily paid several thousand dollars for my services. Jessie Lee and her daughter Dannie continued as my clients until I left the private practice of law.

BANKRUPTCIES were not as common to law practice as they are today. By happenstance, I handled several no-asset bankruptcies during my first two years of practice and thereby became the Firm's specialist for such matters. I remember organizing a corporation for a fast-food restaurant call the Pizza Pie, doing several years of legal work for it, and then taking it through bankruptcy—a cradle-to-grave business client.

Our Firm represented Burlison Packing Company, which had been in the meat packing business in Wichita Falls for years. Clyde Fillmore was a close friend of Hap Burlison, the owner. Hap was my neighbor on Buchanan Street, and his son Merlin was a debate partner in high school. The company fell upon hard times, and Texas Bank and Trust (TB&T) filed an action to put the packing company into bankruptcy and foreclose the bank's mortgage. This would have been the end of an old family business and client. The Firm asked me to represent Burlison, and I solved the problem and saved the day, by discovering Chapter 11 of the Bankruptcy Code. Chapter 11 allows a debtor to file a plan; and if approved by the bankruptcy judge, the debtor pays something to its creditors and remains in business. Creditors are barred from foreclosing. When I filed the counteraction for Chapter 11, it was a great surprise to TB&T because this remedy was seldom, if ever, used in Wichita Falls at that time. As it worked out, TB&T was paid in full, without interest; and Burlison Packing lived on for 15 more years. Impressed with my work, TB&T later asked me to join its board of directors. All's well that ends well.

One other bankruptcy is memorable. Ernest Medders and his wife moved to Muenster, Texas, in 1965. Although likable and seemingly well heeled, the origin of their wealth was a mystery. They purchased a small ranch, prize cattle, and lots of expensive items, all on credit. A party barn was built on their property where they entertained high-profile political and business leaders from Dallas, Wichita Falls, and elsewhere. As it turned out, the Medders did not have money. Ernest was an illiterate mechanic and his wife a practical nurse back in Tennessee where they convinced the Poor Sisters of Charity that they were the long lost heirs to a Spindletop oil fortune. The Sisters advanced substantial sums of money on the hope—and prayers, as time passed—that much of the lost Spindletop fortune would eventually be donated to their charitable and religious endeavors. Even Lyndon Johnson heard of the Medder's generosity and attended one of their parties. At the party someone who introduced the Medders to Lyndon became confused and said, "Mr. Vice President, I want you to meet the Muensters from Medders." Unfortunately, the Medders were credit "monsters," and the house of cards fell in on Neiman Marcus, the Sisters, several Dallas banks, the City National Bank in Wichita Falls, and other unsuspecting creditors.

Bad loans, including the one to the Medders, prompted the City National Bank in Wichita Falls to hire Harold Jones away from our law firm to serve as its president. The Medders filed bankruptcy to stop foreclosures, and Harold hired the Firm to recoup the losses of City National. Clyde Fillmore and I did the legal work to recover a part of the bank's loan. I will never forget Ernest Medders's testimony at one of the bankruptcy hearings in Gainesville, Texas. When Ernest testified he could not read, write, or sign his name—except with an "X"—it was believable. Clyde wisely opted not to cross-examine Ernest, and he proved the bank's secured claim by other means. The case received significant state and national publicity and put Muenster on the map and the Medders back into a more humble abode. The Poor Sisters were poorer for the experience.

EDUCATION LAW: From 1967 to 1975 I did most of the legal work for the Wichita Falls Independent School District (WFISD), which acquainted me with the Texas Education Code and aspects of constitutional law that was invaluable when I became General Counsel for the University of Texas System. I tried cases in U.S. District Court for other area school districts, as well as the WFISD. My primary adversary was East Texas attorney Larry Watts, who specialized in suing school districts in connection with non-renewal and termination of school employee employment contracts. I won most of my cases against Larry's clients and argued appeals for several of them before the U.S. Fifth Circuit Court in New Orleans and Houston.

Judge Sarah T. Hughes

WORKER'S COMPENSATION: Although benefits for an injured worker were much smaller than today, the law favored the claimant. Most of the cases were settled, but I tried several before a jury and lost most of them. One interesting compensation case was in federal court with Bob Wilson before Judge Sarah T. Hughes. This case was unusual in several respects, including venue in federal court, the preexisting handicapped condition of the claimant, and the case being tried for a second time after a hung jury in the first trial. After the jury was out longer than usual, Bob grew nervous and complained to Judge Hughes that he had never lost a comp case. I responded that I had never won a comp case; she found my response humorous. Despite the lack of surprises in the retrial, the jury found no injury. Bob lost his first comp case.

RAILROAD ABANDONMENT: A railroad abandonment before the Interstate Commerce Commission (ICC) in Paducah, Texas, and Washington, D.C., was one of the more unusual cases I handled. The St. Louis and San Francisco Railroad (the Frisco) owned the Quanah, Acme & Pacific Railroad (QA&P). It was a short-haul rail line that served as a bridge between the Santa Fe Railroad and the Frisco in better times. The volume of traffic had dwindled and the line was no longer profitable. The Frisco filed an application to abandon its track between the towns of Acme and Paducah, prompting wheat farmers and small businesses in Paducah to protest the abandonment. They contacted me about representing them. I had no experience with railroad abandonments, but neither did anyone else in Northwest Texas. Although my Senate representation of the area did not extend to providing free legal service, I agreed to help for a small fee and expenses.

Attorneys and officials for the Frisco did not expect a fight when they came to Paducah. They were surprised to see me and the farmers when they arrived at the Cottle County Courthouse, where an Interstate Commerce Commission (ICC) Hearing Examiner from Washington, D.C., called the proceedings to order. With the help of Tom Bacus, a young attorney in our firm, we contacted wheat and cotton farmers, chamber of commerce officials, and small-business leaders of the area to testify against the abandonment of this "lifeline" of transportation, which was running one train over the 43.5-mile stretch each week. Frisco officials were not fully prepared for our protest, but they submitted evidence about the diminished traffic and availability of independent truckers to haul the seasonal grain harvests and smaller shipments of commercial goods for the dwindling population of Paducah. I called a banker from Floydada to refute the testimony about the reliability of independent truckers in this region of Texas. This banker witness gave the classic opinion of my trial experience when he testified, "I have known many independent truckers in the area. It has been my experience that the only thing between an independent trucker and bankruptcy is a flat tire."

The ICC Hearing Examiner ruled against abandonment, and the railroad appealed to the full ICC in Washington, D.C. We prepared and filed briefs in support of the Examiner's decision. I flew to Washington and argued the case for the farmers before an ICC panel, which affirmed the opinion of the Examiner, and Paducah kept its railroad—but not for long. Congress deregulated the railroads and the Frisco filed another petition to abandon within a year. This time the farmers decided not to fight, and the QA&P was abandoned.

CRIMINAL CASES: Wichita County had no public defender, and each practicing attorney was periodically appointed to provide counsel for indigent defendants charged with felony offenses. I received my share of appointments and did the best I could for clients in this circumstance. Few indigent defendants could afford bail. I visited them in jail, investigated the case as best I could, and determined whether the defendant wanted to try the case or plead guilty. Most of the defendants wanted to enter a guilty plea if I could negotiate an acceptable plea bargain. I took this responsibility seriously and learned a lot about the criminal jurisprudence system.

During the summer of 1962, I was appointed to assist fellow attorney Jim Jameson with the defense of Tommy Lee Walker. Tommy was charged with the murder of James Adams by shooting him on February 10, 1962. The District Attorney was seeking the death penalty, and the situation did not look good for our client. Tommy fled to Michigan where he was found with the gun that killed Adams. Two other young black men, who were with Tommy during the robbery, testified that Tommy Lee shot Adams after they cleaned out the cash register. They said Adams recognized our client and said, "Tommy, why are you doing this?" Tommy was black, Adams white, and both were younger than 20 years of age.

Though Jameson was more experienced than I, neither of us had defended a capital murder case. Jim's father had been Sheriff of Montague County, and he was no stranger to the Texas criminal justice system. We both worked hard to provide the best defense we could, but it was extremely difficult.

We presented evidence about a disastrous childhood. Tommy was abandoned by his mother at an early age. His natural father was Lieutenant Lacy. I presumed that Lacy was an Air Force officer, like me. Our investigation revealed that he was a chronic alcoholic simply named "Lieutenant" who had never accepted any responsibility for his illegitimate son, but would occasionally show up to embarrass or humiliate Tommy. A fundamentalist black minister took Tommy into his home and tried to raise him in the way of the Lord. Like most adolescents, our client was not a model church member. The preacher, his family, and congregation drummed Tommy out of the church for his sinful ways, with actual drums and public castigation. He was on the street again.

Our argument to the jury was that Tommy Lee was young and abused and had no prior criminal record, and that nothing would be gained by giving him the death penalty. Jim had recently read an article about the pain and horrors of electrocution, then the Texas method of execution. He shared the contents of this article with the jury in his closing argument, urging mercy and the alternative sentence of life imprisonment or a lesser number of years in prison.

The jury deliberated for the better part of a day, and then came a knock on the door. They had reached a verdict. Judge Walter Friberg ordered Tommy brought from the jail, and we stood anxiously while the judge opened the envelope and read the verdict: "We find Tommy Lee Walker guilty of murder with malice aforethought and assess his punishment at 99 years in the state penitentiary." We were greatly relieved. Tommy did not wish to appeal, and the case was ended. As I left the courtroom, the sister of the murder victim accosted me, expressing her disappointment that the verdict did not assess the death penalty. I could not help but think about the murder of my brother, and our sadness about the verdict in that trial 15 years earlier. I understood her hostility, but I had no regrets about helping to save Tommy Lee's life.

During the time I served in the State Senate, some of my better legislative work was in the field of civil and criminal jurisprudence and juvenile justice. You can talk all you want about law and order, justice, and property rights, but once you have had the responsibility for someone's life, you are more likely to see the whole picture and reach more studied conclusions.

Campaign for the State Senate:
1973–1974

You just don't understand politics, Doc. You don't
understand what makes the mare go.
—Robert Penn Warren's Willie Stark in *All the King's Men*

B Y 1973 I THOUGHT I understood politics. With work experiences for elected officials and volunteer efforts in the political campaigns for others, I was no stranger to the process. Family responsibilities and work obligations had tempered my youthful ambitions, and early visions of running for a series of public offices, culminating with an election as governor had faded away. At age 40, I was not ready to get "down in the mud" or seek elected public office for myself.

But then a strange thing happened on the way to the forum, or in this instance, the State Senate. Jack Hightower, the incumbent state senator since 1965, announced he would not seek reelection but instead run for Congress in 1974. A vacancy would occur in the 30th Senatorial District (the District) that included Wichita and 28 other Northwest Texas counties. The only likely candidate to succeed Hightower was State Representative Charles Finnell of Holiday, Texas. Charles had the advantage and disadvantages of being in the Texas House of Representatives since 1967, where his record was less than stellar.

As a Democratic leader in Wichita County, I visited with several attorneys, suggesting they run for the anticipated vacancy. Ben G. Oneal was the last person from Wichita Falls to serve in the State Senate, and that was from 1931 to 1939. None of my prospective candidates were interested, but several thought I should run for the office. My response was the same as theirs: I don't have time; too many commitments to law practice, partners, and family. However, friends planted the seed, which started me thinking about making the race for State Senate. What if I did, and what if I didn't? A big decision had to be made.

THE DISTRICT AND THE DECISION

No decision could be made to run, or not run, for state senator of the District without knowing more about what was involved in making the race. I had never been in half of the 29 counties constituting the District, and I didn't know anyone in 20 of them. Wichita County was the largest, but only one-third of the voters lived there. Finnell represented a part of Wichita and all of Archer, Clay, and Young counties in his House District. Charles was the subject of criticism in *Texas Monthly* magazine, where he had been listed as one of the ten worst legislators; however, he was accomplished at running for office and getting reelected. He had laid plans to succeed Hightower for several years prior to the election, long before I ever thought of it.

So how do you make an assessment of whether an unknown candidate would have much chance of winning an election in the other two-thirds of the large rural district? How many votes would my opponent get in Wichita County, particularly the part he represented? Some might suggest hiring a consultant and taking a poll, but I had no money for a consultant, and a poll at that time would have shown I had no chance whatsoever because I was unknown outside of my hometown. In addition, the smaller towns and cities comprising the rest of the District were suspicious about anyone from the "big city" of Wichita Falls.

In my quest for the answers, I started visiting as many people as possible in Wichita Falls and elsewhere, gathering names of contacts in far-flung places like Big Spring, Plainview, Snyder, Sweetwater, Vernon, Stamford, Floydada, Memphis, Henrietta, Turkey, Haskell, Munday, Knox City, Throckmorton, Albany, Hamlin, Seymour, Childress Quanah, Paducah, Spur, Colorado City, Aspermont, Baird, Silverton, Matador, Jayton, and other towns and byways within the District.

Lynn Darden was one of the attorneys in Wichita Falls whom I encouraged to run for the State Senate. Lynn was the area campaign manager for

30th District with 29 counties and the candidate, primary mail piece, April 1874

Governor Dolph Briscoe and had managed the Congressional campaign for Graham Purcell. Although Lynn declined, he and his wife Margaret suggested that I run. They invited Helen and me to attend an area dinner in Stamford, Texas, honoring Bob Strauss and his brother Ted. The Strauss brothers grew up in Stamford and went on to fame and fortune. Bob Strauss was then serving as Treasurer of the National Democratic Party, and a large number of political leaders from the District attended the dinner. We met many of them, including Representative Pete Laney of Plainview and Charles Stenholm of Stamford; both invited me to come and visit about the State Senate race. I did so before making my decision.

Nelda and Pete Laney lived on their farm near Hale Center. With some difficulty, I found the farm and had a good visit with Pete. I inquired why he didn't run for the Senate, and he said

Candidate with Garland Smith (Hale County Dem. Chair) and Rep. Pete Laney, 1974

he had given it some thought, but felt his future was in the House. Apparently it was, because he was elected as Speaker of the House for five terms, from 1993 to 2003. Pete said he could not get involved in my race if I chose to run because he was currently serving with Charles Finnell, but he suggested the names of several persons I should visit in the northwestern part of the District. Pete also advised me to make a prompt decision, because Finnell was hard at work getting commitments and raising money. I spent the night at the Laney farm. Nelda prepared a hearty breakfast of ham, eggs, biscuits, and gravy before I started back to Wichita Falls by way of Plainview, Floydada, Matador, and Paducah, where I called on Representative Bill Heatly.

William S. (Bill) Heatly served as chairman of the powerful House Appropriations Committee for several terms prior to our meeting, and he was known as the "Duke of Paducah." Although he had lost the chairmanship of the Appropriations Committee, Bill was still the most powerful politician in Cottle County and surrounding area. Like Laney, Heatly wouldn't get involved against a fellow House Member, but he gave me names of leaders in the central part of the District that I should see. Bill also advised me to decide quickly whatever I was going to do. After his death, Cottle County commissioned a life-size statue of Mr. Heatly that stands in the town square of Paducah, but Bill Heatly was bigger than life back then, and twice as mean. Fortunately, Bill never got mad at me—except in the middle of the campaign.

Big Spring in Howard County was the second largest city in the District. I had never been to Big Spring and knew no one who lived there. The only time I ever viewed it was in the movie *Midnight Cowboy* when Jim Buck, played by Jon Voight, boarded a bus there to seek his (mis)fortune in New York City. Fortunately for me, a good friend named Tom Locke had lived in Big Spring for several years before being transferred to Wichita Falls. As manager of the electric company in Big Spring, Tom knew all the folks one needed to know for a successful campaign in Howard County, and he gave me their names and phone numbers.

It takes the better part of a day to drive the 234 miles from Wichita Falls to Big Spring, but the trip was worth it. At the time, Big Spring had more organized labor voters than Wichita Falls and voted heavily Democratic. With Tom's list, and dropping his name here and there, I made friends across the political spectrum of Howard County—and that was a wide swath. I

Charlie Stenholm, circa 1995

stopped in Sweetwater and Stamford on the way back home. In Sweetwater I visited with Temple Dickson, a former House member, and received great encouragement to run for the Senate. (Dickson was later elected to the State Senate and served from 1989–1991). Charlie Stenholm was optimistic about the prospects for Jones County, which included the towns of Stamford, Anson, and Hamlin. (Stenholm was elected to the U.S. House of Representatives in 1978 and served in Congress until 2004.)

The next question was whether I could raise more than $100,000 dollars to fund a winning campaign for the primary race. Ray Clymer said he would help raise the money if I ran, and Jerry Estes agreed to be my campaign treasurer, an important responsibility for compliance with campaign reporting laws. With the help of Bill Hobby and several friends in Austin, we determined that some money could be raised from political action committees and lobbyists, but limited because I would be running against an incumbent House member. Responses from Wichita Falls and friends around the state were more encouraging.

During all of this travel and time on the phone talking about the possible Senate race, I maintained my law practice, attended board meetings, and met family obligations. Any decision to run was a family one, and Helen was extremely helpful in trying to make the right assessment. We took the boys to California in August 1973. The opportunity to get away was worthwhile, and we made the decision to run for the State Senate while on the family trip, somewhere between Los Angeles and San Diego. According to Helen's notes:

Aug. 10–19—California w/ kids-Ray decides to run
Sept.–Oct.—Campaign Begins

Although the decision was made on or about August 15, and the campaign got under way in September and October, I did not formally announce my candidacy until December 12, 1973. Helen joined me, and we flew to Big Spring, Abilene, Plainview, and back to Wichita Falls, announcing for office in each of the District media areas. We were on our way, but not without a few bumps in the road and second thoughts.

THE PRIMARY ELECTION, MAY 4, 1974

My first campaign was homegrown, without paid political consultants, ad agencies, or seasoned experts. The headline of a feature article in the *Wichita Falls Record News* captured the unique nature of our first effort when it said, "Farabee Dining Room Table Center of Family Life, Campaign Planning." Helen served as press agent, poster designer, and organizer for everything from mass mailouts to fund-raisers. We designed the first letterhead, push cards, yard signs, emery boards, matchbooks, bumper stickers, newspaper ads, and even the billboard advertisements. (The printer failed to put the required political advertising disclaimer on the emery boards. Recalling my "Hemphill's # 3 experience at UT, we spent several nights stamping on the required words.)

Every person running for office, particularly on the first go-round, must have a campaign phrase that differentiates him from his opponent. My slogan was "Ray Farabee is a concerned citizen, not a perennial politician." Because of negative attitudes about lawyers and being perceived as a "liberal," I described myself as a "businessman and attorney," emphasizing such business connections as being a bank director and officer in several non-profit corporations. Another requirement is a good family photo, preferably with

All-American family campaign picture by Ron Gleason, Fall 1973

a dog. Ron Gleason, a friend and director of the local museum, took more than 100 pictures. We gleaned several family pictures from his efforts, even though Fred, the dog, was not very cooperative. Finally, it helps to have your picture taken with the Governor or some other high official. Governor Dolph Briscoe, with a little help from Lynn Darden and Rhea Howard, was more cooperative than Fred.

Max Sherman, my friend from

student government and bible-selling days, was in the State Senate at the time, and his district was very similar to mine. Like me, Max did not run for public office before his election to the Senate; I sought his advice on how to field a winning campaign. Max said the most important part of his first effort was district organization from the county level down to the precincts. I followed the advice, and by February 1974 we had one or more campaign coordinators in each of the 29 counties.

The primary elections were scheduled for May 4, 1974, and I spent most of my time from January until that day organizing, traveling, raising money, and attending as many meetings across the wide area as possible. I remember nearly falling asleep at the wheel when I was driving to Big Spring one night. On another evening I was flying back to Wichita Falls from Plainview in a borrowed single-engine airplane. I had an experienced pilot who confirmed with the regional weather station that all was clear for the flight back. We flew into a thunder cell over King County in the least populated part of the District. The plane unexpectedly dropped for several hundred feet, but it seemed like a thousand or more at the time. It crossed my mind more than once that a plane crash or serious car wreck would be a hell of a price to pay for a $600-per-month job in Austin. Several friends, including Jay Cantrell and Monty Deatheridge, helped with the driving on some longer trips.

Meetings and gatherings were occurring across the District throughout the year—service clubs (Lions, Rotary, etc.), county fairs, rodeos, recognition dinners, pancake breakfasts, fish fries, barbecues, Farm Bureau, Farmers Union, 4-H livestock shows, electric co-ops, and more. The meetings of preference, however, for candidates seeking office are annual chamber of commerce dinners. All of the community leaders within each of the small towns gather for a meal of roast beef or chicken, green beans, mashed potatoes, and speeches, with recognition of that year's outstanding man and woman.

Charles Finnell was the champion for attending chamber dinners. Of course, he started several years ahead of me. I hardly knew what a chamber of commerce was, except for the Wichita Falls Board of Commerce and Industry, *Charles Finnell, circa 1974*

which didn't have an annual dinner at the time. I became very proficient at attending chamber dinners with my wife whenever possible. Charles would usually be there with his wife Meryl, and sometimes his brother Les. The problem occurred when two or more of the many chambers of commerce met on the same night. This was less of a problem for Charles because his brother Les attended one meeting and Charles the other. Les looked just like Charles, and I initially thought they were identical twins, but later determined there is a two-year age difference. Nevertheless, it took me a long time to distinguish Les from Charles, and I suspect some of the other chamber attendees had a similar problem.

Although Charles had the advantage of being an incumbent legislator, some problems came with the job, beyond having a voting record. One problem was the Constitutional Convention of 1974 that was comprised of the sitting members of the 63rd Legislature. The Convention convened on January 8, 1974, and did not adjourn until July 30 of that year, nearly three months after the primary. If Charles missed very many days of the Convention, he would be subject to criticism for shirking his duties. If he attended, he could not be on the campaign trail. To a degree, he was boxed up in Austin, and I was rambling all over the 30th District. After seven months, the Convention failed to reach any sufficient consensus to submit a new constitution to the voters, but that did not become an issue in the Senate Election since the Convention had only been wrestling with the difficult issues of constitutional law for four months by the date of the primary.

Charles apparently sought to communicate with that part of the Senate district outside of his State Representative District on the telephone, and that did become an issue, thanks to the *Abilene Reporter News*. The headlines read something like, "State Representative Finnell Makes the Most Long Distance Phone Calls Outside His District on State Phone Lines" with the strong suggestion that state property was being used for political purposes, unrelated to state business. The same article identified me as being an up-and-coming candidate in the Senate race. I had no prior knowledge of the phone calls and did not utilize the innuendo in my race. It was one of those *res ipsa loquitor* (the thing speaks for itself) matters, but I think it was a turning point in my race against Charles.

A problem arose with the newspaper disclosure. The state representative coming in second for the most calls outside his district was Bill Heatly. To say the least, the Duke of Paducah was not pleased with the *Reporter*

Bill Heatly, "The Duke of Paducah," 1975

News article, and his initial response was to blame me. He called me (whether on a state line or not, I do not know) and was hotter than hell about it. I explained that I knew nothing about the article before it appeared and had nothing to do with it. Bill cooled down after a short time and did me no harm, and, in fact, was helpful in some indirect ways.

Although I did no door-to-door campaign work in residential areas, I went to every small town, walking up and down the main streets shaking hands, passing out my push cards, and asking people to vote for me. I first did this with George Morey in Childress, Texas. George was the owner of the local radio station and knew everyone in the city of Childress and most of the folks in the county. He observed me trying to perform this necessary task for about ten minutes and then pulled me aside, explaining that I was never going to make it in the small West Texas towns unless I loosened up, did a better job of making small talk, and pressing the flesh. George said, "Watch me" and he proceeded to walk along the main street of Childress shaking hands, asking people how they were doing, introducing me (as I should introduce myself), all with great ease, warmth, and familiarity. After ten minutes, he said, "OK, now you do it." I did it and passed the George Morey test. I kept on doing it until November 4, 1974, when I was elected State Senator. Initially, it was no more natural for me than knocking on doors and selling bibles. Once I got into the "roll and go" of the experience, I actually enjoyed it—at least on the good days.

Helen and I stopped at the radio station in Vernon one night while returning to Wichita Falls from a reception in Paducah. The station manager wanted interviews with me and Charles Finnell. Charles did his interview earlier in the day, and the radio announcer suggested I listen to it before my interview since my opponent had "gone on the attack" and he wanted to ask me about it. We nervously listened to Charles explain that his opponent (without mentioning my name) was "the thinly veiled voice of the new left." Although I was disturbed by Finnell's accusation, I did my interview and we headed home in the night. On the way I expressed my concern to Helen, and she wisely observed that it was doubtful that anyone would know who or what the "thinly veiled voice of the new left" meant.

During another long day on the road, I encountered more rumors that I was "too liberal" and arguments that I could not represent rural areas outside Wichita Falls. By the time I got home, I was tired; convinced we could not win the primary; and having second thoughts about my decision to run. It was still early in the campaign, but I did not have time to practice any law. I suggested to Helen that we pull out of the race and return the campaign donations. She was more positive about our chances and suggested we call Ray Clymer. Clymer came to our home, and they reasoned with me, asking whether I wanted to be a state senator. I said "yes." We had fewer than four months to go before the primary election, and they thought I could win. Although I wasn't so sure, I agreed to stay the course, and we plowed on through the primary campaign.

As we entered the last two months of the campaign, everything seemed to come together. Our billboards and yard signs went up. The county coordinators put placards all over the telephone polls, and I stapled up a few myself along the byways. Newspaper ads were purchased and sent to all the weekly papers and the few dailies. We recorded radio and TV commercials for the last week before the primary election. Some cities like Vernon and Childress had phone banks to get out our vote. The largest investment was a direct mail piece, which featured the family photograph, sent to all Democratic voting households. My picture was sandwiched between Howard, Scurry, Hale, and Floyd counties, distanced from the urban threat of Wichita Falls, our slogan about not being a "perennial politician," and a comparison of the two candidates, featuring me as the good guy.

It's hard to know what makes the difference in an election that should have been very close. Charles focused his organization on the courthouses, particularly county commissioners. Although I campaigned in all 29 courthouses, my political organization was made up of community business, civic, and education leaders. We reached out to all groups in the vast area of the 30th District—farmers, ranchers, merchants, laborers, minorities, educators, bankers, lawyers, doctors, and retired persons. My law partners and clients were helpful, not just for sticking with me through the months that I was not as available, but by contacting voters, contributing, and sending letters to friends and fellow professionals.

Although Bob Wilson was frequently an adversary in my law practice, he was the closest thing we had to a consultant. Bob was our phrase maker, poll taker, and political strategist. To my knowledge, Bob was never tempted to run for office himself, but he loved a good political fight as much as working up a winning plaintiff's case. Bob Wilson's input was more valuable than the Beechcraft Bonanza he made available on several occasions.

Newspaper picture, morning after the primary election with Steve on his paper route, May 4, 1974

When primary election day finally came on May 4, 1974, we had given it our best shot, and we hit the bull's eye. A total of 62,423 votes were cast in the State Senate race with 38,283 (61.33%) for Farabee and 24,140 (38.67%) for Finnell. Charles carried only four counties (Archer, Baylor, Throckmorton, and Shackelford), and I won the rest. The counties giving me the largest percentage of votes were Howard (Big Spring 73%), Fisher (Roby/Rotan/Roscoe 71%), Scurry (Snyder 68%), and Nolan (Sweetwater 69%). I received more than 60% of the vote in eighteen counties, including 61% in Wichita County. I was up early the next morning to help Steve throw his paper route and deliver the good news to Precinct 22. See picture above.

Charles Finnell ran against Rep. Tom Cartlidge in 1976 and regained his former position as state representative for the 53rd District. He served in the House for 22 more years until he lost to Rick Hardcastle, a Republican from Vernon in 1998. Despite our spirited political race for the Texas Senate in 1974, we remain friends and worked together on matters affecting the counties we both represented.

THE GENERAL ELECTION, NOVEMBER 5, 1974

Mary Virginia Kirchhoff (Mary) of Plainview was the Republican candidate for State Senator of the 30th District in the General Election. Mary was an attractive schoolteacher who was married to John J. Kirchhoff. They had two children who helped make an attractive family picture for the campaign. John was a gregarious chap from an old wealthy family in that area, and they lived on an irrigated soybean farm overlooking Plainview. The Kirchhoffs were longtime Republicans, and Mary proudly related entertaining many public dignitaries in their home, including then-President Richard M. Nixon.

Texas was changing politically in the early 1970's, but it was still a one-party state when it came to state and legislative officials—all Democrats except for a sprinkling of Republicans in the Legislature and U.S. Senator John Tower from Wichita Falls. Nixon's overwhelming defeat of George McGovern in 1972 was an indication of things to come, and we would hear

Arm in arm with Mary Virginia Kirchoff, 1974

lots about George McGovern before the State Senate race was over. I think Mary and her party reasoned that if the state could elect John Tower from Wichita Falls, why wouldn't the 30th District elect an attractive Republican candidate? The fact that Richard Nixon overwhelmingly carried nearly every county in the District bolstered that reasoning and explains the nefarious ad that Mary used against me in the last two weeks of the campaign.

Although the economic fortunes of the Kirchhoffs had floundered in recent years before the general election, Mary fielded a vigorous and well-funded campaign. John Tower, Margaret Bridwell Boudle, and other wealthy Republicans in Wichita Falls and across the District contributed generously, but most of her funds came from Republican political action groups. Mary did not attend as many meetings as Charles Finnell, but she traveled across the entire District and was present at most of the ones that counted. The Kirchhoff push cards, billboards, and newspaper and radio ads were not homegrown—they were the products of professional ad agencies and campaign consultants, including one out of Denver, Colorado.

During the last two weeks of the campaign, the Kirchhoff campaign got down in the mud and came out with full-page ads across the District, assailing my years with the National Student Association as the work of an ultra-liberal with a radical left-wing organization. Worse than my "thinly veiled liberalism," I had voted for, and was, a George McGovern delegate to the Wichita County Democratic Convention in 1972! My efforts for McGovern were actually more related to stopping the George Wallace delegates from taking over our precinct and the County Convention, but such subtleties were ignored for innuendos that I was not trustworthy. The Denver group was thorough in its research about my "dark political past" and printed blown-up copies of my precinct vote for McGovern.

Like Elvis's song, I was "all shook up" and worried about the effect of this negative advertising and direct mail piece. I took the Richard Nixon picture from my student leader days to Plainview, where I suggested we run the picture with the current President's inscription proclaiming me to be a great American. At the time, Nixon was on his way to impeachment, and Plainview was heavily Democratic. The cotton farmer advisors looked at the picture, scratched their heads and said, "Ray, we think that picture of you and Nixon would do a lot more damage than Mary Virginia's ads." They were right.

When the votes were all counted on the night of November 5, I carried every county in the District, including Plainview, and garnered 78.85% of the votes. I did not have either a Democratic or Republican opponent during the remainder of my 13 years in elective politics. I guess that's what Nixon meant when he wrote to me as president of NSA, "with every good wish for the years ahead, from Dick Nixon"—even though he later visited the Kirchhoff's home in Plainview.

CONSIDERATION OF HIGHER OFFICE AND OTHER POLITICAL MISADVENTURES

Once a person has been elected to the State Senate, particularly if you get good marks and press, people ask when you are going to run for governor or some other "higher office." When I went to the Senate, I did not have my eye or ambitions on serving in any higher office. The only campaign I anticipated was for reelection in four years.

In 1982, with seven years' experience in the State Senate, I was approached about running for Texas Attorney General (AG). Mark White was then AG, and he let it be known he was leaving that office to run against Bill Clements for Governor. Because of my long involvement in the practice of law and with jurisprudence issues, the AG's office was very attractive to me; I commenced an exploratory effort to determine what support I might have, if I chose to run for that office. I talked to Mark White about the office and the leaders of various groups to determine the likelihood of their support. I called friends across the state—not on the state telephone line—to check

Ben Barnes from his book Barn Burning, Barn Building, *2006*

their reaction. Positive responses came from liberals like fellow Senator Oscar Mauzy to conservatives like George Christian. Ben Barnes said he didn't know why I would want to leave the Senate where I had more power than the AG, but said he would support me.

At the time, two other potential AG candidates were also roaming the state for support: Dallas Congressman Jim Mattox and former State House of Representative John Hannah from East Texas. John was a member of the Dirty Thirty and a consumer advocate. To my surprise, I received a call from Max Sherman saying he had decided to leave his post as President of West Texas State University and run for AG.

It was apparent to me, and probably to Max, that we would split the conservative and West Texas vote, killing the chance for either of us to make a runoff election in the Democratic primary. I had done enough exploratory work to know that Mattox would run strong with organized labor and in the larger cities like Dallas. I also determined that John Hannah had stronger support in East Texas than I could muster. A successful statewide race for AG would require well over a million dollars, and that alone was enough to chill my ambitions for higher office. I decided not to run for AG, and it turned out to be a wise decision.

Although Max indicated several years later that he probably would not have run had I made the race, he did me a favor by choosing to run. Max ran an organized and well-financed campaign for AG, but he came in third behind Mattox and Hannah. Jim Mattox won the runoff handily and served two terms before running for Governor and losing to Ann Richards. John Hannah served as Secretary of State under Richards and was later appointed U.S. District Judge for the Eastern District of Texas. Although I didn't know Mattox or Hannah at the time, I became acquainted and got along well with both of them during the remainder of my tenure as State Senator. More important, I learned that Barnes was right. I had a better job as a state senator and chairman of the State Affairs Committee, and later as General Counsel of the University of Texas System.

In early 1984 I became interested in presidential politics, not as a candidate, but the campaign of Gary Hart, who won the New Hampshire primary with a margin of 10% of the vote over Walter Mondale. Hart was a very bright U.S. Senator from Colorado, and I felt he had a better chance of winning the Presidential race than Mondale. I made a political contribution to his effort and let my feeling be known to Hart's Texas campaign manager. Before I knew it, I was a Hart delegate to the National Democratic Convention in San Francisco. It was the first and only National Convention for Helen and me, but we believed in our cause and had a good time. Walter Mondale won the Democratic nomination; however, he lost to Ronald Reagan in November 1984, carrying only his home state of Minnesota.

Gary Hart, from book cover of Hart and Soul, *1986, Farabee's Odyssey*

Hart announced he would not run for reelection to the U.S. Senate in 1987, and would seek the Democratic nomination for president again. He was the clear frontrunner. Because of my early support in 1984, I became one of the Texas leaders for the Hart campaign. I introduced him in the Texas Senate and helped secure the endorsement of Bill Hobby (who never let me forget it). I attended a weekend meeting in East Texas with Gary and his wife Lee at Arthur Temple's (Temple-Inland) piney woods retreat.

Everything looked good for Hart, and I could see a future in Washington D.C., but a strange thing happened on our way to the White House. There were rumors of extramarital affairs, and Hart challenged the press to "Follow me around. I don't care. I'm serious. If anybody wants to put a tail on me, go ahead. They'll be very bored." Two reporters took him up on the challenge and observed an attractive woman coming out of Hart's Washington, D.C., townhouse. Later, the *National Inquirer* published a picture of Hart with a young model named Donna Rice on his lap, aboard a yacht named *Monkey Business*. Although the "monkey business" survived to make every daily newspaper in the country, Gary Hart's campaign sank with the bad press.

Hart tried to call me on the telephone after the news event; but I was so mad about his getting that close to the nomination and blowing his chances, I did not return the call. I cooled off after several years, and Hart preserved his marriage with Lee. They live together in Colorado. I learned three important lessons from my Gary Hart misadventure: First, don't challenge the press to follow you; and second, stay away from the monkey business. Finally, I really didn't want to leave the State Senate and move to Washington, D.C.

The longer I served in the State Senate, the less I was interested in seeking "higher office," elected or otherwise. In an August 4, 1985, feature article in the *Austin American-Statesman*, I summed it up when I said:

> I don't rule it out, but I'm not willing to get out there and spill my guts for it either. If you start running for another office, it has a tendency to skew how you vote, react, and articulate the issues.

Holding Office: The State Senate Years, 1975–1988

[A good Legislator] must be a student of the process—
its rules, its rhythms, its reins of power—and the
better student he is the more respect he earns.
—Paul Burka, *Texas Monthly,* July 1987

THE OPPORTUNITY TO SERVE in the Texas Senate is a rare privilege—rare because the Senate has only 31 members, making it the smallest among larger states and one of the smaller of the 50 states. The small size means that a senator's voice in public policy and state government is greater, if he or she chooses to use it. It is also easier to learn and understand the rules, rhythms, and reins of power in a smaller legislative body than, for example, the Texas House of Representatives, which has 150 members. As Senator Grant Jones often reminded me, I was not "House broken" because I didn't come to the Senate by way of the House. Bent, but not broken, I quickly became a student of the process.

My wife Helen and Bill Hobby were important in whatever success I achieved during the Senate years. Helen kept family and home together while I was holding down the two full-time jobs of serving in the Senate and practicing law in Wichita Falls. In addition, she introduced me to Bill Hobby three years before I was elected. Helen later emerged in her own right as a remarkable volunteer citizen advocate for human services, the mentally ill, and health care for indigent Texans.

In this chapter I share some information and recollections of the Senate years. Chapter Eleven outlines what I view as the most important legislation authored or sponsored by me while in the Senate.

LEARNING THE ROPES

By January 1975 I had spent nearly one half of my life as a student—in the Wichita Falls public schools, at UT Austin, as a student leader with the National Student Association (NSA), and finally as a beginning lawyer learning the practice of law. When I arrived at the State Senate, I became a student again, this time of the legislative process, its rules, rhythms, and reins of power.

Charles Schnabel, the secretary of the Senate, was helpful in teaching me the elementary rules of the Senate. The most important rule is securing 21 votes to suspend the rules for getting a bill up for consideration or securing 11 votes to keep someone else from achieving the magic number to consider their bill. Though math was never my strong suit, I could count to eleven (using one of my toes). I quickly learned the words and phrases for each step of the legislative process and was off and running.

Jessye Brown was my first administrative assistant, and she was a good teacher. Jessye had long experience in the Senate and was highly respected. She quickly introduced me to key Senate staffers like Charles Schnabel, Betty King, and Patsy Spaw. Betty succeeded Charlie Schnabel as secretary of the Senate, and Patsy, who was head of Engrossing and Enrolling (E&E) for years, succeeded Betty when she retired in 2001. In those times, before Palm Pilots, computers, and cell telephones, Jessye would

Jessye Brown, 1975

start me out each morning with a small card that outlined the day's busy schedule during the session. Under her tutelage, I never missed a meeting or an appointment.

A few members of the Senate in 1975 were especially helpful to me as a newcomer. Max Sherman was always available to explain things that puzzled me. Max and I frequently attended the many receptions occurring each evening during my first session; he taught me the practical lessons of making an appearance at multiple events in one evening, gathering

Max Sherman, 1975

our name tags as we went, and finding the better food and drink. Don Adams had a desk on the Senate floor in front of mine, and I learned a lot about the rhythms of the Senate and East Texas from Don. Senator A. R. "Babe" Schwartz taught me the important lesson that I did not have to "go along to get along." In fact, my friendship with Babe was a prime example of this lesson. I was in several major debates and disagreements on the floor of the Senate with him during my first session, but we always emerged as friends. Another important lesson Babe imparted was that I didn't always have to win by a large margin—a smaller margin was adequate, and a loss here or there was okay, if for the right purpose. We didn't always agree on what the "right purpose" was; nevertheless, the lesson was an important one. Senator A. M. Aikin, the dean of the Senate, taught me the importance of keeping my word to other senators, particularly with regard to votes to suspend the rules. Aikin explained that when a senator broke his word, two votes were lost—the one from the broken promise and the vote that was not secured from another senator to constitute the needed 11 or 21 votes. I learned to be careful about giving my word and to explain in advance when I changed my mind. Aikin and Schwartz both taught me a lot about respect for the traditions and the importance of the institution.

The reins of power in the Legislature reside not only in the Senate, but also with the House, the lobby, and the governor's office. As much as some senators may think about their side of the Capitol, a Senate bill does not become law until it passes out of the House and is signed by the governor, or allowed to become law without the governor's signature. When I first arrived in the Senate I knew very few House members, other than the ones from my district. I became acquainted with as many as possible and cooperated with them whenever practical. Bill Clayton and Gib Lewis were the two speakers of the House during my 13 years in the Senate. I came to know and work well with them. Even when I opposed some of their appropriations requests or legislation like a water plan that was Clayton's highest priority, both were very fair with me on other issues and never held our disagreements against me.

Rusty Kelly from Haskell was sergeant-at-arms for the House during my first term and helped me learn many of the mysteries of the west wing. Some senators are fond of taking the floor and castigating the House for doing or not doing something that is near and dear to their legislative program. I never saw any percentage in that practice. I knew that I would soon be walking through the rotunda and into the House to ask for a hearing, a committee vote, or some other favor in order to pass my legislation, and I always dealt respectfully with the House. While I was in the Senate, some of the members of the House who achieved higher office included Kay Bailey Hutchison (U.S. Senate), Rick Perry (Agriculture Commissioner, Lieutenant Governor, and finally, Governor), a dozen congressmen including Tom DeLay, who became Republican Majority Leader, and several U.S. district judges.

The "Third House," that is, the lobby, frequently has its hands on the reins of power, and whatever one's position may be, a legislator must do a certain amount of business with the lobby. I knew very few lobbyists when I came to the Senate. Only a few supported me in my hardest race, the May 1974 Democratic primary, because I was running against an incumbent House member. After a convincing victory, more came forward with offers of support, and throngs of them descended upon me after I was elected. Lobbyists, like members of the Legislature, come in all shapes and sizes, with a variety of baggage, some good and others not so good. Four lobbyists who helped me learn the ropes were Phil Gauss with the Texas Trial Lawyer's Association (TTLA), Gene Fondren with the Texas Automobile Dealers Association (TADA), Ace Pickens with the Texas Medical Association (TMA), and Terry Townsend, who worked for the Texas Motor Transportation Association (TMTA).

LEGISLATIVE SESSIONS

My first legislative session as senator convened Tuesday January 14, 1975, when the four new senators (Kent Hance of Lubbock, Lindon Williams of Houston, Frank Lombardino of San Antonio, and myself) together with the members reelected for an additional four-year term, were sworn in. I served in seven regular sessions of the Texas Legislature, beginning in January of 1975 with the 64th Session and ending with the 70th session in 1988. Additionally, the governor called 12 special sessions while I was a member. Impeachment proceedings are rare, but I participated in two, both involving judges. I was appointed the presiding officer for one of the impeachments, an address proceeding involving Supreme Court Judge Don Yarbrough pursuant to Article XV, Section 8, of the Texas Constitution. Yarbrough resigned before we completed the process, but I received a huge gavel for my limited services as the presiding officer. Unfortunately, Judge Yarbrough's name is misspelled on the gavel, confusing it with that of my former employer U.S. Senator Ralph Yarborough. The voters made the same mistake when they elected the deposed judge.

For each session of the Legislature since 1845, photos of members of the Senate are grouped in panels that proudly hang on various walls of the east wing of the Capitol. Sitting governors, officers of the Senate, and young children of the members are also included in these "public hangings." If one must be hung, particularly the small children, it is better to be strung up in a panel picture on the walls of the Capitol than on gallows or a yardarm. Although it is difficult

Family picture, on first day of first Session, Abilene Reporter News, *January 15, 1975*

to get 150 pictures, with accompanying officials and children, into an 8' × 5' foot panel, House members and their small children hang on the walls of the west wing of the Capitol. Pictures of my son David hang in the east and west wings of the Capitol building, one as a child with his brother Steve on the Senate side, and others in the west wing as a member of the House.

Although the beginning of every legislative session is exciting, my first was the most memorable. When senators are first elected, they draw for seniority in their class (that is, the group of newly elected members), which determines the order of choice for such things as office space, desk location on the floor, and parking spaces. I chose the smallest Senate office space because it was the only one available on the first floor of the Capitol building, across from the Secretary of State's Office where I had my first part-time job in the Capitol while a student at UT in 1952–1953. Although I had more choices of office space as my seniority improved, I stayed on the first floor, moving from office number 116 (now 1E.3 and a telecom room and broom closet) to larger offices in number 120 (now 1E.5) and then to number 126 (now 1E.9). All of the offices were part of the original space for the state comptroller, but my last office included the comptroller's vault, which has been converted to a senator's office. I felt very secure in the vault area, and my staff enjoyed the extra space of the larger office, which has two floors on the first floor of the Capitol.

Many other logistical challenges were presented by each session, like where to live while in Austin for five months. I leased a small unit at the Windridge Apartments in southwest Austin during the first two sessions, and lived in an apartment on Greystone in northwest Austin for the session in 1979. As the children grew older and Helen spent more time in Austin, we leased an apartment in the Penthouse (now condominiums) on Guadalupe and 14th streets on a year-round basis from 1980 to 1984. In May of 1984 we purchased our first house in Austin at 4410 Sinclair Avenue, off 45th Street, but the two-bedroom/one-bath bungalow was crowded when all four of the families were standing in line for the bathroom during the time that our sons, Steve and David, were attending UT and the legislature was in session. In December 1986 we sold the house on Sinclair and purchased 2702 Rockingham Drive near Zilker Park, where I still live.

Another logistical problem was getting to Wichita Falls each Thursday afternoon and then back to Austin on Sunday nights. I usually drove the 600-mile round-trip. During my first session, Tom Cartlidge, the newly elected House member who replaced Charles Finnell, Dave Allred, the House member from Wichita County, and staff member Jay Cantrell accompanied me. Tom was an energetic former marine with a good sense of humor that kept us awake, except for Dave, who was significantly overweight and narcoleptic. Dave rode in the front seat with me and

Rep. David Allred, 1975

would invariably fall asleep, leaning a goodly part of his 350 pounds on my right shoulder. I would push him to his side of the car and drive on through the night to Wichita Falls, dropping Tom off in Henrietta.

During the seven sessions I was in the Senate, I filed 640 Senate bills (securing enactment into law of 246 of them) and sponsored 148 House bills that were passed out of the Senate. I authored 12 joint resolutions that were adopted by the voters and became part of the much amended Texas Constitution.

DOING MY HOMEWORK IN WICHITA FALLS
AND THE DISTRICT

"Homework" consisted of the 30th Senatorial District tasks, law practice, and family—not necessarily in that order; however, those three components absorbed all of my time and commitment during the interim periods between sessions of the Legislature.

"Got a problem?" asked the local newspaper, "Then call your elected officials." My name, address, and phone number were listed along with the city council and school board. I was not sure that some people contacting the Senate district office knew the difference between my responsibilities and those of the city council or school board, but we tried to answer their questions, solve the problems, or direct them to someone who could.

In addition to attending chamber of commerce meetings and other gatherings, I was frequently asked to make speeches and deliver programs across the district. When asked, I did my best to show up and perform, even when it was in the far reaches of the district, like Plainview, Big Spring, and Snyder. Sometimes I drove, and at other times I arranged for a private plane, usually a small single-engine model. I gave my share of commencement addresses, including one to a group of inmates at the Ferguson Unit in East Texas. Some of the inmates had earned GED certificates, qualifying them as high school graduates, and others received junior college certificates. I had a "captive audience," and it was a good experience for my work with criminal justice and corrections.

Texas has always thought of its lawmakers as part-time "citizen legislators," and it pays them accordingly at the rate of $600 per month. The part-time nature of serving in the Legislature may have been adequate in earlier years; however, by the time I was elected, it was often more than a full-time job, particularly in large senatorial districts. Some members are retired, wealthy, or have businesses that carry on while they serve; but this was not true in my case or the circumstance of many fellow legislators. I practiced law on a full-time basis when the Legislature was not in session and part-time when it was.

So how did I support my family, meet obligations to clients and law partners, and carry out the year-round responsibilities of serving in the state Senate? It was not easy, but I did it with a combination of long hours and excellent staff support in Austin and Wichita Falls. During legislative sessions I would drive or fly home on Thursday afternoon and practice law Friday, Saturday, and Sunday mornings.

Night and weekend work at the law office in Wichita Falls

Throughout the year my district staff person did casework, answered the Senate phone, and drafted correspondence for my signature. She made travel arrangements for Senate business in the district and travel back and forth to Austin and elsewhere. As mentioned in Chapter Eight, I owe a lot of the credit for maintaining my law practice to legal assistants Beverly Smith Sloan, Debbie Frazier, and Jean Ann Chasteen.

Some think that members of the Legislature get more business because of their political office. This was not my experience or that of most lawyer-legislators. I had plenty of business when I ran and won the Senate seat. After being elected, I parceled some of the work to partners because of Senate demands on my time or possible conflicts of interest. An example was my work for the Wichita Falls Independent School District, which required more time than I could give it as a senator and involved a local government entity, which received much of its funding from state appropriations.

A legislative continuance law provides a delay mechanism for lawyers who have cases going to trial. I seldom, if ever, used it. In fact, I cut back on the litigation part of my law practice because of the unpredictability of my schedule and my embarrassment during voir dire, when the opposite attorney would quiz prospective jurors if they knew me, heard of me as their state senator, and whether my being a senator would make any difference. As I think about it, the opposing attorney might be doing me a favor, but no one ever responded that they could not be fair to my client because he, she, or it was represented by that ##*!%! politician.

COMMITTEES

Most legislative work is done in standing committees of the House and Senate. For those who want to play an important role in making laws, good committee appointments are very important. During the first two sessions Lt. Governor Bill Hobby appointed me to the Finance Committee, the Jurisprudence Committee, and the Natural Resources Committee. Finance is considered the best committee because it involves the Appropriations Act and state funding priorities. It was (and is) very unusual for a freshman senator to be appointed to the Finance Committee, but Hobby appointed Kent Hance and me to that committee at the beginning of our first term.

In January 1979, I was appointed chairman of the Jurisprudence Committee. With a chairmanship comes additional office space, staff, and power. The powers include authority to set (or not set) bills for hearing, appointment of subcommittees, and opportunities to carry more legislation affecting substantive matters. The number of bills I introduced doubled during the five sessions I was chairman of a major committee, and the number of my bills enacted into law more than doubled.

I was appointed Chairman of the State Affairs Committee in January 1981 and retained that position for the duration of my time in the Senate. Although I enjoyed chairing the Jurisprudence Committee because of my legal background, the State Affairs Committee had a broader charge and more exciting bills referred to it by the lieutenant governor.

Boards, councils, and commissions are created by statutes and continue

Farabee will head powerful State Affairs Committee

WF Times Record News *headline, January 1981*

to function from one interim to the next. Some of these organizations have members other than legislators. I served on the following boards, councils, and commissions: the Legislative Budget Board (LBB) from 1977 to 1988; the Sunset Commission in 1986; the Coastal Marine Council, 1975 to 1979; the Texas Judicial Council, 1981 to 1988; the Criminal Justice Policy Council, 1983 to 1988; and the Pension Review Board, 1983 to 1988.

Interim legislative committees are created by a House or Senate resolution or a concurrent resolution of both houses of the Legislature for committees that have both House and Senate members. Some of the joint interim committees I served on include the Property Tax Study Committee (1975–1976), chaired by Representative Wayne Peveto, which led to a major revision of property taxes in Texas in 1977; the Select Committee on the Judiciary (1983–1985), leading to substantive changes in Texas judicial administration; the Commission on Sentencing Practices and Procedures (1983–1985) that I chaired, contributing some solutions for Texas prison overcrowding and compliance with the Federal Court order involving our prison system; the Joint Special Committee on Cogeneration in Texas (1985–1986) co-chaired with Rep. Pete Laney, a committee that was the stimulus for the first major changes in Texas law to encourage cogeneration of electrical power; the Joint Committee on Liability Insurance and Tort Law Procedures (1985–1986) making recommendations for general tort reform; the Select Committee on Worker's Compensation in Texas (1987–1988) that I chaired until my departure from the Senate. Senator Bob Glasgow succeeded me, and the work of the committee produced major changes in the Workers Comp Act during the 1989 session.

I served on several interim committees created by Governors William C. Clements and Mark White, including the Blue Ribbon Commission for the Comprehensive Review of the Criminal Justice Corrections System (1981–1982), Select Committee on Higher Education in Texas (1985–1986), and the Texas 2000 Commission (1981–1982).

A conference committee is appointed when a bill comes back from the other house in a form that is not acceptable to the house that originally passed it. Most conference committees meet and quickly resolve the differences, but this does not always happen, particularly with complex legislation and the General Appropriations Act for the next biennium. I served on more than 100 conference committees, and reports of the conferees may be found in the House and Senate journals for the years of my service.

Reports of the interim committees listed above and of the Jurisprudence Committee and the Senate State Affairs Committee for the years I served as chairman can be found in the Legislative Reference Library in the State Capitol. Some are included with my papers at Midwestern State University.

STAFFING SENATE AND COMMITTEE OFFICES

I hired approximately 50 staff members for my Capitol, committee, and district offices at one time or another. These were some of the most important decisions I made. One of the challenges was assembling a larger staff for the increased workload of the five-month legislative session. When the session ended, the budget for staffing was significantly reduced, and more than two thirds of my staff for the session would be without a job. Some returned for the next session, but most moved on to other employment. Despite the turnover, I consistently had one of the best and brightest legislative staffs in the Capitol.

When I first came to the Senate, I had seven employees during the session and two during the interim. The administrative assistant for the Capitol office and my district office manager worked year-round. During my last session in 1987, I had 15 employees—eight in the Capitol office, six in the State Affairs Committee office, and one in the district office.

Jessye Brown retired after my second session, and Janet Tanner from Vernon became my administrative assistant in 1979 and for the session in

My first Senate Staff, (left to right) Randy Hollums, Jessye Brown, myself, Debbie Rutherford, Jay Cantrell, Billie Glenn, and Lorraine Woodward (Mary Ann Bloodworth not pictured), 1975

1981. Atelia (Lia) Clarkson was my administrative assistant from late 1981 until I left the Senate in 1988. Lia joined me as an administrative assistant at the UT System Office of General Council (OGC) from 1988 to 1998. She was a leader in computerizing my Senate offices and OGC. She also worked two years with Helen at the Special Senate Committee on Delivery of Human Services—a total of 17 years with the Farabees.

Mary Ann Bloodworth was the first manager of my district office in Wichita Falls. In addition to the routine work of answering telephones, handling Senate correspondence, and making travel arrangements, Mary Ann and her successors handled extensive casework involving constituent services. When Mary Ann and her husband, Louis, moved to Washington, D.C., I hired Joyce Powers, who was succeeded by Janice Sons when Joyce moved to the West Coast. The assistance of Mary Ann, Joyce, and Janice was invaluable in helping me function as an effective state senator.

Randy Hollums of Floydada and Jay Cantrell of Iowa Park joined my staff as legislative assistants for the 1975 session. Jay interrupted his college work to serve again as my legislative assistant and media person for the 1977 session. He worked his way through college as a radio announcer and did an outstanding job in my first and second sessions with news releases and the production of a weekly radio program for district stations. Other legislative assistants working during subsequent sessions were Paul Podraza (1979), Chris Cruz (1981), Art Anderson (1983), George Scott Christian (1985), Lisa Anderson (1985 and 1987), and David Wingard (1987).

My Senate and committee staff, 1985 (left to right) Maria Dickson, Norma Lopez, Lynn Allison, James Spearly, Shanna Igo, Lisa Anderson, Rhoda Swanner, Mike Hutson, Atelia Clarkson, myself, Mel Hazlewood, Melanie Thompson, Leah Gardner, George Scott Christian, Eleanor Cochran, Staci Wages, and Janice Sons.

When I was appointed chairman of the Jurisprudence Committee in 1979, I hired Jim Dodds as general counsel for the committee. Jim was a graduate of the UT School of Law and the LBJ School of Public Affairs. He continued as general counsel for the State Affairs Committee from 1981 until 1984 when he entered private law practice. I hired Mel Hazlewood in 1984 as General Counsel for the State Affairs Committee, and he served in that position until 1988. Mel joined me at the UT system, first at OGC and then with UT Government Relations. Later, Mel left law practice and governmental relations to become a Methodist minister.

With a full-time, year-round committee staff, I could handle more complex legislation and interim work. In addition to Jim and Mel, I was fortunate to have several outstanding committee clerks, including Sue Staber (Jurisprudence 1979), Allison Dickson (1981 and 1983), and Shanna Igo (1985 and 1987) for the State Affairs Committee. The responsibilities of a good committee clerk greatly exceed the typical clerical duties of sending out notices and keeping minutes. The work by Sue, Allison, and Shanna helped make the Jurisprudence and State Affairs Committees successful under my chairmanship.

Toni Hunter (1981–1984), Laura Smith (1987), and Pam Beachley (1987) were committee staff attorneys, and their work was invaluable in legislative and appropriations matters involving prisons, mental health, workers compensation, and juvenile justice. Jim Spearly was the Legislative Assistant for State Affairs from 1983 to 1986 and a specialist in mental health issues. He held a law degree from Yale and was completing his doctorate in psychology at UT Austin. Though physically frail, Jim was one of the brightest persons I have ever worked with. He went on to become a college administrator in Colorado, but he contributed more than will ever be known toward improving Texas mental health programs. Jim died as a result of a brain tumor in 1994.

Thousands of letters, cards, and phone calls came to my Senate and committee offices during each session. Thanks to my AA's and administrative staff, practically every letter and many of the cards received a response. With everything else going on in the typical session, it would have been impossible to deal with the workload without dedicated staff. Melanie Thompson, who worked as a secretary for State Affairs for six years, deserves special mention for her fine work. Many of the staff members, including Jessye Brown, gathered in my home in May 2005 for a reunion, in which I reiterated that no state senator ever had better staffing and support. Jessye died in February 2006.

STATE BUDGET AND TAXATION

Bill Hobby has said on numerous occasions, "The state budget is 90% of the Legislature's work, and the rest is poetry." I'm not sure I agree on the exact percentage or the poetry characterization, but there is no doubt that adoption of the Biennial Appropriations Act is the most important thing that the Legislature does in its regular sessions, or special sessions when it fails to pass the 400-plus-page spending bill in the regular session. It is the one bill that must be passed and signed by the governor; otherwise, state government will shut down. Those who are more skeptical of government might not think that would be a bad thing, at least until the public schools and universities shut down, prisons close, mental health services cease—putting more mentally ill on the streets, nursing homes quit taking Medicaid patients, et cetera, ad infinitum. Perhaps Hobby was right about the 90%, particularly when the Legislature's work is judged on the basis of substantive importance.

The Finance Committee in the Senate and the Appropriations Committee in the House wrestle with spending priorities for the state. I served on the Finance Committee during each of my seven sessions in the Legislature. Senator A. M. Aikin from Paris, Texas, was Chairman of Senate Finance during my first four years; he was also the Dean of the Senate, that is, the longest-serving Senate member. Senator Aikin was old, wise, a perfect gentleman, and one of my mentors. He chaired the committee with fairness, and few cared to cross him. Unlike Bill Heatley, who chaired House Appropriations during several sessions before my arrival, Aikin never outwardly threatened anyone or played politics. He loved the Senate and frequently expressed that sentiment in words and deeds.

All 13 members of the Finance Committee seemed to have their favorite budget items when we were passing out the money—usually state institutions or highway projects in their respective districts. Aikin had few state institutions in his district and fewer favorites. He was very partial to M. D. Anderson Cancer Center in Houston and open about the fact that Anderson treated and prolonged the life of his brother. I was surprised when

With Sen. A. M. Aikin, 1975

he advised the president of M. D. Anderson to "be careful for what you ask, because whatever it is that you want, we are going to give it to you." When I exercised my conservative prerogative and suggested we pare back some request of the hospital, I received a questioning eye from the chairman, but we remained good friends throughout our years of service together. M. D. Anderson is consistently rated as having the best cancer treatment in the world, and I have no doubt that A. M. Aikin is responsible in part for that achievement.

When A. M. Aikin retired in 1979, Grant Jones of Abilene was appointed Chairman of the Senate Finance Committee, and he served in that position until 1989, when defeated for reelection by Temple Dickson of Sweetwater. I worked with Grant throughout my tenure in the Senate. Jones and Aikin are the only Senators who have served five terms as Chairman of the Finance Committee. Bill Hobby said that if I had remained in the State Senate, he would have appointed me Chairman of the Finance Committee in 1989. I have no regrets. I enjoyed all of my work on budget and finance, but I liked the breadth and substantive of the State Affairs Committee better than the number crunching and "log rolling" in Senate Finance. I doubt that I would have had the patience of Grant Jones, and most certainly not that of A. M. Aikin.

Despite the foreboding rumors and campaign ads of my political opponents in 1974 about being a "liberal" (whatever that may have meant), I quickly became identified as a conservative Democrat, in part because my work on the budget showed that I held the line on unnecessary expenditures. After my first session, *Texas Monthly* reported that my work on the Senate Finance Committee impressed my colleagues and my "skill and sensitivity on budget matters proved he has the ability to challenge the system of pork barrel trade-outs that has long been the bane of the appropriations process in both houses."

In 1977, after only two years in the Senate, I was appointed to the

Legislative Budget Board (LBB). The LBB is a permanent joint legislative committee composed of four Senate members appointed by the Lieutenant Governor and five House members, including the Speaker. The LBB was then chaired by the Lieutenant Governor with the Speaker of the House serving as Vice Chairman. (Now the Lt. Governor and Speaker are co-chairs.)

Of all the interim committees, the LBB is the most important because it writes the legislative appropriations bill that is filed in each house at the beginning of the session. The governor submits an appropriations bill, but it is the LBB report that serves as the pattern for work by the Senate Finance

Discussing budget and taxes with Senators Grant Jones and John Montford, 1987

and House Appropriations committees. The LBB commences its hearing and work on the proposed budget each year before the upcoming session, which for its members means more travel and time in Austin during the interim. I learned more about state government during my eleven years on the LBB than from any other board or committee.

By the end of each regular session both the House and the Senate usually have passed an appropriations bill, but numerous differences always exist between the two versions. The differences must be resolved in a conference committee, and that is where the final appropriations act is drafted. I served on the Appropriations Bill Conference Committees during each of my last five sessions. The resolution of several hundred differences in a limited period of time is never easy, particularly when many involve favorite agencies, special items, and rider language that tells the agencies how to spend (or not spend) the money. Despite the shortage of time, complexity of issues, rancor between members, and invariable lack of funds to do everything that some may want, the job gets done.

My work on the Senate Finance Committee, the LBB, and the Appropriations Conference Committees presented opportunities to help fund programs that I felt were underfunded or more important. My priorities were: improved delivery of mental health services at both the community and state hospital levels; alternatives to prisons, such as increased probation and parole services; family planning that, as a part of Title XX, had an 80% match of federal dollars; child protective services; the juvenile justice system; and a variety of other human service programs.

Taxation is the other side of the spending coin, and no discussion of budget matters would be complete without mention of this politically disagreeable aspect of government. It was my experience that people want good schools and universities, more prisons, quality health care for all, the best highways, strong law enforcement, and decent protection and care for neglected children; however, few want to pay the bill with more taxes. Texas was and is a low tax/expenditure state. Except for nine states, including Texas, the other 41 states have a broad-based income tax. Because it does not have an income tax but has all of the needs and problems of a large state, Texas has increased the sales tax and put more burden on local communities and school districts, causing some of the highest property tax rates in the country. It is not easy as an elected public official, particularly in a conservative West Texas district, to talk about taxes. However, I think officeholders can articulate priorities that most people agree with and remind constituents that someone has to pay for the programs they seem to want. I found that people understood a little better when I said, "If it's worth doing, it's worth paying for." My office developed a brochure to dispel what I called "Myths about Texas Government." Myth #1 was that we were overtaxed, when in fact we had one of the lowest tax burdens of any state. I frequently used a quote from Robert Penn Warren's *All the King's Men,* in which Willie Stark poses the question, "Do you think it's honorable to want something and not be willing to pay the price for it?" In effect, I said to my audiences, "Do you think it's honorable, or realistic, to think we can have good schools, highways, prisons, law enforcement, and all the other things you seem to want and not be willing to pay for them?"

A WIFE'S WORK: AT HOME AND IN THE LEGISLATURE

During the 1975, 1977, and 1979 sessions, Helen was not very involved with the Legislature except for the swearing in, participation in the Senate Wives' Club, and a few weekends with the kids in Austin. Both Steve and David were at those critical stages that come with adolescence—junior high and high school. I recall receiving a long distance call from Helen one evening when the Senate was still in session. She told me we needed to buy a boat that would provide a recreation and sports focus for Steve. I had never owned a boat except a canoe at Lake Winneconne in Wisconsin, which would not pull a water-skier. It took me a day to come around, but I reluctantly agreed. When I arrived home for the weekend, I found a shiny new deck boat with an outboard motor big enough to pull two skiers. Helen was exactly right. As compared to less constructive diversions, the boat provided an important alternative for both boys.

On another occasion when Helen was with me in Austin over a weekend, we received a call that David had been in a one-car accident. The one car was our new Buick, which we had left at home in Wichita Falls. David apparently decided it was time to learn to drive, and he took the Buick around the block a couple of times too many and hit a tree, getting a bad knot on his head. Fortunately, he was not seriously injured, but the family car was totaled. This experience seemed to discourage David from further driving until he was qualified for driver's education and the lessons nervously administered by his parents.

Steve went on to become an expert water-skier. He was captain of the ski club at UT and was nationally ranked as a collegiate water-skier. Though Steve tried his hand at drag racing on Kemp Boulevard, neither he nor his brother became race car drivers. David strayed along the way and got into politics, but I don't think we can blame that on the ski boat or his head injury—but maybe on the parents.

Helen's involvement in state policy making changed with the passage of Senate Resolution 67 by the Second Called Session of the 65th Texas Legislature in August 1978. The Senate established the Special Committee on Delivery of Human Services with the charge to make a thorough study of the human services delivery systems in Texas and report back to the

Bill Hobby confers with Helen Farabee in Senate Chamber, 1979.

Legislature not later than January 1, 1981. Lieutenant Governor Bill Hobby appointed Helen to chair the committee. This appointment was the first of her three appointments to chair major committees and task forces leading to substantial changes in the delivery of human service, including mental health, mental retardation, and indigent health care services in Texas.

SPECIAL COMMITTEE ON DELIVERY OF HUMAN SERVICES: This committee was unusual in several respects. It was not a joint interim committee, but only a Senate committee. However, only four senators were on the committee (Chet Brooks of Pasadena, who was appointed Vice Chair and also chaired the Senate Standing Committee on Human Services; A. R. "Babe" Schwartz of Galveston; Pete Snelson of Midland; and Bill Meier of Tarrant County). The other eight members were some of the strongest and best-known leaders in the state, including Ann Richards (then a county commissioner for Travis County), Morris Atlas, Dr. Joaquin Cigarroa, Jr., Max Sherman, and Frank C. Erwin. The committee was well financed with an excellent staff headed by Dr. June Hyer. The work of the committee, including extensive hearings, took more than two years. Two committee members (Frank C. Erwin and Dr. John E. Codwell) and executive director June Hyer died before the work of the Committee was completed. Lia Clarkson succeeded Hyer. Frank Erwin, who became famous as Chairman of the UT Board of Regents, was the only member Helen was skeptical about, but he turned out to be an excellent participant and a good friend. When Frank died, Helen and I attended the memorial service for him, which was held in the Frank C. Erwin Events Center at UT. It was one of the largest and more memorable services I have attended.

Despite the loss of June Hyer, Dr. Codwell, and Frank Erwin, the committee finished its work on time and issued a comprehensive report entitled *The Potential in the Patchwork: A Future Pattern for Human Services in Texas.* The report made 72 recommendations and presented the most comprehensive analysis of human services ever made in Texas. The recommendations included ways to improve, design, construct, systematize, and plan for more efficient, cost-effective, and coordinated delivery of better services to more people. Lieutenant Governor Bill Hobby placed a high priority on enactment of the proposals into law, and 53 (74%) of the total recommendations were implemented in one form or another. Details of the recommendations and their implementation may be found in the committee's *Action Report*, published in September 1981.

MENTAL HEALTH CODE TASK FORCE: The Board of the Texas Department of Mental Health and Mental Retardation established the Mental Health Code Task Force in 1981 to review and recommend a comprehensive revision of the 1957 Texas Mental Health Code and asked Helen to serve as chairperson. Unlike the Delivery of Human Services Committee, this task force was large, with 45 members who served as representatives of all the groups that had a stake in mental health treatment. Although the Legislature was responsible for adopting any changes to the Mental Health Code, no legislators served on the task force. Psychiatrists were fighting with psychologists, state mental health hospitals and all of their allies were lined up against mental health centers and community treatment, county judges had a variety of ideas about commitment proceedings that were in conflict with the opinions of lawyers and social workers. The conflicts among providers, consumers, and public entities seemed irreconcilable, but Helen brought order out of chaos and produced a comprehensive set of recommendations to the 1983 session of the Legislature.

With no legislators on the Mental Health Task Force and an abundance of conflicting interests, few members of the 68th Legislature in 1983 were crazy enough to carry the bill that would rewrite the Mental Health Code. Two of us stepped forward. I introduced SB 435 in the Senate and Representative Tom DeLay of Sugar Land filed the companion bill in the House. Since my wife was chairperson of the task force, I had a good excuse for

Former First Lady Rosalyn Carter, Helen, and Governor Mark White after bill signing, 1983

doing so, but it is unclear to me why Tom DeLay either stepped forward or was talked into carrying the 64-page bill, with no fewer than 100 sections, that required the authors to explain and defend the provisions and reconcile some of the conflicting interests. SB 435 passed out of the Senate on March 23, 1983, and was sponsored in the House by DeLay. It was finally passed and signed by Governor Mark White on April 27, 1983, in the Senate Chamber in the presence of former First Lady Rosalyn Carter, Betty Jo Hay (President of the Mental Health Association), Tom DeLay, Helen, myself, and others.

TASK FORCE ON INDIGENT HEALTH CARE: The Delivery of Human Services Committee and the Mental Health Code Task Force were hard acts to follow, but in September 1983 Governor Mark White, Lieutenant Governor Bill Hobby, and House Speaker Gib Lewis asked Helen to serve as chairperson of the Task Force on Indigent Health Care in Texas. This task force was composed of 71 members including elected officials, physicians, medical school faculty, hospital administrators, other health professionals, community health and mental health center staff, business and labor leaders, individuals from advocacy organizations, consumers, and representatives of state health agencies. The elected officials served as the executive committee and decision-making body for the group. State leadership asked the task force to address four main issues regarding any program to provide indigent health care: scope of service; eligibility criteria; administrative structure; and methods of finance.

After extensive research, hearings, and input from all of the various health care and governmental entities involved, the task force issued its final report in December 1984. The report presented the results of extensive research concerning the medically indigent with findings about the role of local and state government, public hospitals, and investor-owned hospitals and the problems of uncompensated care in hospitals. The task force made 50 recommendations, ranging from allocation of responsibility for indigent care to prioritizing the types of health services to be provided.

Bills were introduced in the 69th Legislature (1985) to implement many of the recommendations of the task force. The bills were carried by legislators who served on the task force, primarily Senator Chet Brooks of Pasadena and Representative Jesse Oliver of Dallas. I worked with them and supported the legislation, but passage was much more difficult than that of bills concerning the delivery of human services in 1981 and a new Mental

Health Code in 1983, particularly the measures requiring funding to meet the needs of uninsured and/or indigent Texans. The Texas Primary Health Care Services Act (HB 1844), the Maternal and Infant Health Improvement Act (HB 1023), and HB 1963, which called for the prohibition of "patient dumping" and the refusal to take indigent cases in emergency rooms, passed in the regular session, but the centerpiece, which provided funding and coordinated the other legislation, failed in the House on the last night of the Regular Session.

Bill Hobby moved "hell and high water," and Governor Mark White immediately called a Special Session that held the Legislature over. Senator Chet Brooks refiled the Indigent Health Care and Treatment Act (SB 1) and the Senate passed it out by noon of the first day of the Special Session, sending it to the House. The House took up the bill that afternoon in committee and passed it to the floor, where it was debated into the evening. Finally, a vote was taken, and it resulted in a tie of 74 for and 74 against the bill. Speaker Gib Lewis broke the tie and hammered his gavel down on the most dramatic passage of any bill in my recollection. Senate Bill 1 appropriated $22,000,000 for indigent health care in fiscal year 1986 and $41,000,000 in fiscal year 1987, together with other important provisions defining county and state responsibility for indigents. It was a good day's work, and the bill was signed into law by Governor White in the Rio Grande Valley during June 1985. Legislation flowing from the task force set the stage for subsequent progress, and it would never have happened without Helen's leadership.

Helen is recognized for her work with the above committee and task forces in the *Handbook of Texas History*. She was inducted into the Texas Women's Hall of Fame later in 1985 in recognition of her contributions to the state as a volunteer. The December 1985 issue of *Texas Business* magazine named Helen and me "Texans of the Year," with an article about "The Team of Helen and Ray Farabee" that discussed Helen's outstanding leadership as chairperson of the Indigent Health Task Force and other volunteer work.

Texas Business *magazine recognition of Helen, Dec. 1985*

PRESIDENT PRO TEM OF THE SENATE

Article III, Section 9, of the Texas Constitution states that the "Senate shall at the beginning and close of each session . . . elect one of its members President Pro Tempore, who shall perform the duties of the Lieutenant Governor in any case of absence or disability of that officer." On the first day of the 69th Legislature in 1985, I was elected by my fellow senators to be President Pro Tempore (Pro Tem). "Pro tempore" is a Latin phrase meaning "for the time being." My time for being Pro Tem was January 8 to May 27, 1985, and then it was Senator Carlos Truan's time for serving as such. Although it is an honor to be Pro Tem, it is a consequence of seniority and is passed on to the next senator according to seniority of service.

Fortunately, Bill Hobby was seldom absent and never disabled during my term as President Pro Tempore or any other time during his 18 years as lieutenant governor. During the times when Hobby was absent from the chair for purposes like meeting with the Speaker, twisting arms, or answering important phone calls, I took the chair and presided over the Senate. The Senate had a very good parliamentarian named Camilla Bordie, and she would whisper all of the right words and phrases that I needed for compliance with the rules. I don't recall any complex points of order on which I had to rule.

When the governor is absent from the state or otherwise unable to serve, the lieutenant governor assumes responsibilities of the governor. Following the logic of the relevant constitutional provisions, a time-honored tradition called "Governor for the Day" has emerged whereby the governor and the lieutenant governor absent themselves from the state on a mutually convenient Saturday during the term of each president pro tem, and *voila*, the Pro Tem is the acting Governor of Texas! My day was May 4, 1985.

The Governor for the Day is a wonderful time for family, friends, and constituents to gather in Austin (though a few, including Max Sherman, have observed the big day in their home districts), heap praises on the head of the Pro Tem, shake hands, and eat barbecue. Eleanor Cochran was the planner for my day in the sun, and a good time was had by all.

Both of our sons, Steven and David, were enrolled at UT Austin at the time and were sanitized by pledge training so that their hair was cut and they were well dressed and on good behavior. Helen made a wonderful first lady, knew practically all the folks from Austin and the district, and had

The First Family, May 4, 1985

done more in her own right than many of the real first ladies of the past. Family members came from near and far, including Helen's mother and brother from Wisconsin. Along with the pomp and circumstance, we had a family reunion in the Governor's Mansion. (It was the first and last Farabee family reunion until September 2004 at Lake Buchanan.)

The grand event reached its crescendo on Saturday morning for the inauguration. The Midwestern State University Symphonic Band presented pre-inaugural music in the Capitol rotunda; the UT Longhorn Band provided inaugural music; Helen and I walked down the Senate chamber aisle beneath the shining swords of the Ross Volunteers of Texas A&M; Dr. Louis Rodriguez, President of Midwestern, gave the invocation; Austin College of Sherman provided selected music; Senator Grant Jones made introductions, and Senator Babe Schwartz and Ray Clymer made remarks about what a great American I was. Finally I was sworn in by my old friend, Judge Don Morgan, and a 19-gun salute was fired off by the National Guard that rocked the Capitol building. After all that, my response was anticlimactic, except for well-deserved praise of Helen, family, and staff.

After the inauguration and coronation, I proceeded to the lobby of the Capitol for a reception with constituents and Austin friends, then a festive

Grand Entry with Pomp and Circumstance in the Senate
Chamber under swords of Ross Volunteers

barbecue with entertainment from the district, including a reenactment of frontier lawlessness by the Red River Renegades. Filled with barbecue and wonderment at the size of the crowd, we proceeded to the Governor's Mansion across the street, where I shook hands with hundreds of people. At the end of the day, the UT System gave a reception for my family and closer friends at the Bauer House in West Austin. At the time, I didn't know that I would be frequenting the Bauer House more often after 1987 when I left the Senate to go to work for the UT System.

If one did not have the bighead before a Governor for the Day ceremony (and many would claim the swollen ego is a common malady among state senators), he or she would have one afterwards. The stars in my eyes were only exceeded by the amount of pain in my right elbow for several months after the big day. I mentioned this physical condition to Gene Fondren, who explained that it was tennis elbow, resulting from my shaking several thousand hands on May 4. Gene apparently developed a similar condition when he first ran for election to the House of Representatives in 1962. My tennis elbow finally went away and the swollen ego shrunk by the push and pull of the closing days of the 69th Regular Session and three called sessions thereafter.

FILIBUSTERS AND OTHER UNUSUAL OCCURRENCES

A few of my experiences in the State Senate were unique or so out of the ordinary that they deserve mention.

LONGEST FILIBUSTER IN HISTORY: *The Guinness Book of World Records* reports that State Senator Bill Meier of Euless, Texas, holds the record for the longest known filibuster, which occurred May 2–3, 1977. Guinness does not mention that it was my SB 1275 that sustained 43.5 straight hours of talk and criticism by Meier and then passed by a vote of 23 to 7. When one considers that Meier had to talk continuously (except for some friendly questions from colleagues and various announcements); that he could not sit, lean on his desk, eat, sleep, or go to the bathroom except in a bag attached to his body, his endurance was a remarkable feat. Since it was my bill, I got very little sleep. Fortunately, Senator Oscar Mauzy, a co-sponsor, kept watch for several hours each of the two nights while Senator Meier droned on, allowing me a few winks on a couch in my office. By comparison, Senator Strom Thurmond holds the record in the U.S. Senate for his filibuster against the Civil Rights Bill in 1957 that lasted only 24 hours and 18 minutes.

The only other time I had a bill that was the subject of a serious filibuster was in 1983. Port Arthur annexed an offshore gas well that was 10.5 miles from the coast and proceeded to levy city taxes on it, although no city services were provided to the property. Senator Carl Parker defended

Roy Acuff making a point to me and Senator Bill Meier, March 1977.
Acuff did not return for the world's longest filibuster in May.

the rights of his hometown, and filibustered my SB 551, which would limit coastal annexations into the Gulf of Mexico. Carl talked about ten hours, and I finally worked out a compromise to limit offshore annexations by coastal cities to areas no more than one league (about 3.5 miles) from shore. Carl sat down, and I passed my bill. The moral to this story is that getting two thirds of a loaf is better than enduring a longer filibuster on the Senate floor—for me and for Carl.

THE SAGA OF THE KILLER BEES: The filibuster is one way to slow, and sometimes kill a bill. Another parliamentary maneuver is the defeat of a quorum (two thirds of the elected members) for consideration of a measure. In the 1979 Regular Session 12 Democratic senators succeeded in breaking a quo-  rum for consideration of a bill to change the date for the presidential primary in a manner that they felt would favor former Governor John B. Connally in his unsuccessful quest for the Republican nomination. I stayed in Austin with 14 other Democrats and the four Republican members, but 19 does not make a quorum. A call was placed on the Senate and the Department of Public Safety, and the Texas Rangers were dispatched to round up and bring back the errant 12, who became known as the "Killer Bees." Although the Rangers looked high and low across the state, the Bees could not be found, and their flight and unknown whereabouts dominated the media. As it turned out, most of the Bees were crammed into a small garage apartment with only one bathroom, located two miles from the Capitol. A compromise was reached that allowed the Bees to return after their five-day hideout, so that we could get on with more important business than having a separate presidential primary for John Connally (who was soundly defeated in his campaign for the Republican nomination by Ronald Reagan). I could go into more details, but it was a "stinging experience." If anyone won, it was the Bees.

CAPITOL BUILDING FIRE OF 1983: On Sunday morning, February 6, 1983, I received a call from my administrative assistant who excitedly told me the Senate side of the Capitol building was on fire, and the fire might spread to the rest of the structure. I drove immediately from Wichita Falls to Austin. When I arrived, the fire had been contained, but billows of smoke were still pouring out of the east end of the second and third floors of the building. The lieutenant governor's apartment, where the fire started, was gutted, along with the offices and hallway behind the Senate chamber. One young man who was staying in the lieutenant governor's apartment died in the fire, and a fireman later succumbed from the effects of smoke inhalation. Electricity and heat were not restored to the Senate chamber for more than a week, but we proceeded with our business in more darkness than usual, bundled in sweaters and overcoats. An investigation determined that the fire started from a defective television set in the lieutenant governor's apartment and also revealed how vulnerable the whole building was to other fire hazards. The fire of 1983 led to the creation of the State Preservation Board, extensive Capitol restoration and expansion from 1990 to 1995, and the installation of a comprehensive sprinkler system.

REDISTRICTING is one of the most difficult tasks the Legislature must accomplish after the national census taken at the beginning of each decade. The Legislature is required to redistrict not only itself but also the congressional districts for the state. Ordinarily state and federal lawmakers go their separate ways, not paying much attention to the other, but a majority of Texas congressmen came by my office and those of other legislators in 1981 with advice about drawing the new maps for their respective districts. Since all of the growth, then and now, is in urban areas, redistricting is particularly difficult for the rural and smaller city areas of the state. I filed a joint resolution that proposed an amendment to the Texas Constitution to expand the number of senators from 31 to 33, but it went nowhere, not even out of committee. Maps and estimates of demographic populations poured forth from a giant computer in the basement of the Capitol, and we finally produced bills to redistrict the House and Senate, but to no avail. A federal court invalidated the bill that redistricted the House, and Governor Clements vetoed the bill redistricting the state Senate. As a result, the Legislative Redistricting Board drew the new lines. I lost three counties (Howard, Hale, and Nolan) and gained five more, including Grayson and Cooke counties, and the northern third of Denton County.

ADVICE AND CONSENT: Appointments by the Governor are subject to the "advice and consent" of two thirds of the Senate members present. An unwritten rule called "senatorial courtesy" exists whereby the governor must secure prior approval from the senator of the district where the prospective appointee resides. Senators vary on how much they exert their influence to defeat an appointment from their district. I never blocked a gubernatorial appointment by Dolph Briscoe, Bill Clements, or Mark White,

Gov. Clements gives advice about my tie; I consent, 1987

but I came close to it in connection with a proposed appointment to fill a vacant district judgeship in Haskell and several adjoining counties. Governor White's appointment secretary contacted me to secure my approval of Joseph Thigpen from Haskell. Although I did not know Thigpen, I was surprised by this proposal because he had just been soundly defeated in his race for reelection as District Attorney for the 39th Judicial District. Thigpen was the brother of Anita Perry and the brother-in-law to then–Democratic State Representative Rick Perry. I got along well with Perry and his family, but I expressed my concern about approving this appointment. The governor appointed another Haskell attorney named Charles Chapman, rather than Thigpen (Chapman was reelected on several occasions since that time before his retirement). Perry apparently heard of my concerns and was disappointed. Later he changed political parties, and he currently serves as Governor of Texas. On several occasions I have visited with Governor Perry and his wife Anita; they have always been very cordial and gracious. Now Perry has to wrestle with the advice and consent of the Senate and the unwritten rule of senatorial courtesy.

THE BUDDY HOLLY STORY: One of the more unusual pieces of legislation I handled in the Senate was the Buddy Holly Bill (HB 834), which I passed out of the Senate in May 1987. The bill added Chapter 26 to Title IV of the Texas Property Code. At the time a deceased person's name and fame (like that of Buddy Holly, who was killed in a plane crash with the Big Bopper) was not protected and could be used for the promotion of a cause or product without permission of surviving heirs and payment of royalties. Maria Elena Holly, Buddy's widow, contacted Representative Al Granoff, who authored HB 834. Al passed the bill out of the House and asked me to sponsor it in the Senate. I did, and its passage made Maria Elena very happy and wealthy. Maria Elena has been an aggressive enforcer of her rights under the Buddy Holly Bill, which is documented by Joe

Nick Patoski in an article entitled "The Widow's Pique," *Texas Monthly*, February 2001.

A SURPRISE BIRTHDAY PARTY: On November 22, 1982, I turned 50. Both Helen and I were in Austin for meetings, and I assumed that we would have a quiet dinner celebrating my attainment of the half-century mark. After a meeting of the LBB, Bill Hobby suggested that we go over to the Quorum Club, which was then located on the top two floors of the United Bank Building. When we arrived, a crowd of well-wishers greeted me with jokes and derision about my new status as a "senior citizen." Helen arranged for the surprise birthday party that still remains one of my most memorable life events. Governor Mark White, Treasurer Ann Richards, and many other friends and officials attended. Helen secured the services of a belly dancer and "Nurse Feelgood," who checked my heartbeat and blood pressure. I passed all the tests. Oh, to be 50 again!

Nurse Feelgood gives her diagnosis on my 50th.

RECOGNITIONS, HONORS, AND AWARDS

All members of the Legislature receive an abundance of plaques, certificates of appreciation, and awards during their tenure, and I was no exception. By 1988, when I left the Senate, I had received over 100 plaques, desk sets, and certificates—more than I had wall space for hanging them. The failure to mention most of them reflects no lack of appreciation, but several come to mind that stand out.

Texas Business magazine named Helen and me as "Texan(s) of the Year," featuring our picture on the front page of its December 1985 edition. The four-page article by Dennis Holder began with the statement: "In tandem, Senator Ray Farabee and his wife, Helen, have, to a surpassing degree, altered circumstance and affected lives statewide in 1985." Although the magazine is no longer published, the recognition of us as a team and as separate individuals was particularly meaningful.

Texas Monthly magazine named me in 1977, 1981, 1983, 1985, and 1987 as one of the ten best legislators at the end of the legislative sessions during those years. I'm not sure anyone, including myself, could live up to some of the positive comments that *Texas Monthly* made about my performance as a state senator, but I greatly appreciate them, then and now. My favorite phrases were: "The compleat senator. Operates on a different level from anyone else, even the good ones: acts not a representative of a single district but as a trustee of an entire state." (July 1981); "The most respected member of the Legislature: carries the best bills, runs the most important committee, and has the longest vision . . ." (July 1983); "Ray Farabee is the sort of person who could give politics a good name . . . Remarkable above all for his fairness." (July 1985) A copy of each segment concerning me is attached in the appendix to this chapter.

Two other recognitions received in 1987 come to mind. One was being named Outstanding West Texan by the West Texas Chamber of Commerce. Former Attorney General John Ben Shepperd, who helped me get my first job in the State Capitol building, received a similar award. The other recognition was from the Texas Corrections Association, which presented its annual Hall of Honor Award to me for legislative work in connection with criminal justice and corrections. I was given a life membership in the association.

TEXAS MONTHLY "TEN BEST" ARTICLES

Ray Farabee: the Senate torch is passed

JULY 1977: Ray Farabee, 44, conservative Democrat, Wichita Falls. All the clichés fit this rising Senate star: observers describe him as conscientious, hardworking, smart, fair, independent, someone who does his homework. These qualities apply to at least a score of legislators; yet there is something about this soft-spoken, scholarly looking senator that sets him apart—an air of inner strength, of incorruptibility, which suggests that a true legislative craftsman may be in the making.

Earned his spurs by soundly thrashing Senate heavyweight Babe Schwartz in the floor fight over medical malpractice. Their clash was the session's most dramatic moment: the veteran with the wisdom and skills accumulated over two decades against the upstart newcomer in his first major test. Senate historians may mark Farabee's victory (he carried the doctor's amendments to a trial-lawyer-backed compromise bill) as the moment the torch was passed to the upcoming generation of senators.

Carried a small but important legislative program, including a bill to provide a method of financing the revitalization of blighted downtown areas. Conceived, drafted, and passed a "natural death with dignity" bill for terminally ill patients: it was one of the few major bills to become law without the help of organized support—mainly because Farabee lobbied it through the House himself. Also carried a crucial worker's compensation bill that required delicate handling in both houses.

One of a regrettably small handful of senators who can't be seduced, coerced, or otherwise convinced to support sleazy bills (voted against loan sharks, insurance sharpies, and the more outrageous realtor positions). If he has a flaw, it's that he is still unsure of himself. Showed signs last session of resisting the logrolling and pork barreling so prevalent in the appropriations process; performed well on the Finance Committee again but no longer seemed willing to question the system. Like Max Sherman, tends to be less conservative than his district (though neither is a liberal by any stretch of the imagination) but, unlike Sherman, hasn't learned how far to follow his instincts. (Page 93)

JULY 1981: Ray Farabee, 48, conservative Democrat, Wichita Falls. The compleat senator. Operates on a different level from everyone else, even the good ones: acts not as a representative of a single district but as a trustee of an entire state.

Nowhere was his overriding concern with public policy more evident than in final negotiations over the state budget, when Farabee stood his ground against House members bent on destroying social programs.

Farabee: more statesman than politician.

Single-handedly fended off attacks on welfare and prison appropriations. Overcame objections to state-funded birth control counseling by exploiting House members' moralistic impulses ("This program is one of the best controls against abortion and child abuse and, frankly, in the long run, welfare"). When the House wanted to stonewall the court decree to end overcrowding in state prisons, Farabee responded with calm appeals to logic ("We should be as concerned about overcrowding as the court is"). On the twelfth day of combat, the House abandoned the siege.

Not a do-gooder but a do-righter. At the same time that he was fighting for better prisons, Farabee was passing law-and-order bills to improve the management of the Board of Pardons and Paroles and to relieve the burden on the Court of Criminal Appeals.

Follows Senate protocol as though he wrote it. Never grandstands, never claims credit where none is due (he soft-pedaled the effect of his bill implementing teacher competency tests while House supporters were trumpeting it as an educational millennium), never shows disrespect for his colleagues. Inherited the chairmanship of the powerful State Affairs Committee from defeated Senate pooh-bah Bill Moore and, to no one's surprise, put an end to the panel's reputation as a burial ground for legislation.

Back in 1977 we said of Farabee, then making the Ten Best list for the first time, ". . . there is something about this soft-spoken, scholarly-looking senator that sets him apart—an air of inner strength, or incorruptibility, which suggests that a true legislative craftsman may be in the making." Consider him made. (Pages 103–104)

JULY 1983: Ray Farabee, Democrat, Wichita Falls. The refutation of former U.S. Speaker Thomas Reed's observation that a statesman is a politician who is dead. The most respected member of the Legislature: carries the

Farabee: the session's hidden persuader.

best bills, runs the most important committee, and has the longest vision, though the competition in this category is limited. Not a technician to equal Bob McFarland or a master compromiser to equal Kent Caperton, but has a higher role to define, by example, what a senator is supposed to be.

A case in point: his handling of a bill that, depending on your point of view, either protected struggling offshore oil operations from annexation by greedy coastal cities or protected greedy offshore oil operations from annexation by struggling coastal cities. Senate regulars, whose frequent pastime is the inspection of Farabee's feet for evidence of clay, hinted that he had sold out to Big Oil in furtherance of his suspected ambition to seek statewide office. Some sell-out. By the time his bill reached the floor, Farabee had already cast the tie-breaking vote in his State Affairs Committee to keep alive an unrelated bill Big Oil was sworn to kill. Then he agreed to a compromise on the annexation bill despite having the votes to run over the opposition. "If I were in a fight to the death at the Alamo, I wouldn't want Farabee as my second in command," griped one observer. "He'd be out cutting deals with Santa Anna." But the Senate got the message: consensus over confrontation.

Involved in everything, though not always visibly. One of the few senators who will work just as hard for a bill that doesn't bear his name as for one that does. Farabee's own achievements bore the same low-profile but high-import stamp: the first major revision of the mental health code in 25 years, three prison reform bills, and a constitutional amendment to allow garnishment of wages for child support. Once again the Senate got the message: substance over show.

Reached his peak—as usual, without advance fanfare or ensuing glory—in the final negotiations over the state budget. Sat aloof from the usual haggling, hoarding his chips for a raise in Texas' paltry welfare spending (forty-ninth in the nation). Up against tradition, which dictated putting off welfare until the very last—when, not coincidentally, there is never any money left; also up against unsympathetic colleagues eager to claim dwindling dollars for their own purposes. Farabee pounced at exactly the right time in exactly the right way, slipping welfare into a package that incorporated all the loose ends, including the solution to an impasse over state employee raises. This time the whole Legislature got the message. (Pages 112–113)

JULY 1985: Ray Farabee 52, conservative Democrat, Wichita Falls. What else is left to be said about this good, gentle man? That he has more virtues than Mother Teresa? No, we listed a lot of them—conscientious, hardworking, smart, fair, independent, an air of inner strength—back in 1977, the first time he appeared on the Ten

Farabee: a Lord among the Commons.

Best list. That he operates on a different level from anyone else, not as the voice of a single district but as the trustee of an entire state? Nope. Said it in '81. That he is the most respected member of the Legislature, who defines by example what a senator should be? Sorry. That was '83. So leave it at this: Ray Farabee is the sort of person who could give politics a good name.

Everybody wanted Farabee to carry their bills, though his floor skills are just ordinary, because, in the words of a Senate staffer, "having him as your sponsor is like the *Good Housekeeping* seal of approval." His legislative program would have sunk a supertanker: judicial reform, blue law repeal, toxic waste regulation, computer crime control, protection for time-share purchasers, securities deregulation, a bond procedures act, fine tuning of parole procedures, indigent health care. Passed most of it despite refusing, as usual, to use his chairmanship of the busy State Affairs Committee as a lever to shift votes, as other chairmen have done since time immemorial.

Remarkable above all for his fairness. Never has a hidden agenda, never gets petty, never tries to get even, never overlooks the weak and helpless. As a member of the Senate's budget-writing team, looked out for agencies aiding delinquent youth, abused children, and the mentally ill. Has a deep-rooted faith in the process of compromise; seemed genuinely offended by the give-no-inch attitude of House budget negotiators, lecturing them that "the act of compromise is not just coming up here to sign off on the House bill," and helped fashion the final agreement.

His one shortcoming, if it is that: he's too trusting in the process, too aloof from winning or losing. But he's doing better. When he was informed that three of his judicial reform bills had died in the House after he had worked on them for a year and a half, Farabee actually threw down his ballpoint pen. On the session's closing night, he even risked exposure to the teeming House floor to inquire after the fate of indigent health care. "They're killing our bill," someone shouted to him amid the pandemonium.

But there was nothing he could do. He was out of his element, a Lord among the Commons. (Page 117)

JULY 1987: Ray Farabee 54, Democrat, Wichita Falls. Poor Farabee, everybody kept saying. He's having his worst session. Well, maybe he did. When you've spent a decade in the rarefied air of the Senate's ionosphere (this is his fifth appearance on the Best list), you can't fall back to the stratosphere without causing talk. But from our vantage point on the ground, he's still pretty high up there.

Certainly there was no drop-off in his work load; he had more credits than Laurence Olivier. Without fanfare, Farabee labored on the cutting edge of the state's biggest problems: *prisons* (he overhauled the much-lambasted parole system), *tort reform* (he provided badly needed protection from lawsuits for charities and their directors and volunteers), *AIDS* (he revised the state's communicable disease laws, establishing how to test for and report AIDS), and *state debt* (with the investment community getting nervous about Texas' financial condition, he established a bond review board to get the state's fiscal house in order).

Nor did he fail to exhibit his usual scout's oathful of virtues. In the ill-fated conference committee on the budget, which degenerated into a Babel of name-calling and rhetoric between House members and senators, Farabee steered the discussion away from personalities and back to numbers. When his own bills came under attack in the Senate, he lived up to his nickname, "Fairabee," by being quick to compromise. His bill allowing flexibility in rate setting of local telephone service started out as highly controversial; after Farabee agreed to amendments backed by consumer groups, it passed with hardly a murmur.

So what went wrong? For one thing, his major issue, merit selection of judges, never got off the ground. For another, he suffered a rare public humiliation when a utility bill he carried proved to be full of mousetraps for consumers and went down to a 20-10 defeat on the Senate floor. Most obvious, however, is that Farabee is no longer looked to as the role model for what a senator should be. He is calm, deliberative, concerned above all about what's best for Texans. The torch has passed to a younger group that is highly partisan, intensely ambitious, and given to showboating and political gamesmanship, and the Senate and the state are the less for it. (Pages 116–117)

Legislation Making a Difference:
1975–1988

O F THE 640 BILLS I authored, 246 passed and became law. I filed my share of local bills arising from the needs of the 30th District, authorizing hospital districts, county juvenile boards, new courts, and even such consequential matters (at least to the hunters) as changing the time for quail hunting in Cottle County. In addition, I carried various "housekeeping" bills for state agencies that helped them perform their functions. All of these bills were important to constituents or the daily operation of state government but not within the purpose of this chapter.

The purpose of this chapter is to identify measures I consider the most important bills that I authored that became law and had a substantive impact on the lives of people across the state of Texas. In some instances, the House companion bill arrived before my bill moved out of the Senate, and I carried the House bill to final passage.

Some of my bills were ahead of the times and died unceremoniously in committee or with more fanfare on the floor of the Senate. The most important in this category concerned judicial selection, and I discuss that legislation, although it did not become law.

LIFE AND DEATH MATTERS

TEXAS NATURAL DEATH ACT: SB 148 (1977). I followed the lengthy 1976 debate in the California Legislature that led to the first "right to die" law in this country. The legislation authorized persons to sign a written document, sometimes called a "living will," directing physicians, hospitals, and relatives to avoid additional medical treatment when their death is imminent and they are not otherwise capable of making treatment decisions. I authored the Texas Natural Death Act patterned after the California law. My bill was opposed by leaders in the Catholic Church and the Right to Life movement.

Although I had no organized support for the bill, I secured passage; Governor Briscoe signed it into law on June 15, 1977. Texas was the third state to authorize this important right. Most states and the federal government now have similar laws allowing, even encouraging, end-of-life decisions by advance written directives. As witnessed in the recent Terri Schiavo case, the concept is still controversial. I worked with Rep. Bob Bush in subsequent sessions to simplify the prescribed forms and make this important procedure more patient-friendly. Some people said I was making a mistake getting involved with the issue. Based on experience with my mother's last month of life and a strong personal belief that such decisions should be those of the patient, I have never regretted taking this initiative.

Op-ed column by John Robertson Austin American-Statesman, *March 28, 2005, about Schiavo case.*

STATUTORY DEFINITION OF DEATH: SB 8 and HB 12 (1979). The Right to Die bill led me to other significant life and death legislation. With emerging medical technology, physicians can keep an otherwise dead person's heart beating and substitute oxygen tubes for lung function. Texas had no statutory definition of death; the most common method for determining death was the lack of a heartbeat—even when qualified neurologists and neurosurgeons said a person was "brain dead." In November 1978 Representative Henry Allee of Houston and I filed companion bills establishing a legal standard for determining death. The House bill passed first and I carried it to final passage in the Senate. At the Senate committee hearing, I called a neurosurgeon and neurologist to testify about the need for the bill and difficulty in using the old standard of cessation of heartbeat and respiratory function. In my interview with the doctors prior to their testimony, they kept referring to "harvesting" organs for transplants. I knew such words, though commonly used among doctors, would have a negative impact on my efforts to pass the bill. Upon my advice, they minimized the "harvest language," and the bill passed and became law.

ORGAN TRANSPLANT LEGISLATION: SB 32, SB 33 (1985), and SB 16 (1987). Through my work on the Determination of Death bill, I developed an interest in organ transplantation as one means for continuation of life. Significant medical progress was made during the 1980's in the frequency of organ transplants, but a serious shortage of organs and tissue existed. In the 69th Session I authored and secured passage into law of SB 32 and SB 33. Senate Bill 32 expanded existing law involving cornea transplants to cover the taking of tissue and organs upon consent, or presumed consent under limited conditions. Senate Bill 33 prohibited the sale of organs for a profit. Testimony showed sales of organs would limit access for persons in greatest need of a transplant. Many lives have been saved and improved as a result of greater availability of tissue and organs resulting from these two laws. I authored SB 16 in 1987 requiring hospitals to make an inquiry whether, under appropriate circumstances, family members wish to consider a donation of tissue and organs of a relative after death has occurred. A similar federal law was later adopted. One day when several of my organ bills were on the intent calendar, Gov. Hobby announced that he would hold an "organ calendar" right after Morning Call, rather than just prior to lunch. He didn't want to spoil anyone's meal with my grizzly descriptions of liver, tissue, and heart transplants.

CHILD WELFARE AND JUVENILE JUSTICE

CHILD SUPPORT LEGISLATION: SB 105 (1981); HJR 1 and HB 2 (1983); SCR 58 (1983); SB 632 (1987). Child support may not be a life and death matter; but for many children, it means the difference between hunger and health, shelter or the streets, and day care or being home alone. I carried more than a dozen measures enacted into law to improve child support collections. The most important was voluntary wage assignment (SB 105) and garnishment of wages (HJR 1 and HB 2) providing new methods for assuring payment of support. My work transferring state child support enforcement from the Department of Human Services to the Attorney General's Office (SCR 58 and the Appropriations Act) greatly improved the collection of delinquent support payments.

DAY CARE: SB 826 and SB 827 (1987). I was "home-schooled" by Helen about the importance of day care for working mothers. When the Department of Human Services proposed stringent regulations for all entities offering day care services, I was an advocate for flexibility to accommodate small providers caring for three or four children and short-term charitable programs. As larger corporations began to provide day care service for their employees, we asked, "Why not state agencies?" I introduced and passed SB 826 that was the first authorization to use space in state-owned office buildings for child care. Senate Bill 827 authorized the Texas Employment Commission (now Texas Workforce Commission) to provide technical assistance to employers offering child day care as an employee benefit and established a state Child Day Care Advisory Committee.

Senate backs garnishment of wages

By ARNOLD HAMILTON
Austin Bureau

AUSTIN — The Texas Senate voted to lift a 107-year constitutional ban on wage garnishment records of child support col in the country." With voter approval

Dallas Times Herald *article about child support legislation, May 18, 1983*

JUVENILE JUSTICE: SB 247 (1975); SB 421 (1983); SB 253 (1985). When I was growing up in Wichita Falls, a former Texas Ranger handled complaints involving juvenile offenders. "Big Jim," the juvenile officer, was not overly concerned about due process and was rumored to freely use corporal punishment. Children could be treated as serious offenders for lesser offenses and held without bail or representation in the county jail with adult criminals. Even in 1975, juvenile offenders had few rights or alternatives to what my mother called the "reformatory." Three bills that I authored addressed such problems: SB 247 required basic legal rights for alleged juvenile offenders, including the right to remain silent, have counsel, and terminate an interview at any time before waiving rights; SB 421 authorized the creation of juvenile boards in each county without a special law, specifying the duties for juvenile boards and requiring appointment of a citizen advisory panel in each county to assure the input of interested citizens about juvenile crime and punishment;

and SB 253 directed the State Juvenile Probation Board to set minimum standards for the detention of juveniles, for example, not keeping children in county jails or within close proximity to adult inmates.

PUBLIC SCHOOL EDUCATION: HOUSE BILL 72 AND THE SEA CHANGE

During the Second Called Session of the 68th Legislature I was in my Wichita Falls law office on a Saturday afternoon catching up on legal correspondence when the phone rang. No one else was in the office, so I picked it up. It was Ross Perot calling to thank me for my efforts on behalf of HB 72, which was the product of the Select Committee on Public Education in Texas chaired by him. Perot was the richest man in the United States at that time, and I was impressed that he was also working in his office on the weekend. He said, "This is the most important thing I have ever done in my life, and I think it's the most important thing we can do for Texas schoolchildren." I agreed.

Working with Ross Perot on House Bill 72, 1984

HOUSE BILL 72 (June 4–July 3, 1984): Though I did not author or sponsor HB 72, it was the most important bill I worked on and voted for during my 13 years as a legislator. The bill involved those persons and things nearest and dearest to my constituents and most Texans: our children, public schools, and pocketbooks. House Bill 72 made the most far-reaching changes in Texas public education since the Gilmer-Aikin Act of 1949, and required the largest tax hike during my time in the Senate. After the Senate made substantial changes to the HB 72, it went to conference committee. I served as Chairman of the Senate conferees. After nearly a week of negotiation, compromise, and contentious meetings, we came to a consensus that was adopted by each house of the legislature. Then came the hard work, passing a tax bill to pay for the reforms and equalization of funding between poor and rich school districts (the birth of the "Robin Hood" redistribution of property tax wealth). During the last day of the session,

Senator John Leedom, a very conservative Republican from Dallas County, threatened to filibuster until midnight, thereby killing the tax bill. I helped work out a compromise that avoided the filibuster and allowed passage of the 4.8-billion-dollar tax package.

TEXTBOOK SELECTION: SB 27 (1983). Before the era of the Christian Right, one ultra-conservative couple dominated the selection of textbooks for Texas schoolchildren: Mel and Norma Gabler of Longview, Texas. Irrespective of their philosophical position, it did not seem right that two people should have so much power over what my children or others should read. I filed SB 27 to allow greater participation in the textbook selection process for Texas, which, because of its size, has a disproportionate effect on the rest of the country's textbooks. Although I suspected greater controversy and opposition, the bill was passed into law with strong support from even more conservative newspapers. The lead editorial in the November 21, 1982, *Dallas Morning News* was representative of the broad support for the bill. Nobel Laureate Stephen Weinberg testified for the bill, and it was supported by the State Board of Education. Senate Bill 27 did not stop the Gablers, but it slowed them down and assured an open process.

HEALTH ISSUES

I authored more legislation involving health issues than any other subject matter. Some, like medical ethics and liability that affect the quality, availability, and cost of health care, are discussed under other segments of this chapter. Many of my local and uncontested bills involved hospital districts and local health authorities. The bills I identify in this segment were emerging health issues that still present significant challenges.

MENTAL HEALTH: SB 435 (1983); SB 626/HB 1256 (1985). Senate Bill 435 updated the Texas Mental Health Code, enacting many of the recommendations of the Task Force chaired by Helen. It also addressed protective custody issues in response to a federal

Helen and I discussing Senate Bill 435 with former First Lady Rosalyn Carter, 1983

court decision holding then-existing provisions unconstitutional. The most important aspects of the legislation encouraged community care and treatment, as compared to the traditional Texas approach of commitment to various state hospitals. Senate Bill 626 and its House companion HB 1256 expanded emergency detention and protective custody options for those who suffered from severe emotional distress and deterioration.

FIRST TEXAS AIDS/HIV LAW: SB 1072/HB 1829 (1987). During the last week for filing bills in the 70th Session, the Texas Department of Health (TDH) requested me to file legislation proposing multiple amendments to the Communicable Disease Prevention and Control Act. I already had a full plate of bills for the session, but TDH assured me it was non-controversial and would not consume much time. I agreed to carry the bill partly because it covered tuberculosis, which had plagued my mother's life and terrorized me as a child. The bill made no reference to a new communicable virus called Acquired Immune Deficiency Syndrome, better known as AIDS, and its early stage component known as HIV. The "non-controversial" house bill became the vehicle for a series of amendments addressing the growing problems of AIDS/HIV in Texas. A general lack of knowledge about the disease existed at the time, and the Legislature exhibited its share of ignorance. The final bill that was passed on the last day of the session contained important amendments to protect the public and persons with AIDS/HIV.

URBAN DEVELOPMENT: A TAXING EXPERIENCE

TAX INCREMENT FINANCING ACTS OF 1977 AND 1981: SB 635 and SJR 44 (1977); SB 16 and SJR 8 (First Called 1981); SB 641 (1983). Dick Brown, the principal lobbyist for the Texas Municipal League, brought my office a proposal for financing improvements in blighted urban areas. Although more than half of the states had adopted similar legislation, I didn't know what it was nor did most Texans at the time. I understood the importance of the concept for a Texas that had, unlike my district, become more urban than rural. Simply stated, the concept allows a city to freeze property taxes in blighted areas (where the tax base is sliding downward) and sell bonds secured by the projected growth of tax values resulting from public improvements paid for with the proceeds of the tax increment bonds—not exactly the easiest concept to explain and sell to a bunch of skeptical legislators; but we did it. After we did, the excrement began to fly. As it turned out, counties and school districts didn't like cities fiddling with their tax base. Developers loved the program, but this sometimes raised questions of propriety. To top it off, the proposed constitutional amendment accompanying the initial legislation in 1979 failed to pass at the polls.

Lesser men and lobbies would have been discouraged (and I was), but Rep. Steve Wolens of Dallas and I filed the Tax Increment Financing Act of 1981 and a new proposal for amending the Texas Constitution to resolve any legal doubts. With the help of the cities, Ray Hunt of Dallas, and Lloyd Hayes (former mayor of Port Arthur), both SB 16 and SJR 8 passed the Legislature. The constitutional amendment was approved at the polls in November 1981. I was considered a hero by the cities and developers; but I continued to catch flak from the school districts and counties. I authored legislation in 1983 that remedied some of the unintended consequences, but three sessions of tax increment (and excrement) was enough!

Gov. Bill Clements signing Senate Bill 16 in 1981 in presence of me and Rep. Steve Wolens of Dallas

PROPERTY REDEVELOPMENT AND TAX ABATEMENT ACT: SB 17 and SJR 8 (1st called 1981). The Kemp-Garcia Enterprise Zone Act was under consideration by the U.S. Congress during the summer of 1981, and Rep. Jack Kemp and President Ronald Reagan argued that enterprise zones were the answer to inner-city unemployment and urban blight. It appeared Texas would be in a better position to receive federal assistance with its urban redevelopment programs if it had a tax abatement law. Tax abatement authorizes cities to encourage reinvestment through tax abatements on improvements. Cities contract with individual owners allowing tax abatements for five-year periods. Contracts may not be renewed for more than 15 years. The additional authority has been important in attracting new industries to Texas. Without it, Texas cities could not compete with cities in other states that utilize this tool to attract new industries and jobs.

An amendment of the Texas Constitution was necessary for the use of tax abatement, and the electorate overwhelmingly adopted SJR 8.

CONSUMER LEGISLATION

All legislation should be in the public interest, but many bills benefit one group, while limiting others. Some bills are very specific in their focus, such as those affecting only the people in one area, group, or profession. I authored various bills that had the purpose of protecting and/or benefiting Texans as consumers of goods and services. Examples of my legislation in this category include the Business Opportunity Act, which helped protect against fraudulent franchises (SB 533 in 1981) and the Texas Timeshare Act that established a framework for regulating the sale of time share interests (SB 92 in 1985). The bills that had the greatest public impact were the elimination of the Texas Blue Law and authorization of cogeneration of electrical power.

REPEAL OF TEXAS BLUE LAW: SB 674 and HB 533 (1985). At the time I filed SB 674, one poll showed that 70% of Texans opposed the Texas Blue Law and three lower courts had held parts of it unconstitutional. Texas laws governing Sunday shopping were a confusing mess. Parents could buy paper diapers, but not cloth ones. You could buy nails, but not a hammer or saw. A majority of churches, labor unions, and local merchants were opposed to the repeal, and I didn't have the votes to get my bill out of the Senate. David Cain, then a House member from Dallas, filed the House companion bill and secured passage to the Senate on May 2, 1985. Since the bill was referred to the State Affairs Committee, I received a prompt committee hearing, which occurred on a Sunday afternoon in the Senate chamber. Austin was under a storm warning, and a flash of lightning occurred near the Capitol. A clap of thunder shook the building. Some suggested it was the voice of the Lord registering His opposition to my bill—and possibly to working on Sunday. Austin had one of the worst floods in recent history. I took it as an omen that stores needed to be open on Sunday to help storm victims. With my vote, the bill passed out of the State Affairs Committee.

I still didn't have 21 votes to suspend the rules or a majority of the Senate to pass it, but I plowed onward. Two things occurred that helped secure the few additional votes needed. I compromised with the Automobile Dealers

Senators John Traeger (left) and John Sharp (right) after debate on SB 674, April 17, 1985

Association, which was one of the strongest opponents, by exempting them so that they were still required to close on Sundays. I presented economic data showing that repeal of the Blue Law would stimulate additional sales tax revenue that could be used for indigent health care; this secured approval of the bill by the Catholic bishops of Texas and some progressive Protestant denominations. My co-sponsor, Senator Oscar Mauzy, reduced the pressure from organized labor, and I added additional worker protections. We had a long debate with blistering questions by Senator John Traeger of Seguin who kept asking me, "Senator, do you want to turn them loose and let them run?"—which I didn't understand, but it sounded bad for my bill. I got my 21 votes to consider the bill and a majority of the Senate passed it. The consumers of Texas got their right to shop until they dropped on Sundays, except for automobiles.

COGENERATION OF ELECTRICAL POWER: SB 141 and SB 142 (1987). During the interim between the 69th and 70th Sessions, Representative Pete Laney and I co-chaired the Joint Special Committee on Cogeneration in Texas. Based on the findings and recommendations of the committee, we filed bills to expedite the cogeneration of electrical power in Texas. Cogeneration is the sequential production of electric power and heat energy from one source, most commonly natural gas. When unused heat from a refinery in Houston or a molten glass plant in Wichita Falls is not used for secondary purposes, energy is lost. More efficient uses of unused heat help reduce the cost of electricity. Senate Bill 141 authorized contracts between electric utilities and cogenerators or small-power producers, and SB 142 reduced the regulatory lag time for transmission line certification. These were the first laws in Texas encouraging the cogeneration of electrical power.

JUDICIAL SELECTION; COURT JURISDICTION; AND ADMINISTRATION

Most states select judges on a nonpartisan basis. Texas is one of only nine states that elect judges on a partisan basis, that is, through political parties in primary and general elections. As a practicing attorney, I was aware of the problems caused by our political system for selecting judges and tried to do something about it. My efforts were not successful; however, I felt so strongly about reform in our methods of judicial selection that I kept advocating changes while I was in the Senate.

My legislative program for improving the efficiency and administration of the Texas court system was more successful. The following bills and SJR's chronicle what I consider to be some of my more important work in the Legislature on this subject—even the ones that did not pass.

JUDICIAL SELECTION: SJR 9 (1977); SB 706 (1981); SB 28 (1983); SJR 4, SB 55, and SB 56 (1985); SJR 2 and SB 12 (1987). I started my campaign for reform with a modest proposal for selecting only appellate judges on a merit basis, rather than the partisan election, where very few voters have any knowledge about the candidates on the ballot. At the time, the appellate courts were 100% Democratic, and most people voted on name identification. Judge Calvert, a retired Chief Justice of the Texas Supreme Court who favored my proposal, testified that although he was a teetotaler, he owed his success at the polls to the Calvert Distillery Company, which always had billboards across the state advertising its whiskey and inadvertently the judge's name. Don Yarbrough, then under criminal investigation and later deposed by an impeachment proceeding, was elected because his name sounded like that of U.S. Senator Ralph Yarborough. The Democratic Party activists didn't care because they had all of the appellate judges, and Republican leaders didn't want to change the flawed system because they saw a brighter day—which soon arrived with a 100% Republican Supreme Court and most of the judges on the Courts of Appeal also on that slate.

Since I determined that many Texans felt that electing judges, particularly at the local levels, was sacred, I tried proposals for nonpartisan nomination and election. Those skeptical of an appointive system could vote out the rascals and judicial activists. Although I did get one of my nonpartisan selection bills out of committee, I could not garner enough votes to suspend the Senate Rules and take it up—the political parties and lawyers who liked the partisan elections sunk my boat. I finally tried broader merit system plans and limitation of campaign contributions to judges. At the time, Texas had received national attention on CBS' *Sixty Minutes,* when South Texas litigator Clinton Manges contributed more than $200,000 to a Supreme Court candidate who might well be hearing his multi-million-dollar appeal. Still no luck, but I received strong editorial endorsements and support for my efforts. I did cause people to think about a system that had become a national embarrassment for Texas, and that made the effort worthwhile. Some of the problems of the Mississippi judicial selection system, similar to that of Texas, is dramatized in John Grisham's 2008 book *The Appeal.*

COURT ORGANIZATION AND JURISDICTION: SJR 36 (1979), SB 265 (1981). In 1979 all appeals of criminal cases went to just one court, the Texas Court of Criminal Appeals in Austin. Appeals of civil cases went to fourteen separate Courts of Civil Appeals in different geographic regions of the state, with an avenue for further appeal to the Texas Supreme Court. The criminal appellate system was antiquated and inefficient. Civil appeals took less than a year; appeals of criminal cases took much longer. Convicted felons with money for bail used the slow criminal appeals system to delay punishment; those without funds languished in jails, even when they might later be determined innocent. Criminal justice was greatly delayed and often denied. In January 1977, Chief Justice Joe Greenhill asked me to author an amendment to the Texas Constitution that would update and streamline the state appellate court system. I filed SJR 36 and secured passage in the Legislature; the proposal was adopted by the voters on November 4, 1980. I filed SB 265 in 1981; it proposed a comprehensive reorganization of the appellate court system, changing the names of the intermediate Courts of Civil Appeals to the "Courts of Appeal" and giving them jurisdiction to consider all civil and criminal appeals. The Court of Criminal Appeals was given the same discretionary authority as the Texas Supreme

Court to accept or reject applications for further and final appeals. The restructure of the appellate system resulted in a significant reduction of time required for final appeals in criminal cases—from three or four years to an average disposition time of ten-and-a-half months. (See article by Judge Greenhill in the 2002 *Texas Tech Law Review* Volume 33, Number 2, for additional details about the history and results of SJR 36 and SB 265.)

COURT ADMINISTRATION: SJR 36 and SB 428 (1979); SB 586/HB 1658 (1985); SB 18/HB 27 (1985 Second Called); SB 687 and SB 1108 (1987). Helping the judiciary improve court administration became another priority while in the Senate. Case loads were burgeoning and the time of final determination for many civil and criminal matters lagged further and further behind. One answer was to create additional courts, but I felt a more important answer was to provide for better court administration. Amending the constitution with SJR 36 allowed the Legislature to give the Texas Supreme Court authority to improve the performance of our courts. I was the Senate author of the Court Administration Acts of 1985 (SB 586/HB 1658) and 1987 (SB 687).

LIABILITY AND RESPONSIBILITY

Insurance is the principal mechanism in our country for meeting financial responsibility for damages caused by someone's negligence. When there is little or no insurance, a person damaged by a driver, doctor, corporation, or others is less likely to recover damages resulting from the failure of another to exercise ordinary care under the circumstances. It is an imperfect system and people love to hate insurance companies—except for the people who work for them, agents selling the policies, and insureds having their claims promptly adjusted. Because of my law practice, I was well acquainted with the merits and shortcomings of the Texas liability system. A medical malpractice insurance crisis in 1975 provided the opportunity to win my Senate spurs early.

I began my career in the Senate with far-reaching tort reform proposals involving medical liability and finished it during the last session with legislation involving the responsibilities of charitable organizations and Texas' first law encouraging risk management, that is, trying to prevent accidents before they occur.

MEDICAL MALPRACTICE BILLS: SB 635 (1975); SB103 and HB 1045 (1977). Physicians, like everyone else, make mistakes. Back in the days when doctors made house calls, no one would think of suing a physician or hospital, even though mortality and error rates were higher then. As the delivery of medical services became more complex and less personal, the number of lawsuits alleging medical malpractice increased. Physicians and hospitals needed medical liability insurance, and insurance companies entered the market with coverage for medical malpractice. Larger jury verdicts occurred; amounts paid for settlement of malpractice claims increased; and related premium charges ballooned. In 1974 several malpractice insurers decided to leave Texas, and many Texas physicians could not find medical liability insurance, even if they could afford the higher costs. The situation was bad for patients, medical doctors, and hospitals.

The biggest issue during the 64th Session in 1975 was medical malpractice insurance. The Texas Medical Association (TMA) proposed three solutions that had worked in other states: 1) creating a joint underwriting authority (JUA), which would assure coverage underwritten by Texas doctors when other insurers failed to provide coverage; 2) state regulation of the rates for all companies selling medical liability insurance in Texas, similar to auto and homeowners policies; and 3) comprehensive tort law reform in connection with all malpractice claims and medical liability lawsuits in Texas.

Senator A. R. "Babe" Schwartz, chairman of the Jurisprudence Committee, agreed to carry the JUA and insurance regulation bills, but he was not interested in handling tort reform. Although I was a freshman and an untried legislator, Ace Pickens, lobbyist for the TMA, brought the tort reform bill to me. I may have been the senator of last resort, and others had turned it down, as the doctor's "impossible dream." All knew it would be a nightmare because of the opposition of the Texas Trial Lawyers Association (TTLA), a powerful lobby composed of plaintiff's lawyers, some of whom made substantial income from malpractice cases.

I filed SB 635 (the TMA bill) on March 11, the last day for filing bills without special permission. The title of the bill was the "Patients' Compensation Act of Texas," but TTLA called it the "Doctors' Compensation Act" and feared it would destroy much of their compensation. Representative Pike Powers filed the companion bill in the House, and the fight was on. Both of our bills were referred to subcommittees, where they languished

until my bill was reported out of committee on May 1, leaving only one month to
get it passed out of the Senate, over to the
House, through its committees, and up
for floor debate. No one thought it could
be done, but I secured the bare minimum
votes to suspend the rules and debate it on
May 13. After rancorous debate between
me, for the bill, and Babe Schwartz, Lloyd
Doggett, and Oscar Mauzy against it, I secured passage to third reading with some
amendments. The bill passed out of the
Senate on May 15, leaving two weeks to
wind its way through the House. SB 635
was reported from the House committee
with more amendments, but it still had

*Senator Schwartz excoriates SB 635
on floor of Senate, May 13, 1975*

to go through the Calendars Committee. Governor Briscoe helped with a
message to the House designating the measure as an emergency bill, but the
Patients' Bill failed in the emergency room of the House floor on the night
of May 28 by one vote. For the lack of a vote, the Patients' Act was lost.

The Governor considered calling a special session, but declined in favor of creating the Medical Professional Liability Study Commission (the
Commission) to study the problem and make recommendations to the
65th Legislature in January 1977. Dean Page Keeton of the UT law school
was named to chair the Commission. State and national experts named to
the group included Ted Stowell, former Insurance Commissioner for the
State of Ohio and husband of Helen's first cousin Janice. Babe Schwartz
was named to the Commission because he was Chairman of the Senate
Jurisprudence Committee, but I was not appointed because I was still a
newcomer. The Commission heard testimony by experts from all parts of
the country, studied what other states had done to relieve the problem, and
issued its report with recommendations, many of them similar to SB 635.

Senator Schwartz authored several bills that enacted some proposals of
the Commission but not those involving tort reforms. I filed SB 103, which
would enact 14 of the 18 recommendations of the Commission and some of
the provisions from SB 635. My bill was favored by TMA but strongly opposed by TTLA, which had strengthened its forces after near defeat in the

1975 Session. Senate Bill 103 languished in the Senate Jurisprudence Committee chaired by Schwartz. Although the bill received several public hearings, there was never a vote, which was another way of killing it without angering the doctors or consumers with a "no" vote. In the meantime, Rep. Tom Uher introduced and passed HB 1048 that was touted as a compromise plan to resolve the medical malpractice crises; however, the bill had practically none of the Commission recommendations for tort reform.

Senator Schwartz carried HB 1048 in the Senate and secured prompt passage through the Jurisprudence Committee that he chaired. Dean Page Keeton and I were critical of HB 1048 because it failed to address the tort reform recommendations of the Commission. TMA and other health provider groups opposed it for the same reason. When Schwartz suspended the rule for consideration of HB 1048, my colleagues and I submitted several tort reform amendments that were adopted. Action and debate on the amended bill took seven hours, the longest Senate debate of that session. Senator Schwartz became so angry that he said he was no longer sponsoring the bill and dramatically threw it into his wastebasket. Without a Senate sponsor, the bill would die. The Lieutenant Governor, over strong objections by Schwartz, appointed me to carry HB 1048. I quickly ushered the bill to final passage in the Senate, and it was returned to the House. The House refused to concur in the Senate amendments to its "compromise bill," which sent it to conference committee. I was appointed as chair of the Senate conferees. We were now in the last month of the Session. The conference committee met many times, but it was deadlocked. The House members were uncompromising, and it appeared that no medical malpractice bill would pass. The Lieutenant Governor asked Don Adams and Max Sherman, who were also on the conference committee, to try one more time on the last day of the Session to work out a compromise. They secured some agreements from the House conferees, but much fewer than I felt appropriate. A conference committee report was finally adopted during the last hours of the Session on a split vote. I voted against it and removed myself as a sponsor of the bill—not with the drama of Senator Schwartz. Don Adams assumed sponsorship and secured adoption of the conference committee report by a vote of 29-2. I was one of the two "no" votes. Dean Page Keeton agreed with me that the final bill fell far short of the recommendations of the Commission, but the Senate and leadership felt it was better to get some bill, rather than no bill; and in retrospect, I agree.

Despite my defeats on the medical malpractice bills, I came out a winner. My efforts led to the first real tort reform in Texas, and *Texas Monthly* magazine (July 1977, p. 93) named me one of the ten best legislators, stating:

> [He] earned his spurs by soundly thrashing Senate heavyweight Babe Schwartz in the floor fight over medical malpractice. Their clash was the session's most dramatic moment: the veteran with the wisdom and skills accumulated over two decades against the upstart newcomer in his first major test. Senate historians may mark Farabee's victory (he carried the doctors' amendments to a trial-lawyer-backed compromise bill) as the moment the torch was passed to the upcoming generation of senators.

If anyone was "thrashed" in a battle with Babe Schwartz, it was probably me, but I appreciated the kind words from the *Monthly*. Before anyone feels sorry for Babe, it is worth noting that the other two senators to make Ten Best that year were Babe Schwartz and Max Sherman.

CHARITABLE IMMUNITY AND LIABILITY ACT OF 1987: SB 202 (1987) Non-profit charitable organizations, like churches, Boy Scouts, and the Red Cross, were protected by limited immunity from tort liability under Texas common law until 1971. In that year, the state Supreme Court set aside that doctrine and held that such organizations were liable for negligent acts of their employees and volunteers. By 1987 nonprofits were

Conferring with Senator Kent Caperton about Senate Bill 202 in 1987

experiencing difficulty recruiting volunteers and securing liability insurance. Some were cutting back on services, particularly day care and youth activities. Helen and the United Way of Texas brought the problem to my attention. My staff and I drafted SB 202. Senator Kent Caperton and TTLA were initially opposed to the bill, but we worked out changes that assured passage. The new law made the services of volunteers, directors, and officers of qualified non-profit corporations immune from liability for good faith, charitable acts; it limits the liability of charitable organizations to a ceiling of $1,000,000, if the organization maintains liability insurance in that amount. Liability associated with the operation of motor vehicles and delivery of health care service is not covered by the act. During the 1st Called Session of the 70th Legislature, I authored SB 5, which authorized the creation of the Texas Nonprofit Organizations Liability Pool to facilitate accessibility of liability insurance for nonprofit groups.

CRIME AND PUNISHMENT

In legislative matters of crime and punishment, I took the less-traveled road of "corrections," rather than punishment. As for crime, I was more interested in new approaches to old problems and solutions for new offenses. Because of my chairmanships and interest in corrections, I authored many bills dealing with the criminal justice system. The following are the ones I consider my best efforts on this subject:

TRIPLICATE PRESCRIPTION LAW: SB 394 (1981) and SB 137 (reenactment in 1985). Before Ross Perot undertook reform of the state public school system, he chaired the Texas War on Drugs Task Force. It recommended a broad legislative agenda involving drug trafficking and addiction. Rick Salwin, who was the principal attorney and lobbyist for Perot's anti-drug program, asked me to carry several of the proposed bills arising from the task force. I was skeptical about further enhancements of punishment, but I was interested in the findings and recommendations to stem illegal prescriptions of addictive medications. Texas had laws regulating such prescriptions but no effective way to determine when and where the laws were broken. Senate Bill 394 required three copies of prescriptions for Schedule II drugs (addictive substances) rather than two, with data from the additional copy of analyzed by DPS computers to identify unusual patterns. The bill included patient privacy protections, targeting those few physicians and pharmacists who seriously abuse Texas prescription laws. The law was scheduled to sunset in 1986 but was easily reenacted in 1985 because of its success in reducing illegal prescriptions.

INSANITY DEFENSE: SB 7 (1983). In 1980 a Wichita Falls woman killed her infant daughter by cutting out the child's heart; she was trying to exorcise a devil she perceived to possess the child. A jury acquitted the defendant on the basis of an insanity defense; and my constituents were outraged when the woman went free. This local event occurred near the time that John Hinckley shot and nearly killed President Reagan. I agreed to file a bill narrowing the insanity defense and did so with SB 7. However, the more my staff and I studied the problem, the more we realized how very complex it can be. The Wichita Falls woman was suffering from a postpartum depression syndrome, and I concluded the jury was correct in its finding.

The problem was not so much the Texas law as it was the inadequacy of mental health services and lack of supervision to prevent future incidents by mentally ill offenders. With the help of Jim Spearly, my staff person working with mental health issues, and members of the bar, we drafted the bill to limit the insanity defense to severe mental disease or defect where the defendant did not know his or her conduct was wrong. The bill gave trial courts more discretion to require appropriate supervision and medication when defendants are released under the insanity defense. (For additional information about the insanity defense and my bill see *South Texas Law Journal,* Vol. 24, No. 3, page 671 et seq.)

HABITUAL CRIMINAL AMENDMENTS: SB 603/HB 1048 (1983). By 1983 Texas prisons were overcrowded and under federal court order to address the problem. One of the reasons our prisons were overcrowded was because of a law that allowed prosecutors to send criminal defendants to prison for life upon a third felony conviction ("three-time losers"). The life sentence was required, even for less serious property crimes, like three hot checks for small amounts (*Rummel v. Estelle*). The district attorneys loved the existing law, but it made no sense for protecting the public from more serious offenders. SB 603 and its companion House Bill proposed allowing a jury to provide a lesser sentence than life imprisonment upon conviction of a third felony. House Bill 1048 carried by representative Terral Smith of Austin and myself was finally passed into law giving that latitude.

COMPUTER CRIME BILL: SB 72 (1985). Although the Texas Penal Code contained a multitude of offenses in 1985, it had no laws involving emerging computer technology. At the suggestion of my Administrative Assistant Lia Clarkson, I filed SB 72, proposing the first computer crime law in Texas. The bill made it a criminal offense to breach the security or intentionally make harmful access to another person's computer. As compared to the present time, personal computers were not widely used and the Internet was not available. A few additions have been made to the original law, but it remains intact and can be found at Chapter 33 of the Texas Penal Code.

PRIVATE PRISONS: Senate Bill 251 (1987). One of the more controversial bills I authored during my Senate years authorized the Texas Department of Corrections (TDC) to contract with private entities to construct, operate, maintain, and manage correctional facilities. At the time, only three other states authorized private prisons—Minnesota, Kentucky, and Tennessee. SB 251 was controversial because state employees feared the loss of state jobs; advocates for inmates foresaw a proliferation of unsupervised correctional institutions; and state correctional authorities argued that the discipline functions could not be delegated. None of the dire predictions have materialized. Only a few private prisons exist in Texas, and those provide a competitive model that helps assure better management of state correctional institutions and taxpayer savings. Private jails are different and should not be confused with my private state prison legislation.

ACCESS TO OTHER INFORMATION
ABOUT FARABEE LEGISLATION

Other information about all bills and resolutions filed by me may be found in the ten volumes compiled by my Senate staff entitled *Senator Ray Farabee Legislative Programs for the 64th, 65th, 66th, 67th, 68th, 69th, and 70th Legislatures*. These volumes contain bill histories, analyses, fact sheets, and some news clips about the legislation. Copies of the *Texas Monthly* "Ten Best" articles and the *Texas Business* Outstanding Texan Award are also included in the volumes. These volumes are available at the Texas History Center on the UT-Austin campus, Midwestern State University in Wichita Falls, and the North Texas History Museum in downtown Wichita Falls.

A New Phase with Life-Changing Stages—
The UT System Years: 1988–2000

Phases and stages, circles and cycles . . .
that we've all seen before. Let me tell some more.
—Willie Nelson, 1974

IN 1988 I BEGAN a new phase of my life. I left the State Senate and private law practice and went to work for the University of Texas System (UT System, UT, and/or System). Helen and I moved from Wichita Falls to live in Austin. Occurrences unrelated to the UT System changed certain aspects of my life forever. The new phase and some events in my life were like circles and cycles. Let me tell you some more.

TO LEAVE OR NOT TO LEAVE (THE SENATE)—
THAT WAS THE QUESTION

In December 1987 I was approached by Jack Blanton, Chairman of the Board of Regents for the UT System, and Dr. Hans Mark, Chancellor, who expressed interest in hiring me to fill the open position of Vice Chancellor and General Counsel for the UT System. The former general counsel, Jim Crowson, resigned to become the vice president and general counsel for Lomas Nettleton Company, a large national mortgage banking organization located in Dallas.

During the two years before the UT offer, I had the opportunity to join a large Dallas law firm and an invitation to apply for the position of Chancellor of the University of Houston System. I declined the offer of the

Dallas law firm because I didn't want to do lobby work, which was their primary interest in hiring me. The Houston invitation was more interesting, and I was one of ten finalists for the position. As it turned out, the selection committee for the Houston System wanted someone with a PhD and more academic experience. Based on these two experiences, I was reluctant to leave a law practice developed over 26 years and the State Senate that I still enjoyed, despite the hectic life of balancing two jobs.

However, the UT position was very appealing because they wanted a lawyer, not a lobbyist, and an experienced JD (Doctor of Jurisprudence) rather than a PhD. In spite of my reluctance, Blanton and Mark continued to pursue me about their opening. I met with Jack in Houston and learned more about the UT System. Dr. Mark came to Wichita Falls to learn about my law practice and was persuasive about the advantages of working for the System. I visited the Office of General Counsel at the System complex in downtown Austin. Hans added the prospect of an academic appointment, similar to that of other vice chancellors, even if I never filled the position or decided to teach.

Helen and I talked at length about the ramifications of resigning from the Senate, leaving my law practice, and living in Austin. She emphasized that it was a decision that only I could make and refused to express a preference. I discussed the UT offer with two of my best clients and friends, Jerry Estes and Ray Clymer. They felt it was an excellent opportunity that I should seriously consider.

Helen had been spending more time in Austin. She was president of the United Way of Texas and working part-time as executive director of the Benedictine Health Resource Center, a health policy and advocacy group for indigent health care needs in Texas. Our sons had finished their public schooling, and Steve had completed his degree at UT Austin. David was married and living in our garage apartment with his wife Terri while working part-time and attending Midwestern State University. Despite growing amounts of time spent on Senate work, my law practice with Sherrill and Pace was going well; however, the increasing emphasis on billable hours, characteristic of most law firms then and now, diminished my enjoyment of private practice. Sometimes I felt that an important part of my life was being measured away in one sixth of an hour increments, or multiples thereof.

After a month of doubt, deliberation, and inner turmoil, I concluded that if I was ever to make a change, this was the time and opportunity to do so. Helen would be closer to her work and interests in Austin. I would have new challenges without worrying about billable hours, the stress of politics, and commuting 600 miles each week between two jobs. In mid-January we decided to accept the UT offer. The Board of Regents formally appointed me Vice Chancellor and General Counsel at their meeting in San Antonio on February 11, 1988, to be effective March 14—one day before the Ides of March.

The big decision led to many other actions, including resignations from the Senate, my law partnership, and the boards of directors for North Texas Federal Savings & Loan Assn., Texas American Bank in Wichita Falls, and Wichita Falls Education Translator, Inc. Law clients were notified of my anticipated departure and legal work transferred to other attorneys. Arrangements were made for two principal Senate staff persons to work for the UT System; Lia Clarkson would be my Administrative Assistant at the Office of General Counsel (OGC) and State Affairs Committee Counsel Mel Hazelwood would come to work as an OGC attorney. I helped other senate staffers find work elsewhere.

Responses to my decision to leave the Senate and take the UT vice chancellor position were positive—not glad to get rid of me, but appreciative of my work as a state senator. Of the many letters, receptions, and events, three stand out in my memories. Molly Ivins, then a columnist with the *Dallas Times Herald* and not known for complementing legislators, wrote on January 24, 1988, in an article headlined "Farabee's departure a setback to decency in Legislature":

Molly Ivins column, Dallas Times Herald, *January 24, 1988*

Gentle, soft-spoken, unfailingly courteous and reasonable, Farabee has single-handedly made the Texas Legislature a more civilized place than it will be without him. I'm sure he and his wife Helen, an active force for good in her own right, will continue to play a role in public affairs, but it won't be full time.

On February 6, 1988, I "performed" with the Wichita Falls Symphony in its rendition of Aaron Copland's *Lincoln Portrait* as a narrator of Carl Sandburg's writings about Lincoln, quoting a portion of the Gettysburg Address. On February 12, 1988, the *Wichita Falls Times and Record News* devoted its lead editorial to my Senate work benefiting Texas. My friend Bill Hobby joined with other Senate colleagues expressing appreciation for my work with them.

THE UNCERTAINTIES OF POLITICS AND LIFE:
HELEN FARABEE, NOVEMBER 12, 1934–JULY 28, 1988

I had filed for reelection to the Senate in November 1987, before knowing about the UT position. No others filed in either the Democratic or Republican primaries, and the deadline for anyone else to file had passed by the time I made my decision. When I announced I would be leaving the Senate, a flurry of political activity occurred from several who wanted to succeed me as senator for the 30th District. House members Charles Finnell from Archer County and Steve Carriker from Roby in Fisher County declared their intention to seek the Democratic nomination. Bobby Albert III from Wichita Falls announced for the Republican nomination.

People from the District and elsewhere contacted Helen and urged her to run for the open position. No one was as qualified as her to serve in the State Senate. Bill Hobby was enthusiastic about the prospect. Although we had not considered this possibility before, Helen's opportunity of finally having a vote and larger voice for child welfare and human services was very appealing; she decided to put her hat in the ring.

Ordinarily, the governor would have promptly accepted my resignation and called a special election, but Governor Clements delayed any action for several weeks, which put the special election under a different section of the Election Code. According to Dave McNeely in the *Austin American-Statesman*, the delay intended to "confuse the Democrats and help the Republican candidate." Whatever the purpose may have been, the selection of my successor became incredibly confused. A headline in the *Houston Post* (April 8, 1988) characterized the circumstance as "Replacing Farabee (a) Machiavellian Chore," and it was.

Helen proceeded on the assumption of a special election by the voters of the 30th District in May. She traveled throughout the district, organizing

Helen campaigning for an election that never occurred, April 1988

her campaign for an election by voters in the 30 counties. Political contributions came to her from the District and across the state. Campaign materials were purchased, printed, and ready for distribution when it became apparent that the selection of the Democratic and Republican nominees would be by the members of the respective 30th District Executive Committees, not by the qualified voters of the District. The results were crushing for Helen, and disappointing to me and her supporters. Carriker received 18 votes, Finnell 11, and Helen one—Wichita County. The rural counties felt it was their time to have the Senate seat; and Carriker, a longtime Democratic activist, out-campaigned Helen and Finnell with the votes that counted—the Democratic Executive Committee for the 30th District.

A special election between the candidates selected by the Democratic and Republican executive committees was finally held on August 13. Contrary to the Republican strategy, Carriker, a member of the National Democratic Committee from one of the smallest counties, beat Bobby Albert III from the most populace Wichita County. Carriker was reelected to the Senate position in 1990 but defeated by Republican Tom Haywood of Wichita Falls in 1994. Reflecting the uncertainty of politics, the tides were changing.

Though disappointed, we were relieved to have the confusing political mess behind us. Helen returned to Austin and immersed herself in work for the United Way of Texas and Benedictine Health Resource Center. I was traveling to various component institutions of the UT System and learning about my new responsibilities as General Counsel. Typically, I spent about ten hours a day with OGC work, including social and official functions with Helen. Although as busy as ever, we were enjoying our new life together in Austin.

While campaigning in Graham, Texas, for the election that never occurred, Helen bumped and bruised her right thigh. The bruise did not go away and caused her some discomfort, but not enough to consult a physician. On Saturday June 25, 1988, Helen flew to Appleton, Wisconsin, to visit her folks and attend a high school class reunion. She felt all right when she left Austin but had difficulty walking the long distance from one terminal to another in Chicago O'Hare airport. Pain and swelling in her right leg increased, and she had a sore throat with swelling of the glands in her neck. Helen attended the banquet for her reunion but felt worse the next morning—so bad that she went to the emergency room at Appleton Memorial Hospital across from her parents' apartment. The examining physician concluded that her condition might be more serious than a sore throat or bruised leg, and he advised her to return home immediately and consult her medical doctor in Austin.

Dr. Grover Bynum examined Helen on June 28 and admitted her to Seton Hospital in Austin for treatment and a series of tests to determine her illness. The doctors found that Helen had lung cancer that had spread to other parts of her body. She was not released from Seton until July 10. We consulted specialists at M. D. Anderson Cancer Center and decided on chemotherapy and radiation in Austin, which began immediately. On Sunday, July 24, Helen experienced a sharp pain in her chest, and breathing became much more difficult. An ambulance rushed us back to Seton where she was tested, examined, and placed in the intensive care unit (ICU). Despite all efforts, her ability to breathe continued to deteriorate, even after a tracheal intubation was made to deliver oxygen to her lungs. Helen died at 9:45 p.m. on July 28, 1988, at the age of 53. The cause of her death was respiratory failure, massive pulmonary emboli from the bruise on her right thigh, and lung cancer.

Governor Clements ordered flags at the Capitol and other state offices to be flown at half staff. Helen's body was returned to Wichita Falls for a funeral on Saturday, July 30. The First Presbyterian Church was filled with friends and admirers from Wichita Falls, Austin, and elsewhere in Texas. A memorial service was held at the Covenant Presbyterian Church in Austin on Monday, August 1, where the Rev. Kent Miller, Ann Richards (then

State Treasurer), and Ernie Cortes spoke to a full sanctuary of friends and admirers about Helen and her life, leadership, and contributions for a better Texas.

Articles and editorials appeared in the major Texas newspapers memorializing Helen's leadership and many accomplishments in a life that was all too short. The *Dallas Times Herald* in an editorial said, "She was a selfless, tireless worker whose compassion for others will not be forgotten." The *Austin American-Statesman* cited Helen's legacy in public services that helped people who are poor, disabled, elderly, abused, or otherwise unable to help themselves and stated her work had "improved the lives of millions of other people, most of them strangers." The *Daily Texan* wrote, "A few can make a difference, but Helen Farabees are rare." Sam Kinch of the *Dallas Morning News* praised Helen as a do-gooder who knew backstage politics, stating:

> That's why Helen Farabee was so good. She learned the political system, took control of it in the public interest and helped make it work. She made us all better for it. And, in the process, she established a paradigm for everybody—not just political wives with do-gooder instincts.

Helen J. Farabee

1934-1988

When Helen Farabee moved to Wichita Falls in 1961, the first board to call her was the local Mental Health Association.
Lucky us.
For 27 years Helen championed the cause of mental health and human services, her work touching the lives of millions.
To those in the mental health field, she was a personal friend as well as a public policy friend.

Front page of The Mental Health Advocate, *September 1988*

Helen received many honors during her lifetime, including selection to the Texas Women's Hall of Fame in 1985, the Commissioner's Award for Volunteer Services from the Texas Department of Mental Health and Mental Retardation (TDMHMR) in 1983, and "Texan of the Year" by *Texas Business* magazine in 1985. For several years after Helen's death, additional recognitions occurred, including the annual Helen Farabee Wings Award by the United Way of Texas and the Helen Farabee Volunteer Award given each year by TDMHMR. The Wichita Falls Community MHMR Center was renamed "The Helen Farabee Center" in 1994, and is now the "Helen Farabee Regional MHMR Centers," serving more than 6000 clients in 19

Steve, Nancy, Terri, David, and Worth Farabee at the ceremony renaming the Wichita Falls MHMR Community Center in 1994

Northwest Texas counties. More information about the Helen Farabee Centers can be found at: www.helenfarabee.org. The University of Texas at Austin created the Helen Farabee Memorial Endowed Presidential Scholarship Fund for students in its School of Social Work. Many of Helen's friends and the Farabee family continue to support this endowment, which now provides financial assistance to several students each year.

GRIEF AND GOING FORWARD WITH LIFE

After Helen's death, funeral, and memorial service, I experienced feelings of grief, guilt, and depression. Returning to a home without Helen—my best friend and partner for more than 30 years—was very painful. These emotions were accelerated by such necessary chores as disposing of her personal belongings in Wichita Falls and Austin. I felt the guilt that flows from asking, "Why Helen— why not me?" I reasoned that if I had not left the Senate, Helen would not have bruised her leg in Graham; no emboli would have been breaking away to clog her lungs; and she would have had a better chance of surviving a bout with cancer. In a relatively short period of time I was without my private law practice, the State Senate with offices in the

Capitol, and worst of all, my wife. I was depressed; however, family, friends, work, and travel helped make the transition to new stages of my life.

Family was very important in helping each surviving member cope with the loss we felt as a result of Helen's death. My children were no longer "children" but young men pursuing their own lives. Helen's mother and father were in poor health in Appleton, Wisconsin, and unable to attend the funeral. Despite the distances from Wichita Falls where David lived, we remained a close family and helped each other. Since a part of Helen's life is carried forward by her children and their families, it is worthwhile to know where they were in their lives at the time of her death and the beginnings of their own families.

Steve was still an undergraduate when he went to work part-time for Time Warner Cable, selling and installing cable boxes on a door-to-door basis. He received his degree from UT Austin in 1985 and continued with Time Warner on a full-time basis, living at 2702 Rockingham in 1988. His

presence helped take some of the edge off of my loneliness. In January 1990 Time Warner promoted Steve to a management position in Rochester, New York, where he lived for one-and-a-half years before returning to a similar position in Austin. Steve married Karen on September 19, 1992, and their daughter Sara Helen was born in 1995, named for her grandmother. Steve became the Director for the new Time Warner Roadrunner

Wedding picture of Karen and Steve Farabee, September 19, 1992

product in 1997 and was later named Area Vice President for that division. In 2000 he was promoted to Vice President for Operations of the Austin Time Warner Region—an impressive journey from selling cable TV door-to-door and shinnying up telephone polls to connect new customers. Steve left Time Warner in 2007 and formed his own consulting business, Texas Home Technology.

David attended UT Austin during his first two years of college and returned to Wichita Falls to complete his degree at Midwestern State University in December 1989. In 1987 he married Terri Salmon. They have

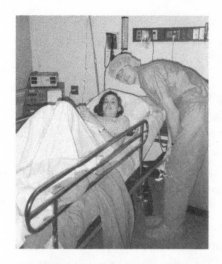

David in scrubs with Terri prior to delivery of my first grandchild, Worth, on May 18, 1990

three children: William Worth (1990); Nancy Helen (1992); and Russell Ray (1994). When David returned to Wichita Falls he first sold life insurance door-to-door and then joined the Boley Featherston Insurance Agency. He is a Chartered Life Underwriter (CLU) and partner in the Boley Featherston Agency. David became active in the community and served on several nonprofit boards and committees, including some his mother had worked with. In 1989 he was elected to the Wichita Falls City Council and served two terms. David was elected to the Texas House of Representatives for Wichita County in 1998 and continues to serve in 2008.

Friends, old and new, were helpful. Some of my closest friends since college days are part of "The Conversation Group" (the Group) that was organized by Carol Hatfield in 1985; the group has been meeting six times each year since then. It was originally composed of Carol and Tom Hatfield, Bill and Mary Arnold, Jim and Eleanor Cochran, Frank and Lynn Cooksey, Joe and Carolyn Osborn, and Helen and me. Members of the Group

The Conversation Group at McDonald Observatory in the Big Bend area, 1992

were the first to check on Helen in the hospital and at our home during her illness, and they shared their friendship and support after her death. Remarkably, only two changes have occurred in the original group: the loss of Helen and the addition of Mary Margaret—no divorces or other deaths as of 2008.

Newer friends from my Senate days and the UT System also came forward to help with my transition. When I told a mutual friend about my feelings of guilt about what might have otherwise happened had I stayed in the Senate, she gave me a small jar titled as a receptacle for "What Ifs" and told me to put all my "what ifs" in it and get on with my life. Former State Senator Ed Howard from Texarkana heard of my depression and invited me to have lunch. Ed left the Senate before I did and assured me there was life after the Senate—and there was. Sadly, Ed died of cancer several years later. New friends at the UT System, including Dr. Charles and Stella Mullins, whom I had known through Helen's mental health work, were helpful.

Bill and Diana Hobby were supportive from the time Helen first entered the hospital through my period of recovery from her loss. They visited Helen in the hospital and frequently checked on her progress. Bill was a pallbearer at Helen's funeral in Wichita Falls. Several weeks after Helen's death, he invited me to fly with them to Diana's family farm in North Carolina where we had a wonderful weekend. Bill and I played racquetball at the UT Austin athletic facilities nearly every week and often had dinner afterwards. It was becoming more fun to talk about what was happening in the Senate than being more directly involved as a member.

My work at UT System kept me busy. I worked longer hours. As a vice chancellor, I received numerous invitations to attend dinners, receptions, football games, and other activities. In fact, I was expected to attend many of these functions, particularly those at the Bauer House. The combination of management responsibilities, a wide variety of legal issues, and social activities left little time to feel sorry for myself or worry about the "what ifs."

Travel was an important part of my work. I visited all of the component institutions of the UT System during my first year, some more than once. I became a frequent flyer on the System plane, Southwest Airlines, and other carriers. Business travel also took me to Washington, D.C., Chicago, and California. I attended the first of many National Association of College and University Attorneys (NACUA) meetings in Chicago and met other new general counsels. I made two trips to California with UT development personnel to gather information about long-term giving programs.

Personal travel was also important. I traveled to Appleton, Wisconsin, several times to visit Helen's parents who were in poor health. While in Washington, D.C., I renewed my friendship with Celia Morris, whom I dated as an undergraduate at UT Austin. Celia and her husband Willie Morris were friends during the two years Helen and I were in Austin while I finished law school. Celia lived and continues to reside in a charming

Hiking the Grand Canyon via the Kaibab Trail, 1989

townhouse several blocks from the National Capitol. We traveled to London, Oxford, Canterbury, and Manchester in October 1989. Celia was and remains a good friend of mine and Mary Margaret's.

Trips to Wisconsin, first to visit the Rehbeins in failing health and then for Mrs. Rehbein's funeral, were reminders that health and life are not certainties. Travel to England renewed my commitment to see more of the world, which really began in 1986 when Helen and I visited Israel and Paris. In 1989 I hiked to the bottom of the Grand Canyon with another friend. Hiking the canyon was important because it proved to me, that however tired I felt or however seemingly impossible the task, by putting one foot in front of the other, I could climb out of the deepest of canyons and depression, going forward with life.

BLUE CROSS/BLUE SHIELD OF TEXAS

In June 1989 I was elected to the board of directors (Board) for Blue Cross/Blue Shield of Texas (BCBSTX). My experiences as a board member of BCBSTX enriched the new phase of my life after the Senate and complemented my work with the UT System. BCBSTX is the oldest and best-known health insurer in Texas. It continues to provide more health coverage for Texans than any other insurance company. Some emerging health care issues and changes occurred during the 13 years I was a director of BCBSTX and its successor Health Care Service Corporation (HCSC) that made my Board service more meaningful.

The most important issues confronting BCBSTX in the 1990's included rapidly escalating health care costs (ergo higher premiums), increased competition from national health insurance giants like Aetna and Humana, the demand by employers for managed care products to offset higher benefit costs, and a growing number of uninsured Texans. As a Board, working with BCBSTX management, we obviously did not solve all of these problems, but we made important decisions that helped cope with the dynamic era of health care delivery.

Dr. Rogers Coleman, MD, was elected President of BCBSTX by the

Dr. Rogers Coleman, President of BCBS of Texas, 1990

Board in December 1990, when John Melton retired. Coleman understood the challenges confronting the company and health care in Texas. One of his first steps was to appoint the two newest Board members, Skipper Dipple and me, to the Executive Committee of the Board; this committee was more involved in oversight of the company and initiatives to cope with emerging problems.

In 1991 BCBSTX organized the Caring for Children Foundation to help address the problem of uninsured children, and I was appointed to its board of directors. I am gratified that more than 6,000 children were covered by health insurance through the Foundation by 1996, when Texas instituted the Children's Health Insurance Program (CHIP). The Foundation then developed a program for free immunizations for children in various communities across the state.

During my board tenure, BCBSTX increased health maintenance organization (HMO) membership; instituted preferred provider organization (PPO) programs; and bargained more aggressively with health care providers for lower payments. None of these efforts won BCBSTX or other health insurers much popularity, but a failure to have done so would have meant higher costs for our insureds and defeat in the competitive marketplace. I also served on the board of directors for the Rio Grande HMO.

The total number of Blue Cross Blue Shield (BCBS) plans across the nation was shrinking because of mergers and conversions from the traditional nonprofit model like BCBSTX to for-profit stock companies. The most prominent examples were the California Blue Cross plan that converted to WellPoint, Inc. and the Indiana plan that became Anthem Insurance Company. When WellPoint and Anthem merged in 2005 to become the largest health insurer in the United States, they had acquired BCBS companies in 12 states.

BCBSTX needed greater access to capital to effectively compete with larger companies. WellPoint and Anthem were both interested in acquiring BCBSTX. The single most important decision made by the Board while I was a member, and arguably during the history of the company, was whether to continue as a traditional nonprofit BCBS plan, merge or affiliate with another nonprofit plan, or convert to a for-profit company and/or merge with one of the giants.

After several years of investigation and considering all options, the Board approved a merger with Health Care Service Corporation (HCSA), a nonprofit mutual insurance company owning and operating the Illinois BCBS plan. HCSA was approximately twice the size of BCBSTX and had a similar vision of maintaining a

Health Care Service Corporation headquarters, Chicago, Illinois

not-for-profit approach with high quality services. After the merger was approved by the insurance regulators of Illinois and Texas, it was announced that the merger would occur on January 1, 1997. Texas Attorney General Dan Morales filed suit, blocking the merger and demanding more than 500 million dollars, alleging that BCBSTX was a "charity" and could not proceed without establishment of a charitable trust similar to the California BCBS conversion.

The merger was postponed and the case tried in 1997. Judge Joe Hart ruled in February 1998 that the merger could occur because BCBSTX was not a charity and the Illinois plan was a not-for-profit mutual insurance corporation. The attorney general gave notice of appeal, and it appeared any merger would be delayed for several more years. I worked with BCBSTX attorney Will Davis and HCSC general counsel Brian Van Vlierbergen to secure an agreement with the attorney general to allow us to proceed with the merger while the appeal was still pending. HCSC agreed to pay $10 million to the Texas Healthy Kids Corporation to benefit uninsured children and to pay $350 million and 5% interest if HCSC lost on appeal. The merger was completed on December 31, 1998, and the Texas and Illinois plans became one company: Health Care Service Corporation, a nonprofit mutual reserve company. The appellate court sustained Judge Hart's decision that BCBSTX was not a charity and the merger was legal; its opinion may be found at 113 SW 3rd 753. Under the court's ruling, no additional sums were owed to the State of Texas by BCBSTX or HCSC.

The road to merger of BCBSTX and HCSC was a long one; however, worth the effort. The combined plans had more than 5.8 million insured members, with revenues in excess of $8.5 billion. The merger elevated HCSC to the second largest BCBS plan at the time. Fears of some that the Texas plan would be swallowed up and neglected were proven unfounded. BCBSTX maintained its identity and management out of Richardson, Texas. Board membership and leadership was shared with the Illinois plan.

I was one of six Texas directors serving on the HCSC board. In 2001 I was elected chairman of the board of directors and served in that position for one year before my retirement in accordance with the bylaws, upon attaining the age of 70.

MEETING AND MARRYING MARY MARGARET

A while after Helen's death I went out with several women for dinner, shows, and parties at the homes of friends. I have been attracted to strong, bright women since high school days, and I was fortunate to know several and become acquainted with others during the three-year interim between Helen's death and my marriage to Mary Margaret.

Deserved or not, friends felt sorry for me and had no shortage of opinions concerning my romantic and marital future. Some were concerned that I might come under the spell of an undeserving or unworthy woman; others had ideas about ladies I should meet. Several women came forward to offer tea and sympathy.

Ed and Helen Baxter were good friends of a woman named Mary Margaret Albright. They concluded that Ms. Albright was a person I should know, and they planned a beautiful dinner party in their home during the month of May 1989 for the purpose of introducing me to Mary Margaret (MM). At the time, I was dating Jodie Richardson, a bright and attractive young attorney with Vinson & Elkins. Not understanding the purpose of the Baxter party, I called and asked if I could bring Jodie. As I recall, Ed may have hesitated but replied that it would be all right. When the Baxters advised MM about my unexpected guest, she altered her plans and did not attend the dinner party, under the misapprehension that Jodie and I were an "item."

Bill and Mary Arnold were also friends of Mary Margaret. When the Baxters told Bill of their failed efforts to introduce me to MM, Bill thought it was an idea worth pursuing. First, Bill had to convince MM that I was not seriously involved with Jodie and then get me to the dinner party on

The matchmakers: Bill and Mary Arnold (l) and Helen and Ed Baxter (r) with bride and groom at the Bauer House, May 25, 1991.

time and unattached. Bill Arnold is, to say the least, a very directive person; he took no chances that I would not show up at their house on Sunday July 16, 1989, for the purpose of meeting Mary Margaret Albright. He contacted my administrative assistant Lia Clarkson and directed her to explain to me in advance the purpose of the dinner and not mess it up. I showed up, as directed, where the Baxters and other mutual friends properly introduced me to Ms. Albright. You might say I got two very good dinners out of the project, with many more to come.

By no accident, Mary Margaret was seated next to me at the Arnold's dinner party. She was, and is, a very bright, attractive woman, and we had a good conversation. At the time, she was Vice President for Development at KLRU-TV, the local public television station that produces *Austin City Limits*. By the end of the evening, I was thoroughly impressed with Mary Margaret. When she asked if I would like to attend the next *Austin City Limits* live show featuring George Jones, I neither hesitated nor asked if I could bring Jodie. I said "yes" and marked my calendar for our first date on August 3, 1989.

I had long admired *Austin City Limits* but never attended a live taping of the program. Mary Margaret worked with the program in connection with her job. George Jones, sometimes known as "No-show George," showed up on time and gave a tremendous concert with all of his favorite songs including "Why, Baby, Why," "White Lightnin'," and "The Race is On"—and it was. Mary Margaret had to work during parts of the production, but when the show was over, I took her to the Green Mesquite for barbeque, and that was our first date, but not the last.

As I saw more of Mary Margaret, I learned more about her. She grew up in North Dallas, graduating near the top of her class at Hillcrest High School in 1957, was a UT Plan II student, and earned a master's degree in American history. Mary Margaret had been married to Dr. James Albright, an able psychiatrist who became disabled from chronic alcoholism. They divorced in 1978, and she raised and educated her two children, David and Patricia. Through employment as a vice president of a bank, a vice president at KLRU, and volunteer activities with historic preservation and nonprofit endeavors, Mary Margaret seemed to know nearly everyone in Austin, and was (and is) universally admired.

We spent more time together, involved with each others pursuits, parties, and problems. After Christmas in 1989, Mary Margaret and I traveled to

Mexico, where we brought in the New Year of 1990 in Cancun. We visited the ancient Mayan ruins of Chichen Itza deep in the jungles of the Yucatan Peninsula. In September 1990 we flew to Italy, rented a car, and drove to Orvieto, Assisi, Florence, and on to Rome. Although we failed to get an audience or his blessing, we saw the Pope in the Papal Basilica of St. Peter. The year was so good that we decided to start 1991 in Puerto Vallarta, on the west coast of Mexico. I think both MM and I were very happy with the time we spent together, but a problem loomed on the

MM sitting on the steps of El Castillo at Chichen Itza, December 29, 1989

horizon for our relationship that culminated at a Blue Cross meeting in Phoenix, which MM attended with me.

An old English rhyme recounts that "For the want of nail, the shoe was lost. For the want of a shoe, the horse was lost," and ultimately the kingdom lost—all for the want of a nail. In my case the shoe fell when Mary Margaret did not have a name tag at the Phoenix meeting. Distressed over confusion that occurred about our relationship, MM let me know, in no uncertain terms, that the kingdom would be lost unless we tied the knot. I quickly proposed marriage and the race was on for a wedding in May. If our marriage was not made in heaven, it was made in Sedona, Arizona, where we retreated to plan the wedding and soothe any hurt feelings for the want of a name tag.

I do not recall my first wedding being as complicated, perhaps because I was at a greater distance from Appleton and traveling for NSA. But this time, when we contacted a local Episcopal priest about the wedding, she advised us that Mary Margaret would have to secure the consent of the bishop for marriage because she was divorced. Widowers were exempt and could marry without such approval. After a counseling session with the priest, our plans to wed in holy matrimony were approved and we proceeded to the altar.

The wedding occurred at the UT System Bauer House on May 25, 1991, and a fine wedding it was. Our families and closer friends attended,

including Mary Margaret's parents and children, my two sons, Terri and
Karen, Chancellor Hans and Marion Mark, Charles and Stella Mullins,
the Conversation Group, Bill and Diana Hobby, Don and Mary Morgan,
Ray and Judy Clymer, Jerry and Claudia Estes, the original matchmakers
Ed and Helen Baxter, Bill and Mary Arnold, and others. After the wedding, we departed for a weekend honeymoon at McDonald Observatory in
West Texas. I promised Mary Margaret that if she married me we would see
the world and outer space together, and we started with the world in Odessa
and a view of the heavens near Ft. Davis. It only got better from there.

Family wedding picture at Bauer House— left to right:
Patricia and David Albright, bride and groom, Steve,
Terri, and David Farabee

The Best Lawyer Job in Texas:
UT System General Counsel, 1988–2000

This has got to be the best job in the state of Texas, especially for a practicing lawyer. It has all of the elements of a broad legal practice. . . .
There is a new challenge, if not every day, then certainly every week.
—Ray Farabee, *National Law Journal,* June 9, 1997

WORK HAS ALWAYS BEEN an important part of my life, from early employment delivering newspapers to the private practice of law in Wichita Falls. In this chapter I share some memories about my last and the best lawyer job before retirement in 2000. My new client and employer as of March 14, 1988, was the University of Texas System (UT System or System). I worked in the Office of General Counsel (OGC). I was no longer a senator, but Vice Chancellor and General Counsel. As fancy as it sounds, there were three executive vice chancellors and two other vice chancellors at the time, and even more as I write this in 2008.

Much like my decisions to drop out of college to work for NSA in 1955, and the one in 1973 to run for the Texas Senate, I had some second thoughts about leaving private law

IN-HOUSE COUNSEL
Ray Farabee, The University of Texas

Locking Horns for
His Alma Mater

National Law Journal,
June 9, 1997, page 1, section B

practice and the Senate. However, it was the right decision, and it didn't take long to realize that I had the best lawyer position in Texas—at least for me. I shared that opinion with the *National Law Journal* in 1997, which featured me as a part of its series of articles about in-house counsel. Other general counsel included major corporations, media groups, and large non-profit organizations.

Some history of the System and OGC may be helpful in understanding my new client and position.

BRIEF HISTORY OF THE UT SYSTEM AND OFFICE OF GENERAL COUNSEL

Texas has several systems of higher education, including those of UT, Texas A&M, Texas Tech, Texas State University, and the University of Houston. Unlike the California systems of higher education that are more structured and coordinated, Texas systems have grown up like topsy, and coordination has been a struggle; however, the concept of grouping institutions of higher education into systems has proven a more efficient method for governance, coordination, management, and delivery of services, as compared to multiple stand-alone universities and medical schools. The UT System was the first and largest system of higher education in Texas; it is one of the largest in the United States.

The Encyclopedia of Texas Colleges and Universities states that the UT System began in 1883 with the opening of the University of Texas at Austin and UT Medical Branch in Galveston, both under the same Board of Regents (BOR). Margaret C. Berry is more accurate in her book about UT when she stated, "The University of Texas System was established gradually," that is, with the addition of other medical schools, hospitals, and institutions of higher education in the 1900's, one by one. The Texas School of Mines and Metallurgy, now UT El Paso, was added to the System in 1913, followed by M. D. Anderson Cancer Center in 1941, UT Dental Branch (now part of UT Health Science Center Houston) and UT Southwestern Medical Center at Dallas in 1943. The BOR created the chancellor position in 1950 and appointed Judge James P. Hart to the position. In 1954 the BOR abolished the chancellor position but re-created it in 1960. The UT System is now comprised of 15 institutions, including nine universities, four medical schools, and two hospitals. A more detailed history and chronology of the System may be found on the Web at: http://www.utsystem.edu.

In the beginning, the System had neither a general counsel nor office of general counsel. The first in-house attorney for the System was Scott Gaines, hired in the late 1940's with the title of "Director of Legal Services." His office was located in the west wing of the UT Austin Main Building. Burnell Waldrip was hired in the 1950's to assist Gaines and work on oil and gas matters and the Board for Lease. The first UT System attorney with the title of General Counsel was Richard Gibson who was hired in 1967. Burnell Waldrip continued as Associate General Counsel.

W. O. Shultz, 1998

The Office of General Counsel began when W. O. Shultz left the Attorney General's Office, where he had represented UT in litigation matters, and joined Gibson and Waldrip in 1972— one or two lawyers doth not make an office of General Counsel, but three do, particularly if it includes W. O. Shultz. The new OGC was located on the second floor of O. Henry Hall in space now occupied by the Office of Health Affairs. The OGC moved to the eighth floor of the newly completed Ashbel Smith Hall in 1975. James T. Fitzpatrick succeeded Richard Gibson as General Counsel in 1976. Growth in the size of the OGC commenced between 1976 and 1980. During that time Merrill Finnell Shields (Charles Finnell's first wife), Lin Shivers, Tom Stockton (a former UT Austin football player), Kathy Chapman, Francie Frederick, Jim Irion, Lyn Taylor, and Bob Giddings joined the OGC. Later Fitzpatrick returned to Midland to enter private practice, and Jim Crowson was appointed General Counsel in 1980.

Crowson left the OGC at the end of 1987 to become Vice President and General Counsel of Lomas Nettleton Co. in Dallas. I served as General Counsel from 1988 until October 22, 2000, when I retired. Mike Godfrey succeeded me and served in that position until October 21, 2004, when he returned to private practice. Barry Burgdorf was appointed Vice Chancellor and General Counsel on February 15, 2005, and continues to serve in that position in 2008.

The operating budget of the OGC for my first fiscal year, 1988, was $1,586,771 for 18 attorneys and a support staff of approximately 25 persons, including a geologist–land analyst and a trademark license manager. During the 13 years I was General Counsel the System grew from 13 institutions with 120,000 students and 54,000 system-wide employees to 15 institutions with more than 153,448 students and 79,430 employees. When I retired in 2000, the OGC had an operating budget of $3,617,871 for 24 attorneys and 27 support staff.

MY NEW CLIENTS

As the principal lawyer for the System, I had no shortage of clients. My new clients were the Board of Regents, the Chancellor, System officers and offices, and the UT universities, medical schools, and hospitals.

The nine-member **BOARD OF REGENTS** (BOR or Board) is the ultimate authority for governance of the System. Members of the Board are appointed by the Governor. They are usually closer friends and/or supporters of the governor appointing them, particularly in the instance of the chairperson of the Board. The Board elects a chair every two years, and most of my work with the Board was either through the Secretary to the Board, Art Dilly and later Francie Frederick, or the Chairman of the Board. The chairmen I worked with were Jack Blanton (1988–1989), Louis Beecherl (1989–1993), Bernard Rapoport (1993–1997), and Donald L. Evans (1997–2001). I was fortunate to have a good working relationship with each of them, irrespective of their politics. All were successful, busy, and independent persons, but each was responsive to my

Jack Blanton

telephone calls and legal advice, even when they might have preferred another answer or different legal opinion. It is not easy to tell a board member or chairman that he/she can't legally do something; however, on occasion, I did so and still maintained a good working relationship with them—and avoided unnecessary legal problems and embarrassment.

CHANCELLORS: Although the General Counsel provides legal advice to the BOR, the Chancellor of the System was my immediate boss and principal client. At the time I served, the BOR appointed the General Counsel upon nomination by the Chancellor. In 2004, the BOR Rules and Regulations (Rules) were rewritten; the Chancellor now hires the General Counsel. The Secretary to the BOR, who is also an attorney, now serves as its Counsel. The General Counsel continues to provide legal services to the BOR as needed. Although I did not experience any conflicts between the BOR and Chancellor, the new structure addresses such problems if they occur.

I served with three chancellors while I was General Counsel: Dr. Hans Mark (1988–1992), Dr. William H. (Bill) Cunningham (1992–2000), and R. D. (Dan) Burck (2000). Hans Mark is a physicist and former U.S. Secretary of the Air Force under President Jimmy Carter; Bill Cunningham was

With Mary Margaret and Dr. Hans Mark at the Bauer House in 1992

Dean of the UT Austin College of Business and later President of UT Austin before being appointed Chancellor. Dan Burck was appointed Vice Chancellor for Business Affairs for the System shortly after I became General Counsel. Although I only served under Dan as General Counsel for a part of 2000 before my retirement, I worked as his executive assistant on a part-time basis during 2001–2003. In addition to different backgrounds, each of the three Chancellors had different management styles and personalities. There was never a shortage of legal questions, and my working relationship with each of them was excellent. All remain good friends.

OTHER SYSTEM OFFICERS AND OFFICES: Various Executive Vice Chancellors, Vice Chancellors, and their offices are responsible for running the System. Each officer and office is confronted with legal problems and questions that find their way to OGC. The offices and the officers I worked with were the Academic Affairs (Drs. James Duncan and, later, Ed Sharp), Health Affairs (Dr. Charles Mullin, MD), Asset Management (Michael Patrick and Tom Ricks), Business Affairs (Dan Burck and Kerry

Dan Burck, Vice Chancellor Bus. Affs. (1989–1999) and Chancellor, (2000–2003)

Kennedy), and Government Relations (Gerald Hill and Mike Millsap). When Bill Cunningham became Chancellor, the Office for Development and External Relations was created, and Shirley Bird Perry was appointed Vice Chancellor for that office. The functions of Asset Management were transferred to the University of Texas Investment Management Company (UTIMCO) in 1996, and additional officers and offices have been added to the System Administration since my departure.

UT COMPONENT INSTITUTIONS: The nine academic institutions, four medical schools, and two freestanding hospitals produced the largest segment of law business for the OGC. Employment disputes, student matters, medical liability claims, intellectual property matters such as patents and copyrights, real estate, federal tax, multiple contracts, and varied litigation flowing from the diverse institutions presented daily challenges and problem-solving opportunities. Shortly after my arrival at UT, I made a point of visiting each of the institutions and getting to know their presidents and other officers. All of the institutions were different. UT Austin had 50,000 students, as compared to UT Permian Basin in Odessa, with fewer than 3000 students. UT M. D. Anderson Cancer Center in Houston was and is the largest cancer hospital/research institution in the United States, while UT Tyler Health Center in the piney woods near Tyler is a small facility, traditionally focused on lung and respiratory problems. Irrespective of size and location, each component institution needed all kinds of legal services, and they received them from or through the OGC.

A GENERAL COUNSEL'S WORK

The duties and responsibilities of the UT System Vice Chancellor and General Counsel are many. Since the job was new to me, a quick learning curve was required. W. O. Shultz and Francie Frederick, who had been managing many of the functions of the OGC before and after the departure of Jim

Crowson, were helpful in my quick course of study for becoming the functioning leader for the OGC. Office manager Carolyn Faulkner, my legal secretary Shirley Schneider, and her successor Beverly Page were also of great assistance.

The Board of Regents Rules and Regulations (Regents Rules or Rules) served as the bible for the operation and governance of the System. Like the Good Book, the Regents Rules were seldom read and not always un-

OGC Office Manager Carolyn Faulkner and Beverly Page, 2000

derstood. The two-volume work of my era was without index or word search and subject to changes at nearly every meeting of the Board of Regents. The Rules have now been rewritten, placed online, and are more user friendly. When I arrived, only two people seemed to understand the Rules from alpha to omega; one was Art Dilly, Executive Secretary of the BOR, and the other W. O. Shultz, who helped write most of the amendments during his tenure with the System from 1972 until 2003. W. O. functioned like Merlin the Magician when it came to the Rules. With W. O.'s help, I found Chapter II, Section 8, of the Rules that outlined my duties and responsibilities. The most important functions I carried out in my thirteen years as General Counsel were the following.

LEGAL ADVICE: The principal function of the General Counsel is to provide legal services and advice to the Board of Regents, Chancellor, other administrative officers of the System, and the UT institutions. Considering the size and complexity of the System, that is a tall order, and the job could not be done without OGC attorneys and staff. However, the ultimate responsibility for the legal services, opinions, advice, and related tasks rests in the General Counsel, where the buck stops.

MANAGING THE OGC: The effectiveness of a general counsel is dependent on the strength and capabilities of his or her legal and support staff. I inherited a good staff and made only a few personnel changes, other than the natural attrition that occurs over time. I instituted monthly staff meetings shortly after my arrival and organized the attorneys and support staff into five separate groups with section managers. The staff meetings and sections improved communication and fostered greater involvement and accountability.

SETTLEMENT OF CLAIMS AND LITIGATION: Although other OGC attorneys supervised various lawsuits, I was involved in approving settlements or decisions to try cases. Negotiation skills that I learned in Wichita Falls settling fender benders and hurt backs were helpful, as we did our best to determine what a jury might do in cases alleging damages, sometimes in the millions of dollars. Larger payments required approval of other System officials and the BOR for the largest amounts. Most of the settlements presented to the Board involved medical liability lawsuits, and I had the responsibility for making the presentation to them about such cases.

MEDICAL LIABILITY BENEFIT PLAN: As General Counsel, I was the administrator of the medical liability self-insurance plan (Plan) that insured more than 3000 UT physicians and 1800 medical residents against claims and lawsuits alleging malpractice in their delivery of care at UT hospitals, clinics, and affiliated institutions. The Plan was similar to liability insurance companies. Premiums were set on the basis of loss experience and professional actuarial estimates. Each year the Plan typically paid out 14 to 18 million dollars for settlement of claims and lawsuits and approximately five million dollars for outside legal expense to defend our physicians. The annual operating and actuarial expenses for the Plan averaged $950,000. Premium charges to the practice plans of our medical schools and hospitals were about one third of what similar coverage would have cost in the commercial market. As administrator, I issued annual reports to our insured institutions and their practice plans that quantified the loss experiences of the various medical specialties covered and the financial activities of the Plan.

LEGISLATIVE ANALYSIS AND DRAFTING: Working closely with the Office of Governmental Relations and other System offices, OGC reviewed and tracked approximately 1200 to 1500 bills during each regular legislative session. We were responsible for providing written and online analyses of legislation that would affect any part of the UT System. Lia Clarkson and Mel Hazelwood, who came to OGC with me from my former Senate staff, were extremely helpful as we assumed the additional responsibilities that occurred during legislative sessions.

ETHICS AND COMPLIANCE: The General Counsel was the primary source of advice and information about compliance with ethics laws, related regulations, and opinions of the Texas Ethics Commission.

Government agencies in general, and universities in particular, are held to higher standards of legal conduct and compliance than the private sector. My advice frequently went beyond whether something was legal, by suggesting that some decisions might have an appearance of impropriety, and it was well received.

THE ATTORNEY GENERAL (AG) and his office represent the System and its institutions in all litigation, except medical malpractice cases against doctors covered by our self-insurance plan and a few cases where the AG permits outside counsel. Although some felt that assistant AG's were not as capable as outside counsel, I did not find that to be generally true, and we saved millions of dollars in outside counsel fees by not using outside private counsel. The AG's permission is also required prior to retaining outside counsel for non-litigation matters such as patent, tax, and bond lawyers. As a result, the relationship between the General Counsel and the AG and his office is very important. I made a point of getting along well with all three of the AG's with whom I worked: Jim Mattox (1988–1991), Dan Morales (1992–1998), and John Cornyn (1999–2000).

Mattox and Morales were Democrats, and Cornyn a Republican. I met Mattox while I served as a state senator and seriously considered running against him when he left Congress to run for AG. One of my wiser political decisions was to defer that opportunity to Max Sherman. I knew Morales as a House member during my Senate years, and we worked together on several pieces of legislation. After Morales was elected AG, he asked me to leave the UT System and become First Assistant Attorney General. I considered the offer for a couple of days and wisely and politely declined. I did not know John Cornyn, who served on the State Supreme Court prior to his election as AG, but we worked well together and remain friends.

Jim Mattox ran for governor against Ann Richards, lost, and went into private practice in Austin. John Cornyn was elected to the U.S. Senate, where he contin-ues to serve after being reelected to that office. Dan Morales was indicted on 12 counts alleging mail fraud, conspiracy, and false

Working with Attorney General Jim Mattox, 1988

statements on his tax return and a loan application. Morales plead guilty on two counts and went to prison. Ironically, Morales' problems arose out of his 1996 success in making the largest settlement in Texas history in a lawsuit against major tobacco companies ($15 billion to be paid out over 25 years to the state and $2.3 billion through 2003 to Texas counties and hospital districts).

TRANSACTIONS, TRIALS, AND TRIBULATIONS

Thousands of OGC transactions, hundreds of trials, and many tribulations occurred while I was general counsel. Most of the transactions and trials were routine, but a few come to mind that I briefly describe. The dictionary defines "tribulation" as a trying experience, and I had my share of them. Although my OGC tribulations seemed very serious and often stressful at the time, most were in the normal course of management of more than 50 people and functioning in a large organization. Many tribulations did not involve personnel or management problems but were unique legal problems that never rose to the level of a transaction or trial. In retrospect, some of the tribulations now seem humorous, but others had sad consequences.

Transactions

BRACKENRIDGE TRACT: Shortly after I arrived at the UT System, I was asked to join several other System officials in negotiations with a West Austin neighborhood group about the future of the Brackenridge Tract (Tract). The 500-acre Tract was donated by Regent George W. Brackenridge in 1909 to be used as the future campus for UT Austin, which was outgrowing its original 40 acres in the middle of the city. The Tract, located on and near Lake Austin, was extremely valuable by 1988, but it was primarily used for a 141-acre golf course leased for a nominal sum to the Austin Lions Club, married student housing, a biological field lab, a Safeway store, and a boat dock. The golf course lease was nearing its end, and the West Austin neighborhood wanted the golf course but no further real estate development. The System had a fiduciary obligation to improve economic utilization of the Tract for the benefit of UT Austin.

We negotiated for several months. One of my best friends, Mary Arnold, was the leader of the neighborhood group. Although it appeared at times that no agreement was possible, we finally reached one. The golf course lease was renewed at a fairer rental for UT Austin; 90 acres on the west side of the river known as the Stratford Tract was sold for prime residential lots, and acreage east of the river was developed under long-term leases for restaurants, apartments, and LCRA office buildings. The biological field lab and married student housing continued as they were. Millions of dollars have and will continue to flow into UT Austin endowments for students, faculty, and other purposes because of these negotiations and related transactions. History about George W. Brackenridge and the Tract may be found on the Web through a Google search of "Brackenridge Tract in Austin, Texas."

UT PAN AMERICAN AND UT BROWNSVILLE: The UT System did not have a presence in the Lower Rio Grande Valley when I joined it in 1988. Chancellor Hans Mark realized the importance and future growth of that area. He identified Pan American State University in Edinburg and its branch campus in Brownsville as excellent prospects for becoming part of the UT System. OGC and I worked with Dr. Mark and others to realize the addition of Pan American in 1989 when the Legislature approved the transfer and merger as a UT institution. In 1991 the Legislature created a separate academic institution as UT Brownsville. Priscilla Lozano, who was General Counsel at UT Pan American, joined the OGC staff and remains as one of its most experienced and capable attorneys.

PUF AND OTHER LANDS: The UT System owns and manages 2,100,000 acres of Permanent University Fund (PUF) lands in West Texas,

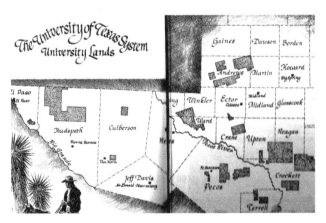

Map from Land, Oil, and Education *by Berte Haigh, showing PUF lands in West Texas*

115,000 acres of endowment lands, and over 10,000 acres of campus lands. OGC provides the legal work for transactions involving these lands, including title work and preparation of deeds, surface leases, oil and gas leases, and easements. The 1000-acre Ste. Genevieve vineyard and winery near Ft. Stockton is an example of surface leases that keep OGC attorneys busy. It is the largest vineyard in Texas and produces the greatest quantity, if not quality, of Texas wine. Wines from the UT vineyards find their way into supermarkets and are blended with other more critically acclaimed wines around the world.

ORGANIZED ATHLETICS: Transactions ranging from hiring and firing coaches, licensing trademarks, and building super-stadiums involved OGC during my years as general counsel. When the addition of luxury suites and a private club was proposed for UT Austin Darrell K Royal Memorial Stadium, some of us were skeptical about the prospects for filling them, but we were wrong. The first suites were built, quickly leased, and more added along with the popular University of Texas Club under the east side of the stadium. The Southwest Conference dissolved in 1996 after more than 80 years as the dominant NCAA athletic organization in Texas and Arkansas. UT Austin, Texas A&M, Baylor, and Texas Tech joined the Big Eight Conference. OGC worked on documents leading to UT Austin's transfer to the Big Twelve Conference, with larger economic returns and more vigorous competition.

TOBACCO SETTLEMENT: Although the State of Texas lawsuit against the tobacco companies was a trial and tribulation for Attorney General Dan Morales, the settlement was a very remunerative transaction for UT health institutions. OGC assisted the AG's office in preparation of the case for trial. When the case was settled, the four UT medical schools, two UT hospitals, and a future regional health center in South Texas received endowments totaling several hundred million dollars.

UTIMCO: The largest transaction to occur while I was General Counsel was the UT System transfer of management for the PUF (other than its lands and minerals) and other funds to the University of Texas Investment Management Company (UTIMCO) in March 1996. UTIMCO is a nonprofit corporation organized by the BOR for the purpose of managing the PUF and other funds. The Vinson & Elkins law firm represented UTIMCO, and OGC represented the UT System in the transfer of management responsibility.

Trials

Over 98% of all civil cases filed are either settled or dismissed without going to trial. The same statistics are applicable in the UT System. Of the hundreds of lawsuits filed against the UT System and/or its institutions, the following trials were the most memorable.

CASE OF THE UNAPPRECIATED THUMB: Phon Van Avong was a Vietnamese fisherman working off the Gulf coast when his thumb became tangled in a net and was torn from his right hand. The thumb was lost, and he was rushed to Houston for emergency care. A distinguished surgeon from a UT medical school was brought in to operate on Phon's hand. Phon spoke no English, and our surgeon spoke no Vietnamese. The hospital retained an interpreter with limited knowledge of Vietnamese language or its culture. The surgeon explained a new procedure for taking a patient's toe and attaching it to the patient's hand to serve as a thumb. Thinking he had approval, the surgeon proceeded to remove one of the patient's toes and attach it to Phon's right hand. The evidence showed that with appropriate exercise and therapy, the new "thumb" would have worked well; but there was a problem. Phon didn't want his toe on his right hand. In Phon's culture, the right hand is the "clean hand," used for eating and other sanitary endeavors. The left hand and the feet are viewed as unclean. Phon was very upset and sued our insured physician. Although the jury found no negligence in the surgical procedure, they found that our doctor failed to secure informed consent and assessed approximately $300,000 in damages, which, with interest after trial delays and lengthy appeal, came to more than $500,000. We lost only two medical liability cases while I was administrator of the Plan, and this was one of them. As W. O. Shultz was fond of saying, "No good deed goes unpunished"—at least in this case.

THE DOG FOOD CASE: Scientists at UT Health Science Center in Houston did research concerning the effects of higher dosages of lysine, an amino acid, when added to food. They used dogs and cats to measure the impact of the food additive on the brain. Although the lysine had no appreciable impact on the cats or humans, the scientists observed significant brain activity and enhanced appetite in the dogs. What started with research about the impact of lysine on humans resulted in U.S. Patent #4,267,195 for "Dog Food Flavors." After the System received its patent, someone at the medical school noticed a label on Ralston Purina dog

See what UT "Dog Food Flavors" can do for your best friend?

food and compared it to an older package. Ralston had significantly increased the amount of lysine in their most popular dog food. For whatever reason, lysine makes a dog biscuit taste like beef steak, and dogs eat more of the lysine-enhanced biscuits. OGC advised Ralston Purina that it was infringing upon our client's patent and that they must cease and desist or enter into a license agreement with UT System for the benefit of our medical school and its scientists who made this amazing discovery. We were promptly rebuffed. Ralston not only denied infringement, but also challenged our patent in the U.S. Office of Patents. We prevailed in Washington, D.C., and filed suit in Austin. After lengthy discovery and months of negotiation, Ralston Purina settled on the morning we were to go to trial for a sum that I cannot disclose under terms of the settlement agreement, but it was the largest patent infringement settlement in OGC history at the time.

LULAC VS. RICHARDS ET AL.: The League of United Latin American Citizens (LULAC) filed suit against the governor and all Texas institutions of higher education alleging discrimination against Mexican Americans living in the 41-county area along the southern border of the state (South Texas) in 1987. After an eight-week trial in South Texas in 1991, a jury found no discrimination based on race but made a finding that South Texas had not received its fair share of higher education funding from the Legislature. The trial court entered judgment for the plaintiffs, holding the entire Texas higher education system unconstitutional. The Attorney General appealed the case to the Supreme Court of Texas, and that court reversed the trial court in November 1993. OGC worked with the Attorney General's Office throughout the trial and appeal. During this same time, the Texas Legislature enacted the "South Texas Initiative Program," which improved funding and new programs for universities in South Texas, including UT El Paso, UT San Antonio, UT Pan American, UT Brownsville, and UT Health Science Center San Antonio. I was called upon many times to explain why the UT System was not discriminatory against

Mexican Americans and South Texas. Some of my audiences were not particularly friendly, but we came out of the whole process with better funding for South Texas institutions and a favorable Supreme Court holding that the higher education system in Texas was constitutional.

HOPWOOD CASE: At the same time the UT System was being sued for discrimination against minority groups and persons, a "reverse discrimination" suit was filed in 1992 in the U.S. District Court by Cheryl Hopwood and three other plaintiffs against the Board of Regents, alleging discrimination against non-minority students by the UT School of Law in its admission policies. The Hopwood Case became a centerpiece for attacks on affirmative action in higher education for the next ten years. UT won the case without a jury in 1994, but the plaintiffs appealed the decision to the 5th Circuit Court of Appeals, which reversed and remanded it back to Austin in 1996. The case was tried again and resulted in a judgment awarding only nominal damages of $1.00 to each plaintiff but enjoining UT from using any consideration of race in its admissions policies. Costs and attorney fees for the plaintiffs of more than $750,000 were assessed against UT. The case continued through another round of unsuccessful appeals after my retirement. The University of Michigan Law School was involved in a similar lawsuit in another U.S. Circuit Court. In *Grutter v. Bollinger, et al.* the U.S. Supreme Court, in a 2003 5-4 decision, upheld the use of limited affirmative action. Hopwood was the highest profile case of my legal career, and my comments about the case were nationally quoted. UT lost its battle, but Michigan won the war—at least for the time being.

Another irony involving Texas Attorney General Dan Morales emerged early in the Hopwood Case. Morales was a graduate of Harvard Law School and likely a beneficiary of affirmative action. Although he was the UT attorney under Texas law, he made public statements and issued an opinion that were sympathetic to the plaintiffs and undermined affirmative action in Texas higher education. Morales did allow UT to use the Vinson & Elkins law firm as our principal counsel. Vinson & Elkins contributed more than two million dollars' worth of pro bono legal services in our defense and appeals of the Hopwood Case.

TITLE IX LAWSUIT: A class action was filed against UT Austin in 1992, alleging violations of Title IX of the federal law prohibiting discrimination against women. The plaintiffs contended that the University did not comply with federal law because the ratio of males to females in athletic programs (77:23) was not substantially the same as male to female under-graduate enrollment (53:47). We argued the law did not require similar ra-tios, only that the University adequately accommodate the interests and abilities of its student body and that UT's programs made such accom-modation. After lengthy discovery and two unfavorable court opinions on similar issues elsewhere in the country, we settled the suit by agreeing to add women's soccer and softball and to increase the percentage of women participating in varsity athletics.

THE LARGEST ADVERSE VERDICT: American Health Advisors, Inc. (AHA) sued the UT System and its three teaching hospitals in 1992, alleg-ing $60 million in damages for breach of contract and an unauthorized taking of its trade secret. The "trade secret" was a federal Medicaid program that was brought to the attention of UTMB by the president of AHA. The teaching hospitals and related UT medical schools received substan-tial sums from the federal government programs; however, the contract for services was not properly approved; and the federal program was hardly a trade secret. Nevertheless, a Travis County jury awarded AHA $10 million in damages for taking its "trade secret." We filed an appeal of the court's judgment but agreed to several mediations. AHA and its president were in difficulty with the IRS, and we finally settled the case for substantially less than the $10-million judgment. The IRS and attorneys got the money, and the AHA official may have avoided prison.

Tribulations

THE GRINCH WHO STOLE THE CHRISTMAS PRAYER: 'Twas the week before Christmas and time for the annual OGC Christmas Lun-cheon, over which I presided each year. It was customary to request a longtime staff employee, who was also a Baptist minister, to offer a prayer of thanks unto the Lord. Jim Evans gave thanks; we gobbled down the ham, turkey, dressing, and the tasty vegetables that my wife Mary Mar-garet brought; and then we proceeded with an elaborate exchange of gifts. A good time was had by all—except one—the Grinch. The Grinch was a lawyer/architect who specialized in construction contracts and disputes. He was a bright, detail-oriented person who did not lack for opinions. My wife and I retired to my office after the party, and shortly thereafter the Grinch stormed into my office and vociferously accused me of violating the

United States Constitution. My constitutional sin was allowing Jim to ask the Lord to bless our food. I politely listened and thanked him for expressing his constitutional opinions. Although the encounter did not enhance my Christmas spirit that year, it did impress my wife and administrative assistant that being General Counsel is not always a piece of cake, not even Christmas cake.

BUDGET TIME: Each year it was my responsibility to develop and present a budget for OGC. In some ways it was easier as a Legislative Budget Board member to set the multi-billion-dollar budget for the State of Texas than OGC's $1.5-million budget that had grown to $3.5 million when I retired. The pain of budget making involves salary decisions and balancing the amount of funds available against the needs and relative merits of each employee. I couldn't, and probably shouldn't, make everyone happy, particularly during years when funds available don't allow appropriate salary increases for some of the most deserving. OGC turnover was very small, and in most cases the salary level was not the principal cause for persons leaving. The assistance of office manager Carolyn Faulkner was invaluable in the complicated and sometimes painful process.

ANNUAL EMPLOYEE EVALUATIONS: Although I had been an employee of one kind or another for more than 35 years, with responsibilities for managing other employees in several jobs, I had not experienced the stress of administering formal annual employee evaluations. It is hard to sit across the table and tell an attorney that he or she is doing poorly, setting a bad example, or performing unsatisfactorily in some other respect. It is much easier to grade everyone high, postpone, or delegate the responsibility to someone else; however, it is not responsible to do so, and it can be disastrous in those few instances when poor performance leads to termination proceedings. I bit the bullet and performed the evaluations of all 24 attorneys and the support staff working directly for me. On occasion, it was painful; but most of the time positive, constructive criticism led to better performance.

HIRING AND FIRING: As in the case of assembling my Senate staff, OGC employment decisions were some of the most important I made. It is neither as easy to hire nor fire government employees, as compared to the private sector where the "employee at will" doctrine generally prevails. Laws ranging from constitutional due process to whistle blower protection are applicable to government employees, including OGC attorneys and support staff. One of the larger parts of OGC's work was advice and assistance to clients who had employment law problems. In one instance, my office manager noticed unusually high long-distance charges to the phone line of one our attorneys. We determined that the attorney was making hundreds of dollars' worth of personal long-distance phone calls at state expense. I required the attorney to reimburse the System for his personal calls and terminated his employment.

Hiring was easier than firing. OGC had little turnover of attorneys while I was General Counsel. When a vacancy occurred, we were fortunate to have good responses to our job postings. On occasion, attorney applicants advised me that they were interested in "slowing down" and would like the job. They never got the job. OGC was not a place to slow down.

LEGISLATIVE SESSIONS: Although I once was one, members of the Legislature and their many bills provided tribulations every other year. Our workload doubled for several months, and some of the legislation, should it pass, would create many more tribulations. Somehow, we made it through each of the six sessions that occurred on my watch. Because of my familiarity with the legislative process, I usually analyzed more bills than other attorneys. One might say it was a form of penance.

RARE BIRDS: 1990 was a year for the birds. I received a call from UT Southwestern Medical School advising that the federal government and

Audubon Society had descended upon them, alleging destruction of the habitat for Great White Egrets. The egrets occupied the treetops of the western part of the campus each year to lay eggs and hatch their young. Southwestern was clearing a few trees to make way for a tennis court for its students. Unfortunately, some of the egrets occupied the trees that were being felled, and unbeknownst to Southwestern and its contractor, the egrets were protected under federal migratory bird laws. We stopped, ceased, and desisted from our nefarious destruction of the bird habitat, and no tennis courts were built for the medical students.

Great white egret and chicks

Several months later, OGC received an emergency call from UT Permian Basin in Odessa with another bird problem. We knew it couldn't be another Great White Egret situation because Odessa is short on tall trees. As it turned out, hundreds of small barn swallows were building their mud nests on the ceilings of the covered walkways, which protected the students from the searing West Texas sun. The nests would not have been a problem except for the voluminous bird droppings, sometimes on the heads of students and faculty. The UTPB maintenance department saw no problem encouraging the pesky barn swallows to seek other environs by scraping down some of the nests with garden rakes. The Audubon Society and the law enforcement officers of Ector County entered the fray. UTPB called OGC, and found, to our surprise, that the barn swallow was also protected. My legal advice was to immediately stop raking the ceilings. My practical advice was to wear a hat when traversing the covered walkways.

PIT VIPERS: Only one snake case occurred while I was general counsel, but it involved the most poisonous of reptiles: the fer-de-lance. One of our professors was working in Central America on an archaeological dig, and a native worker helping him was bitten by this pit viper. Unless treatment is received immediately, the venom of the fer-de-lance is deadly. The accident occurred in the jungle. Our faculty person transported the victim to a local clinic in time to save his life, but the worker lost an arm. OGC attorney Priscilla Lozano handled a series of unusual legal questions on an emergency basis, and we promptly resolved what seemed a life-and-death matter, particularly for the unfortunate worker.

IMPORTANT OGC CHANGES 1988–2000

Many OGC changes that occurred while I was General Counsel would have happened at some point in time, but it was my privilege to personally initiate some of them and assist OGC attorneys and staff in the implementation of others. The following represent the changes I consider most important:

OGC ORGANIZATION AND DIVERSIFICATION OF LEADERSHIP: Prior to 1988 OGC was not organized by legal specialties. The General Counsel and Associate General Counsel W. O. Schulz made assignments of work and supervised all attorneys. Several of the staff attorneys worked in more specialized areas such as oil and gas, real estate law, medical liability, and intellectual property. During my first year I organized OGC into five groups: Claims, Lands (later Business Law), General Attorneys, Medical Liability (later Medical Liability and Health Law), and Intellectual Property. Management responsibility was expanded to include the five section managers I appointed. The percentage of female attorneys increased from 21% to 50%; by the year 2000, four of the five section managers were women, appointed because they were the best qualified for the leadership positions.

REFINEMENT AND EXPANSION OF OGC DATABASE: When I arrived, OGC had a database for current assignments, closed cases, and other information that was on a mainframe computer system. A few attorneys and most legal secretaries had early vintage desktop computers. With the help of emerging technology and the leadership of Lia Clarkson, OGC was one of the first System offices to more fully computerize its operation. In the process, we refined and expanded the OGC database, which made our legal work more accessible, both to OGC staff and its clients. Prior to each monthly staff meeting, attorneys reported the current status of their work and assignments from their desktop computers through the OGC database. We never became a paperless office, but we saved a lot of trees.

Lia Clarkson, an invaluable resource for many of the OGC innovations cited

LEGISLATIVE TRACKING SYSTEM: With the help of Lia Clarkson and her son Gavin Clarkson, OGC developed the first computerized system for analyzing and tracking the status of legislation that might impact the UT System. OGC published a training manual for the tracking system that was distributed throughout the System.

ANNUAL REPORTS: The first *Office of General Counsel Annual Report* was published in 1991. It reviewed the work of OGC in 1990 and provided our clients helpful information related to our legal services. With information from the improved database, we published a similar report each year. The detailed reports fostered a better understanding of the broad range and quality of OGC work.

NEW IN-HOUSE LAWYERS: In response to increased federal tax matters, construction contracts and related disputes, real estate transactions, environmental law, and the volume of requests for collection work, I hired new OGC attorneys to work in these specialties. As a result, the System saved substantial sums of money that would have otherwise been paid for outside counsel, and the delivery of such services was greatly improved.

RISK MANAGEMENT: In 1992 I established the Office of Health Care Quality and Risk Management to develop and coordinate risk management services in connection with our medical liability self-insurance program. OGC created the Office of Environmental Affairs in 1994 to promote proactive compliance with environmental laws and regulations. Although the environmental risk management function was absorbed into other UT System programs, the health care program remains an active component of the medical liability insurance program. The work of Margaret Shifren (an RN and JD) was invaluable in establishing the health care risk management program; the establishment of an interactive website by Muffett Mills (an RN Certified Legal Assistant) was outstanding.

ETHICS AND COMPLIANCE: I was appointed by the Chancellor in 1992 as the first Ethics Compliance Advisor for the UT System. The appointment was in response to a request by the newly established Texas Ethics Commission that all state agencies appoint an ethics officer. OGC instituted the first ethics training programs for the UT System and published the *Standards of Conduct Digest* and other related materials for the System and component institutions.

STRATEGIC PLANNING: During 1992 OGC participated in the formulation of a strategic plan for the UT System. Additionally, OGC professional and technical staff developed a specific strategic plan for the Office of General Counsel. The plan established goals, objectives, and outcomes for the delivery of legal services to the System. Most of our goals were accomplished during the next eight years. A copy of the comprehensive ten-page plan may be found in the *OGC 1992 Annual Report*.

OGC PUBLICATIONS AND ONLINE PROGRAMS: Although everyone is presumed to know the law, they don't. One of my first projects was the development of a series of OGC publications to achieve better understanding of the law throughout the UT System. OGC commenced website and online publications in the mid-1990's. It was one of the first offices of general counsel to do so. By 2000 OGC had published more than 50 reference manuals, policy collections, handbooks, law bulletins, brochures, guidelines, and other printed publications. More than a dozen OGC articles, courses, checklists, and guides were online at the time I retired. Although many OGC attorneys and staff persons contributed to our publications, Lia Clarkson, Georgia Harper, and Beverly Page deserve special recognition. A list of OGC publications may be found in the 2000 Annual Report and on the OGC web page at www.utsystem.edu/OGC/.

RETIREMENT AS GENERAL COUNSEL

As one passes the 65-year age mark, thoughts of retirement occur. I decided in 1998 to talk with Chancellor Bill Cunningham about my retiring in 1999. When I broached the subject, he walked over and closed the door to his office. The Chancellor then advised me on a confidential basis that

he intended to retire in 2000 and asked me to stay on until that time. I respected and enjoyed working with Dr. Cunningham and continued as General Counsel.

When Cunningham retired on May 31, 2000, the Board of Regents appointed R. D. (Dan) Burck as Interim Chancellor and later Chancellor. I worked with Dan in the selection of a new Vice Chancellor and General Counsel. The Regents appointed Michael

Pictured with Dr. William H. (Bill) Cunningham, Chancellor, 1992–2000

Godfrey, and I retired as General Counsel on October 22, 2000. I continued work for the UT System on a part-time basis for two more years as Special Assistant to the Chancellor.

As Special Assistant, I handled assignments from the Chancellor and consulted, as needed, with the OGC. One of my larger assignments involved a special study of the UT Medical Branch (UTMB) health care delivery system for the Texas prison system. I was well suited for the task because of my work with the Texas Department of Correction (TDC) in the State Senate and handling related legal issues as General Counsel. While working with the task force making the study, I visited several prison health clinics in Texas prisons and the prison hospital at UTMB. The study was prompted by a series of *Austin American-Statesman* articles that were generally critical of UTMB's program. In summary, we found, as did TDC and the legislature, that UTMB was providing good health care for the prison system, considering the size and complexity of prison health problems.

With Mary Margaret and Lady Bird Johnson at
retirement reception at the Bauer House, November 30, 2000

The Mary Margaret Years
(1991–)

She is a friend of mind. She gather me, man. The pieces I am, she gather them and give them back to me in all the right order. It's good, you know, when you get a woman who is a friend of your mind.
—Sixo's description of how he felt about the Thirty-Mile Woman in *Beloved* by Toni Morrison

I HAVE BEEN MARRIED to two active, bright, attractive, and strong women. Helen was, and Mary Margaret is, a friend of my mind, gathering the pieces that I am and giving them back to me in better order. This chapter is about Mary Margaret and our life together, travels around Texas and the world, support of each other in good and difficult times, and mutual interests and endeavors.

Second marriages can be difficult, particularly when one's first marriage was a good one and with the second marriage each new spouse has his and her own family, friends, and work. After 17 years of marriage and retrospect, I can say without qualification that my marriage to Mary Margaret (sometimes referred to as MM) has been unusually good. This is not to say we don't have differing opinions, approaches, and personalities. Otherwise, it would have been terribly dull—and it has been quite the opposite. The time we spent together before marriage getting to know each other, traveling, and sharing experiences was important; our life as a married couple has become more important.

YOUR PLACE OR MINE: HOW A HOUSE BECAME A HOME

One of the questions to be resolved prior to our marriage was whether we would live at my place, 2702 Rockingham, or MM's place, 1811 Polo Road.

The Rockingham home is in South Austin, with a large yard to be maintained, while the Polo Road townhouse is in what might be considered the more fashionable west part of Austin, with minimal yard and maintenance responsibility. As a second home, I made very few improvements to the Rockingham house, and most of our friends lived in West Austin. The question of "my place or your place" could have been a big problem, but it wasn't. We settled on 2702 Rockingham and started a series of improvements, some of which I had doubts about. Mary Margaret's ideas were good ones, and my second home became our primary home.

The first step for our home together on Rockingham was making room for Mary Margaret's books. New bookcases were built to the ceiling of the den that became our library. A new bay window was added, enlarging and brightening the breakfast room. Later, the third bedroom became MM's home office with more bookshelves and new cabinetry. Floors and carpets were next on the home improvement agenda. We selected an Italian ceramic tile and a lighter shade of carpet to replace the old vinyl tiles and brown shag. The good news was that no cracks were found in the slab after taking up three layers of vinyl. The bad news was that each level of vinyl had more asbestos in it than the one above. Eventually, the new Italian tile flooring and carpet did wonders to further brighten the old house.

Shortly thereafter, MM proposed a remodel of the kitchen, modernizing and opening it to the breakfast room. The bids came in at more than I had paid for the mansion on Buchanan Street in Wichita Falls. Mary Margaret was very persuasive, and I was the primary beneficiary of her excellent cooking. What could I do? Gritting my teeth and mumbling, I consented to our largest remodel effort to that date. Despite initial doubts and anxieties, the new kitchen was a great improvement, and I did not have to file for bankruptcy or go to the poorhouse.

Many other improvements have been made to our home in South Austin. Mary Margaret has adjusted to crossing the Colorado River several times a day to see friends and do good works. We toil each weekend in the yard and gardens that have also benefited from MM's sharp scissors and opinions. She is the pruner; I am the propagator.

Shortly after our marriage, I initiated a program of gifting my Wichita Falls home to my sons. David purchased Steven's one-half interest, and with his wife Terri, they have raised their three children Worth, Nancy Helen, and Russell in the Martin-Farabee House at 1512 Buchanan. Steven and his wife Karen and their child Sara Helen live south of the river in West Lake Hills. MM has gifted her townhouse on Polo Road to her daughter Patricia, and we are happily at home in South Austin with Miss Lilly, the cat, at 2702 Rockingham Drive.

Miss Lilly, the cat, at work with MM, 2000

MUTUAL COMMITMENTS TO THE COMMUNITY AND BEYOND

After we were married, I suggested that Mary Margaret leave her employment and spend more time pursuing her individual and our mutual interests. She did so, and our lives became even busier with UT receptions and events, Blue Cross meetings, nonprofit volunteer activities, family commitments, and travel. The additional time, free of employment obligations, allowed Mary Margaret to pursue new and creative community projects, and I was glad to help with financial contributions and some of my time. It also gave her time to mentor young people and encourage them to become more effectively involved.

Most of us, including myself, do not like to ask people for money or their time. This is one of the reasons I was not particularly successful at selling Bibles, though I overcame some of these aversions while I was in elective politics. Mary Margaret has not suffered from this fund-raising disability or timidity. Even before she was making a living as Vice President for Development for public TV station KLRU, MM was leading the way to raise funds for historic

Most Worthy Citizen Awards Program

April 3, 1998
11:30 a.m. – 1:00 p.m.
Renaissance Austin Hotel

honoring

Mary Margaret Farabee
Austin's Most Worthy Citizen of 1997

The Austin Board of Realtors selected Mary Margaret as Austin's Most Worthy Citizen of 1994, recognizing her volunteer and public service work.

preservation and other worthy causes in Austin. Examples of her early leadership making a difference include the restoration of the Paramount Theater and the establishment of the Austin History Center. With our marriage, MM became free to pursue new projects for the benefit of others.

Mary Margaret prefers to work behind the scenes and is not particularly interested in public recognition. She seems happiest when she is mentoring younger volunteers, providing pro bono counseling and advice to nonprofits, and tending details for events for which she has responsibility. She has been the idea and energy person behind many worthwhile efforts, but I share only some facts and recollections of the following:

PHILOSOPHERS' ROCK: If you visit Zilker Park near the entrance to Barton Springs Pool, you will see a statue of three icons from the 1930's and 40's engaged in argument and serious discussion while seated on what became known as "Philosophers' Rock." The subjects of the statue are three former UT Austin faculty members and authors: J. Frank Dobie, Roy Bedichek, and Walter Prescott Webb. The bigger-than-life statue was created by world-renowned Texas native sculptress Glenna Goodacre. Author Larry Wright and screenwriter Bill Wittliff asked Mary Margaret to serve with them on a small committee to raise the several hundred thousand dollars to create and place the statue.

Capitol Area Statues of Texas (CAST), a nonprofit, initiated the project shortly after our marriage. No Mary Margaret fund-raising effort is complete without a gala dinner or two. With no thanks to actor Rip Torn, who spoke longer than expected at the Ex-Students' Association, the money was raised, statue completed, and located during the latter part of 1994. I was pleased to make a significant do-

Philosophers' Rock *statue by Glenna Goodacre in Zilker Park. Capital Area Statues photograph.*

nation, and we have a maquette of the original statue. Mary Margaret said it best in the following quote to the *West Austin News*, "It's inviting and touchable. There's so much energy in this statue, and I think children are the first to respond to that. I've been over to see it three times so far this week and there's always a crowd." The Philosophers' Rock project combined three of MM's favorite priorities: art, historic preservation, and literature.

CHARLES MOORE HOUSE AND FOUNDATION: Charles Moore was an internationally recognized architect who came to UT Austin in 1984 to assume the O'Neil Ford Centennial Chair at its school of architecture. Prior to UT, Moore was on the faculties of the University of California at Berkeley, UCLA, and Yale, where he was Dean of the School of Architecture. In 1991, Moore received the Gold Medal Citation of the American Institute of Architects (AIA), its most prestigious and highest recognition. When he came to Austin, Moore purchased a 1930's bungalow in West Austin. He remodeled the house and added a studio for his architectural practice, but preserved the basic structure. The compound became known as the Charles Moore House. The *New York Times* featured the Moore House in its October 20, 1994, Living Arts section.

Charles Moore died unexpectedly from a massive heart attack on December 16, 1993. There was no will, and it was unclear what would happen to the Charles Moore House, papers, extensive library, and folk art collection. The house was mortgaged, and the estate did not have liquid assets to pay off the debts. Because of the size and location of the lot, developers were interested in buying it but not in preserving the historic house. It was hoped that UT Austin would step in and preserve the house and pay off the debts, but UT was not interested in doing so unless someone else raised and contributed a substantial sum to endow the maintenance and operation.

Mary Margaret was asked by several architects and Tana Christie (Tana and her husband, former State Senator Joe Christie, commissioned Charles Moore to design their home in West Lake Hills) to help negotiate a favorable settlement with the heirs. She did so, and they agreed to contribute their interest to a nonprofit foundation, organized to preserve the Moore house. She chaired an ad hoc committee to identify potential donors and leadership for the Charles Moore Foundation. As a result of her efforts, Mary Margaret was nominated and selected by the Texas Society of Architects as an honorary member.

THE SEA RANCH AND A 911 CALL: One of Charles Moore's most celebrated works is the Sea Ranch Condominiums in Sonoma County, California, overlooking the spectacular Pacific coastline. Moore reserved one of the condos for his own use, and the estate made it available to Mary

Margaret and me for the purpose of celebrating our fifth wedding anniversary on May 25, 1996. Ed and Helen Baxter and Jim and Eleanor Cochran joined us for the trip.

We flew into San Francisco, had lunch at the famed Chez Panise Restaurant in Berkeley, and drove up the coast to Sea Ranch. After a late dinner, MM and I retired to our room on the top floor loft of the condo. After midnight, I woke and heard someone moaning. Mary Margaret was not in the bed and I got up immediately and checked the stairwell to find her on the steep stairs that provided access to the closest bathroom. She had fallen, was unconscious, and bleeding from her head. We did not move her for fear that her neck or back might be broken, but immediately called 911. The local emergency medical service arrived shortly and carefully moved her to the ambulance.

The ambulance drove through the night to the nearest hospital in Santa Rosa. Because of the winding roads, sharp curves, and rugged terrain, the 50-mile trip took more than an hour. I was in the front seat of the ambulance, and a male attendant was with Mary Margaret. The first thing MM remembers after the fall is waking up strapped to a gurney in the ambulance. She explained her need to go to the bathroom, which was the reason for her originally traversing the perilous stairway. The attendant said she could not move and provided no help for what seemed a nearly bursting bladder. She felt her head, nose, and bloody hair and asked what had happened. With less than a good bedside manner, the attendant told her that she had probably broken her nose. We finally arrived at the hospital and MM was wheeled into the emergency room. She explained her need to urinate, and the young physician on duty helped her to the bathroom. When she looked at herself in the mirror, she was shocked at her appearance and the dried blood matted in her hair.

The Baxters followed the ambulance in the rent car and comforted me in the emergency room waiting area. During the first hour, the doctors gave very little information about her condition. We were worried and anxious, calling back to the Cochran's at Sea Ranch every 20 or 30 minutes. After a battery of tests, X-rays, CAT scan, the removal of some hair, and several stitches in her scalp, the doctors found no broken nose, neck, back, or bones. They brought her out in a wheelchair with a prescription and advised aspirin and bed rest.

The sun had risen, and our next task was to find a drugstore to fill the prescription. Unfortunately, the drugstores in Santa Rosa don't open until 10 a.m. on Saturdays, so we found coffee for our recovering patient and even toured the city. After filling MM's prescription, we headed back to Sea Ranch. It is a much easier drive in the daylight than through the darkness of night.

When we arrived back at Sea Ranch, the Cochrans and a curious group of neighbors met us to see the patient who had disturbed their sleep with the siren and flashing red lights of an EMS vehicle. Mary Margaret emerged from the rent car, somewhat pale and haggard in appearance with a splotch of her hair missing where the stitches sewed her scalp back together. The hydrogen peroxide highlighted the remaining hair around the wound. Her first remark was, "What time is the party tonight at Jim Daniels?" After an afternoon nap and a few aspirin, we all went to the party, including Mary Margaret. May 25, 1996, is one of the more memorable anniversaries of our marriage.

THE TEXAS BOOK FESTIVAL: Mary Margaret loves books and is an avid reader. As a grade schooler, she caught the bus each Saturday morning to the public library in downtown Dallas where she checked out as many books as she could carry, before taking in a movie and heading back home for a week of reading. Plan II and graduate work at UT further enhanced her reading habit.

Carolyn Osborn told Mary Margaret about a book festival she recently visited in Nashville, Tennessee. The Tennessee festival was held annually over a weekend at the state capitol. It sounded like an exciting idea, and MM approached persons she knew at the Texas State Capitol complex with the idea of a Texas book festival. However, she was advised that the capitol building would not be available for such a program.

1998 program cover by David Everett

In 1994, George W. Bush was elected governor of Texas. His wife Laura was a former librarian, and has the same love for books as Mary Margaret. When Laura Bush heard of Mary Margaret's interest in a book festival, a meeting was arranged to explore the idea for a festival similar to that of

Tennessee. Before long, the idea became a reality. Laura Bush served as the Honorary Chair and Mary Margaret was the Founding Chair of the Texas Book Festival. The first Festival was held in the State Capitol complex on November 15–17, 1996, and it was a great success. It is now one of the largest and best-known book festivals in the United States. Laura Bush moved on to the White House when her husband George W. became president in 2000, but she continues to serve as Honorary Chair of the Texas Book Festival. Mary Margaret served as Chairperson for eight years and remained on the board until 2008.

WHITE HOUSE NIGHTS: One of the first things Laura Bush did as the new First Lady was to plan a National Book Festival. It was designed similarly to the Texas Book Festival. In appreciation of Mary Margaret's leadership in establishing the Texas festival, we were invited to attend the first national festival held in Washington, D.C., on September 7–9, 2001, as guests of the president and First Lady Laura Bush in the White House. We did not stay in the Lincoln bedroom, but we enjoyed three nights immediately above it on the fourth floor. Twelve other closer friends of Laura Bush were also White House guests for the first National Book Festival.

This was not my first visit in the White House. I attended a reception for Texas contributors when Jimmy Carter was president. However, the opportunity to roam through the historic rooms at will, studying the paintings, art pieces, and antiques, and savoring the White House's history was one of the more memorable experiences of my life. Notwithstanding our Democratic orientation, the President could not have been more courteous and friendly. After a private dinner with the President, First Lady, and other house guests on Saturday night, President Bush asked if anyone would like to see the West Wing. Most of us accepted the invitation. The President checked his messages, gathered up Barney (the family dog), and joined us in the Oval Office. We spent an hour or more talking with him about the presidency and various aspects of the several rooms which constitute the work space for that part of the White House. Mary Margaret and I had our picture taken with President Bush while there.

Laura and President Bush rose early on Sunday morning September 9 to attend a nearby Episcopal Church. All of the houseguests were invited to attend the church services with them, and most did so, but we didn't. Since we do not ordinarily attend such services, we instead spent a couple of hours quietly enjoying our coffee, the Sunday *New York Times*, and our

*Mary Margaret and I with President Bush in the Oval Office
of the White House, Saturday evening, September 8, 2001*

new home away from home—another form of worship. A White House reception and brunch was held later that morning for Texans who were attending the National Book Festival. The President joined Laura and spent more time for conversation and photo ops than expected.

We had an uneventful flight back to Austin on Sunday afternoon, but guests and others who stayed over with flight reservations on Tuesday, September 11, were not so fortunate. Two airliners were flown into the World Trade Center in New York and another into the Pentagon several miles from the White House. A fourth airplane may have been headed for the White House, but courageous passengers wrenched control of the aircraft from the terrorists, and it crashed into rural Pennsylvania countryside with no survivors. As we watched our television sets in Austin on 9/11/01, I observed that life and government in the United States would never be quite the same, and it hasn't been.

We received an invitation from Laura Bush to attend the second National Book Festival in 2002 and again stay at the White House. I thought about it and suggested to Mary Margaret that she take her daughter Patricia. I would have enjoyed spending three more nights in the most famous home of our country but felt it was a unique opportunity that should be shared with Patricia. MM and her daughter joined the President and First Lady for Sunday worship that time around.

LADY BIRD JOHNSON AND THE WILDFLOWER CENTER: Lady Bird Johnson was the leader for the Austin Town Lake beautification plan,

Artist's rendition of LBJ Ranch near Johnson City

and Mary Margaret worked with her friends Carolyn Curtis and Maline McCalla to raise funds for the monumental project. From 1998 to 2004 MM was an active member of the board of directors for the Lady Bird Johnson Wildflower Center; she served as Chairperson of the Wildflower Gala Reception and Dinner in 1999, which raised more than $350,000. With Jean Rather, MM instituted a silent art auction in 2004. Through these activities, we became better acquainted with Mrs. Johnson and visited in her Austin home and the LBJ Ranch on several occasions. The most memorable of these visits was in 2003 when Mrs. Johnson invited us and several other guests to have dinner and spend the night at the LBJ Ranch. On Sunday morning, we went to the Episcopal Church in Fredericksburg and took communion with the former First Lady. The next time we took communion was at the Eucharist service in memory of Mrs. Johnson at the Wildflower Center two days after her death in July 2007.

As I stated to the *Wichita Falls Times and Record News* after her death, Lady Bird Johnson was "one of the most gracious ladies I've ever met. She was a Southern lady in the finest sense."

HARRY RANSOM CENTER: In 2003, the Harry Ransom Center (HRC) at UT Austin appointed Mary Margaret to its advisory council. The HRC has one of the best collections of books, original manuscripts, and related memorabilia in the world, and it was getting ready to open its newly renovated facilities. MM and Nancy Inman were named co-chairpersons for the opening, and it was a great success. When the time came to plan for the 50th Anniversary of the HRC, Mary Margaret and

Nancy were appointed the co-chairpersons for one of the most spectacular celebrations in the history of UT.

We traveled to London, Boston, and New York City with the HRC Advisory Board, and visited some of the best libraries, authors, and collections of each city.

TEXAS OBSERVER: Mary Margaret is a longtime admirer of the bi-weekly newspaper *The Texas Observer* (Observer). She truly believes in the importance of its investigative reporting and coverage of issues generally ignored by Texas daily newspapers. Other than being a loyal subscriber, however, MM was never directly involved with the Observer until 2006 when she had an idea about honoring columnist Molly Ivins before her death from the effects of breast cancer. Molly appreciated the idea and suggested that any such event should be fun and humorous, rather than mournful, and it should raise money for the Observer. That was right down Mary Margaret's alley, and planning began immediately for "An Evening with Molly Ivins—A Roast? Hell, No! It's a BBQ" to occur on October 8, 2006.

An Evening with Molly Ivins invitation with Ben Sargent caricature, 2006

The evening was a roaring, star-studded success, featuring Garrison Keillor, Joe Ely, Roy Blount, Jr., Lewis Lapham, Molly, and many more. Over 760 people attended; the event and related efforts raised more than $500,000, which was matched by a foundation in New York for a total of one million dollars to support the Observer. Mollie Ivins died on January 31, 2007. The Texas Democracy Foundation, owner and operator of the Observer, asked Mary Margaret to serve on its board of directors. I suspect that many of the Foundation's board members didn't know what to think about MM when she joined them, but her ideas, energy, and leadership have made a difference in *The Texas Observer,* as it has with Philosophers' Rock, the Charles Moore Center for the Study of Place, the Texas Book Festival, the Lady Bird Johnson Wildflower Center, and the Harry Ransom Center.

IN TIMES OF SORROW AND ILLNESS

Marriage is more than sharing the good times. Stress, loss of loved ones, illness, and disappointments also occur. Whether these times of sorrow fall upon both, or more specifically on one or the other, they are felt and must be dealt with by both. The deaths of my parents and siblings occurred long ago, and I have not experienced any losses within my immediate family since our marriage. Mary Margaret has not been so fortunate.

Mary Margaret's younger brother and sister died prior to our marriage. As the only surviving child, Mary Margaret bore more responsibility for her aging parents in Dallas. When her father died in March 1996 at age 93 after several years of declining health, the weight of those obligations increased. Her mother exhibited great strength during her husband's lifetime; however, her mental and physical health deteriorated after his death.

Mary Margaret's son David Albright was bright and could be very charming, but he had significant drug and alcohol abuse problems dating back to his high school years. Mary Margaret paid for professional care and did everything within her power to help him deal with his drug addiction, but with very limited results. I helped where I could, but with little effect. During one Christmas holiday, David called from the Travis County jail, advising he was being held for a minor probation violation in connection with a prior DWI conviction in Kerr County. As unaccustomed as I was to bailing people out of jail (never in Travis County), I put on my lawyer hat, determined the amount of bail, went to the bank, which was about to close for the holidays, secured a cashier's check, and bailed him out so we could drive to Dallas for Christmas with MM's parents. David and I drove to Kerrville two weeks later, had a hearing, paid a fine, and secured his release and the return of my bail money. Suffice to say, all of this didn't make for pleasant memories of that Christmas season; however, it worked out better than trying to explain David's absence to the elderly grandparents and bearing the knowledge that he spent the holidays in jail.

David, who earned his bachelor's degree at Austin College, wanted to teach, and he earned credits for a teaching certificate at Southwest Texas State University in San Marcos. He did some substitute teaching in Austin but migrated to San Miguel de Allende in Mexico where he secured a job as a teacher's assistant in a private school. He loved the job, the students apparently liked him, and as he became bilingually proficient, it appeared he

*Mary Margaret, David, and Patricia Albright
in San Miguel, Mexico, at the private school
where David worked, 1995*

may have turned the corner to a more self-sufficient life. Unfortunately, this was not the case. He fell in with some wealthy friends from Austin who made heavier drugs available to him, and his addiction led to a termination of his employment at the private school. When he returned to Austin, he was in bad shape and Mary Margaret placed him in a treatment facility. When David appeared sufficiently drug free, he left the treatment facility and returned to Mexico, for the expressed purpose of getting belongings and returning to Austin to find work. He did not return.

In October 1996, Mary Margaret received a call from San Miguel saying that David was back on drugs and in serious condition. Before she could determine the best course of action, we received another call in the middle of the night advising that David had died from an overdose of cocaine. The loss of one's child is devastating, as I witnessed when my own mother suffered the loss of her oldest son, Leroy, who was murdered. As word of David's death spread, friends from all over Austin came forward to help and ease MM's grief. Bonnie Fielder, a friend who spoke fluent Spanish, accompanied Mary Margaret and her daughter Patricia to San Miguel where they made arrangements for the cremation of David's body and return of his ashes.

October is a difficult month for Mary Margaret. Both of her children and her deceased brother were born during that month, which reminds her of the best of times. David died in October and grief for him and her siblings remains.

The first Texas Book Festival occurred approximately one month after David's death, and Mary Margaret was the working chairperson for the event. She plunged her time and thoughts into making it a success in 1996 and for eight years thereafter. Her focus and dedication to this project, together with several others, has helped keep her mind off the sad and troublesome losses of the past. Patricia and I have provided help and support, but it's impossible to forget or overcome the loss of a child, even a greatly troubled one.

Lorraine Manske Carlson, MM's mother, was a complex and needy person. After the death of Dr. Carlson, and with age, her needs accelerated; her moods and physical health became more fragile. Lorraine wanted to remain in her North Dallas townhome, even after she was unable to care for it or herself. MM first arranged for 40 hours of help for her mother each week, and later around-the-clock assistance. No daughter could have been more attentive under the circumstances, with frequent trips to Dallas, parties for her mother on special occasions, daily phone calls, work with caregivers, bookkeeping, and the management required for home care.

Lorraine and Dr. Glenn Carlson, 1992, for Dr. Carlson's 90th birthday

The 1997 family Christmas in Crested Butte, Colorado, is an example of Mary Margaret's efforts to please her mother and keep the family together. We leased a large condominium on the side of a mountain within walking distance of the ski slopes. My family joined us for three days before Christmas, and the Carlson family—MM, Lorraine, and all of her grandchildren—were together for a Colorado White Christmas. It was a happy experience for each family member except Lorraine, who exhibited wide mood swings, including a dinner table declaration that "no one loves me." She was the center of love and attention among those left in her family, but the ghosts of the past haunted her, arguably all of her life. I was reminded of similar statements by my mother, who was haunted by her share of ghosts.

With the progressive decline of her physical and mental health, it was necessary to move Lorraine to a nursing facility during the last year of her life. After a thorough investigation of the available facilities, one of the nicer Dallas care centers, the Forum, was chosen. MM had the unpleasant task of helping her mother make the move, though the townhome was retained, in the event that Mrs. Carlson's condition improved. Mary Margaret visited her mother frequently at the Forum and arranged for additional private care. Lorraine's health continued its decline, and she died on November 8, 2001. We drove immediately to Dallas. MM planned the funeral that occurred two days later. After commencing the complicated tasks of liquidating the estate, we returned to Austin where the sixth Texas Book Festival would get under way in less than a week. As Chairperson, Mary Margaret was on the job, presiding and overseeing another successful Festival.

In our marriage vows, we took each other "in sickness and health." Both Mary Margaret and I have been fortunate to have relatively good health, with a few day surgeries for me and an unexpected appendectomy for her. However, in May of 2008 a routine annual physical examination revealed that MM should have open heart surgery to correct a congenital heart defect. After we secured a second opinion confirming the diagnosis that surgery was needed, Mary Margaret, in her "let's get it done now" manner, scheduled the procedure, and we departed our home in South Austin at 5 a.m. on May 15, 2008, for what was, for me, the longest day of our marriage.

Four hours after Mary Margaret was wheeled into the operating room, the heart surgeon emerged to advise the surgery went well, the defective aortic valve had been replaced with that of an animal (cow), her heart and aorta, except for the defective valve, was in good condition, and I could see her in a couple of hours in the intensive care unit (ICU). Mary Margaret was still under the effects of anesthesia when I first saw her, very pale with tubes in her body and wires measuring her heartbeat, pulse, and blood pressure. My two prior experiences of having loved ones in ICU's were not good—my brother Jimmy, who came out brain-damaged, and Helen, who died. In the ICU waiting room, I overheard a family talking about whether they should pull the life-support systems for their loved one. To say the least, I was scared and worried. My son Steve, Jim Cochran, and several other friends helped me make it through the day.

With the help of medical science, good doctors, and attentive nurses, Mary Margaret made it through the night and beyond. The tubes started coming out, and the wires were removed. After two days in the ICU, MM was moved to a regular room in the cardiac unit, and three days later I drove her home—less than a week after open heart surgery. Our home was overflowing with food, cards, and flowers from friends. Mary Margaret made progress each day and was planning to attend a gala fundraising event that she spearheaded prior to her surgery. While she was in the hospital, a closer friend brought MM an Energizer Bunny doll. Like the bunny, Mary Margaret just keeps going and going—for me, Patricia, others, and worthwhile causes.

TRAVELS WITH MARY MARGARET

Travel together has been an important part of our marriage. It provides opportunities to communicate without the distractions of work, phone calls, and the many activities and obligations that comprise a major part of our daily lives. Some people have the impression that we spend most of our time traveling. More accurately, it would average about a month of the year—not in one place or at one time such as each summer in Colorado, but some long weekends and a couple of weeks on a longer tour. Sometimes we travel by ourselves, renting a car upon destination. Other travel has been associated with my work prior to retirement, closer friends, and several educational tour groups.

Mary Margaret was experienced in organizing tours and trips when we married, and she put these skills to work for the two of us, our families, and friends like those in the conversation group. Over 17 years of marriage we have visited all parts of Texas, the United States, and many foreign countries. It would require another book to fully describe our travels together, and I only set out some categories, places, and dates of travel, with a few of my favorite recollections.

TEXAS TRAVEL: McDonald Observatory and the Big Bend for our honeymoon in 1991; Indian Hot Springs on the Rio Grande south of El Paso, 1991 and 1993; East Texas and the Big Thicket with a canoe trip down Village Creek, 1994; Dolan Falls near Presidio, 1996; Cibolo Creek Ranch in South Texas, 1999; several visits to the LBJ Ranch in Johnson City, including dinner, an overnight stay, and church with Lady Bird Johnson; visiting Edd and Lynda Farabee on the High Plains, 2003; and travel through East Texas with friends, stopping at Jefferson, Caddo Lake, and Marshall.

MM and I canoeing on Village Creek in the Big Thicket, Southeast Texas, 1994

Mary Margaret suggested a new dimension for the Conversation Group: a long weekend of travel each year to interesting places in Texas. With suggestions from the group, MM did most of the planning such as hotel reservations, meals, access, and itinerary. The program was so popular that the group traveled beyond the boundaries of Texas to Sedona, Arizona, in 1997, and Savannah, Georgia, and Charleston, South Carolina, in 1998. Texas trips include: Big Bend and Lajitas, 1992; Galveston, 1993; San Antonio-Castroville-Lost Maples State Park, 1994; Washington County near Brenham where we stayed in a restored plantation and visited Round Top and heard James Dick play the piano in 1995; Port Aransas Lighthouse and the whooping cranes, 1996; Ft. Worth and Granbury, 1999; Dallas and Waxahachie, 2001; and Archer City, where we bought books and visited with Larry McMurtry in 2002.

NEW YORK, NEW YORK, A WONDERFUL TOWN: Mary Margaret and I love New York City. Both of us, long before we knew each other, had experiences in New York that were important to our lives. We have been fortunate to visit the "Big Apple" every year or two since we married. My 66th birthday party in 1998 was the most memorable. Friends from the East Coast, as well as Texas, joined us for a brunch at the Boat House Restaurant in Central Park. Both of us enjoy Broadway plays, museums, and music. We have seen everything from Metropolitan operas with the Cochrans to Mamet off-Broadway, musicals, serious drama, and comedy in New York. One of the more spectacular trips to New York was the opening of "The Gates" exhibit in Central Park by Christo and his wife Jeanne-Claude. The Park sparkled with 7,500 16-foot-tall gates of saffron-colored nylon banners. In 2006 we took my grandchildren and their parents to NYC between Christmas and New Year's Day with hopes that their first visit to the city would be as positive and meaningful as ours have been.

USA TRAVELS: By the turn of the century I had visited 47 states. It became my goal to make it to the remaining three I had not experienced—Alaska, South Dakota, and North Dakota. During the summer of 2002, we cruised down the inland waterway of Alaska from Anchorage to Vancouver, stopping along the way at Skagway, Juneau, Sitka, and Ketchikan. In July 2005 we fled the Texas summer, flew to Rapid City, South Dakota, rented a car, and had more fun than ever expected. We visited Mount Rushmore and Custer State Park in South Dakota, and Theodore Roosevelt National Park and Medora with its spectacular outdoor theater in North Dakota.

Other states we have visited during our marriage include: Arizona multiple times, particularly Sedona and Scottsdale; California in 1991, '96, '97, '98, and 2003; Colorado multiple times; Connecticut, 2001; Delaware, 2001, where we found the grave of the first Farabee, assuming we were originally "Furbees"; Florida, 1993 and 1994; Georgia, 1998 and 2004; Idaho, 2004; Illinois multiple times, primarily Chicago; Louisiana, multiple visits including Mardi Gras in 1994 and a barge cruise up the Mississippi River from New Orleans to Memphis in 2004 with Jim and Eleanor Cochran, stopping in Baton Rouge, Natchez, and Vicksburg; Maine in 1992, '94, '97, and 2000; Maryland, 2001; Massachusetts, multiple visits including Boston, Amherst and Martha's Vineyard where we stayed with Joel and Joann Stearns; Montana, 1995; New Hampshire and Vermont, 2001; New Mexico, multiple visits; North Carolina, multiple visits including weekends with the Hobby's at Diana's family home near Yanceyville, 1993 and '94, Farabee genealogy research in Davidson County, 2002, and two great trips to Asheville in 1997 and 2002; Oregon and Washington, 1997; Pennsylvania, where we visited the Frank Lloyd Wright Falling Water House in 1994 and several visits to Philadelphia; Tennessee, 1996; Utah, 2000; Wisconsin, 2004; and Wyoming in 2004 to hike in Yellowstone National Park and watch Old Faithful.

Scottsdale, Arizona, frontier couple, 2002

MEXICO, CANADA, AND CENTRAL AND SOUTH AMERICA have been important parts of our travel itineraries. Mary Margaret's son David taught school in San Miguel de Allende, Mexico, between 1993 and 1996, and we visited him and other Austin friends several times in that beautiful city. We flew to Cabo San Lucas, Mexico, in 2005, and drove up the Pacific coast to attend a wedding and discover the beauty and charm of Todos Santos and the Baja Peninsula.

Canada was our destination in 1998, 2000 (Canada Day in Quebec City and the Montreal Jazz Festival with the Cochrans), 2001 (Vancouver and Victoria with the Prentices), and a second honeymoon at Niagara Falls and Niagara on the Lake with the Cochrans, 2006. We spent part of our 1992 and 1993 Christmas holidays in Costa Rica. Thanks to Mary Margaret's planning, I celebrated my 65th birthday in 1997 in the Lake Country of Chile with MM, Patricia, and the Cochran Family. From there we traveled on to Santiago, then to Lima, Cusco, and Machu Picchu in Peru.

Our trip to CUBA in 2002 was one of our more memorable experiences. U.S. travel to Cuba was limited at the time, and it is more restricted now. We traveled with an Austin nonprofit that was authorized by the State Department to take groups to Cuba for humanitarian and cultural purposes. Mary Margaret assembled our group of 15 adventurous souls; we embarked from Miami to Havana on February 10 with 500 pounds of medications for needy Cubans to learn more about Cuban history, art, literature and to see what Fidel Castro had wrought. We stayed in the Hotel Florida and visited Cuban homes, schools, hospitals, museums, and enterprises during the six days we were there. Although the Cuban economy was struggling after the Russian departure and from the U.S. embargo and trade limitations, we were impressed by access to health care, improvements in literacy, and our safety on Havana streets at any time of day or night. Suppression of civil liberties such as limitations on free expression in the media, use of computers, and foreign travel was apparent. Although U.S. tourists were few, Europeans and Canadians were abundant. The cigar and rum factories we visited were teeming with free market efforts to sell us their products, and everyone brought back the legal limit of cigars. We visited the Ernest Hemingway farm that is now a museum, smoked Cuban cigars, and consumed mojitos in the famous author's favorite bar in the Floridita Hotel (not the same as our hotel).

*Colonial architecture and old U.S.
cars in Havana, Cuba, 2002*

European Travel with Mary Margaret includes the following trips: London and the United Kingdom, 1991 for the week after Christmas; driving through Kent and the Cotswolds with Jack and Cindy Keever in 1996, ending in London and experiencing Shakespeare at the Globe Theatre as "groundlings" (term from yore for the poor folks who stood throughout the play on the ground between the stage and seated patrons); the 2002 Chelsea Flower Show and theater on our own before joining other members of the Harry Ransom Center (HRC) Advisory Board for a great visit to the British Parliament; driving through Scotland, 2000; Ireland in 1992, for my 60th birthday on the Ring of Kerry and on to kiss the Blarney Stone, and then spending the weekend with Bill Hobby, watching him pursue the elusive fox outside of Tipperary; Belgium and Germany in 1991, where we drove the Romantique Strasse (Romantic Road) in the Rhine Valley in our rented car; Berlin, Strasburg, and Prague in 1994; Switzerland and Northern Italy in 1999 to visit Lucerne and hike in the southern Alps, spending time in Milan, Bellagio, and on Lake Como; a Baltic cruise with the Cochrans, Baxters, and Osborns in 1998, visiting Copenhagen, Denmark, Finland, St. Petersburg, Russia, Estonia, and Sweden, where we were guests of fellow Texan Lyndon Olson, who was then U.S. ambassador in Stockholm; in 1995 we flew to Turkey with the Baxters and Cochrans, and after two days in Istanbul, boarded a small cruise ship with stops in Kusadasi (Ephesus), the Greek Isles, ending in Athens, where we saw the Parthenon

St. Petersburg, Russia, 1998

and other remains of ancient world before flying home; three wonderful days on our own in Paris, France, in June 2001 before joining a Smithsonian tour group for travel throughout Provence; and ten days in Spain (Madrid, Bilbao, and Barcelona) with the Cochrans and a Smithsonian group, 2007.

ASIA, AFRICA, AND ELSEWHERE: In March 2003, we visited China and Japan; South Africa, Botswana, and Zambia in May 2004; Egypt, 2005; New Zealand and Australia 2006; and India during the winter of 2007. All of these trips were Smithsonian education tours, and I will share some pictures and recollections about them in the next chapter, since they were a part of the greater freedom of my retirement.

Retirement and Reflections
(2000–2008)

And the seasons they go round and round . . .
We're captive on the carousel of time.
We can't return, we can only look behind
From where we came . . .
—"The Circle Game" by Joni Mitchell

T HE SEASON OF MY LIFE as a retired person commenced on October 22, 2000, when I left the position of Vice Chancellor and General Counsel of the UT System. I was 68 years old and ready for another round of the stages and phases of my life. Retirement as General Counsel was not an abrupt change because I continued work on a part-time basis as Executive Assistant to the UT System Chancellor for two years. I also spent more time with new responsibilities as a board member of Health Care Service Corporation (HCSC) and contemplated what I would do when I fully retired in January 2003.

CHANGES AND CHALLENGES OF RETIREMENT

Many lawyers never fully retire; they may slow down or discontinue their practice because of illness or disabilities. Jim Cowles is one of those slow to retire; he is still trying the big cases in Dallas and elsewhere, going full steam ahead. If I had continued my private law practice in Wichita Falls, I doubt that I would have retired when I did. Some of my former State Senate colleagues, like Pete Snelson and Babe Schwartz, continue to do lobby work; but as indicated earlier, I was not attracted to lobbying.

At the time I retired from the UT System, I thought about assuming my faculty appointment at the LBJ School; however, the prospect of preparing lectures, grading papers, and meeting seminars was not appealing at this stage of my life. I wanted more time, not only to "smell the roses," but to plant and grow them, read, write, learn new things, travel, pose questions to myself, and ponder the answers.

Retirement has been a busy time, but more on my schedule—not that of the court, client, constituents, employer, or employee. I rise each morning at about the same time as when I was employed. After filling my cup with freshly brewed coffee, I listen to the news on public radio KUT, read the *Austin American-Statesman* and the *New York Times*, and then review the *Wichita Falls Times Record News* online. As much as I enjoyed my work, whether at the UT System, State Senate, or law practice, I don't miss the stop-and-go traffic, breakfast meetings, business lunches, routine problems, occasional crises, trials and tribulations of politics, management, and problem solving.

TECHNOLOGY was my first challenge of retirement. For more than 40 years I was supported by legal secretaries, administrative assistants, and staff to type my letters, answer the phone, and help with multiple tasks that kept the wheels turning. Moving across the street to a smaller office at the UT System, I carried my antiquated Dictaphone and computer with me, reminiscent of Steve Martin in his movie *The Jerk*. I thought I would dictate letters and memos required by my new job, and "Presto!" someone would type them for me. Not so; I had to become more self-sufficient, like the younger attorneys at OGC. It was hard, but with the help of my former administrative assistant, Beverly Page, and Muffett Mills, who worked in an adjoining office, I learned to produce most of my own work. Becoming computer literate and self-sufficient was the most important personal accomplishment during the two years I continued work on a part-time basis.

IN 2003, a very important year, a lot happened, including full retirement; however, a major construction project at 2702 Rockingham was the highlight of the year. We added 500 additional square feet to the house as an office and study for me and larger bath and dressing room for MM. The challenges of the construction, related remodeling, and landscaping are too voluminous to list; but we survived and preserved our sanity. I still had an office downtown in the Colorado Building and worked fewer hours on a pro bono basis, analyzing legislation, consulting, and helping with the disposal of old files. However, I could see a time when the System would need

Some of my Farm Security Administration (FSA) photographs, originally purchased from the Library of Congress for my State Senate office, then used in OGC office and now in my home office.

the office, and I didn't want to make daily or even weekly appearances to justify my use of the space. The new home office has everything I could want—a good desk, bookshelves, computer and printer, cabinets galore, 12-foot built-in credenza (accommodating most of my clutter), a seldom used HDTV with surround sound system, a grand view of our terraced backyard, additional wall space for my favorite art pieces, and a quiet place for reading, writing, and communicating with the rest of the world. Within a year after completing my dream office, I suggested to the UT System that I was not using their office space very much and would be glad to move out. It took only a couple of weeks to accept my offer. I don't miss the downtown office, but I do miss the prime parking space.

SIMPLE PLEASURES are more a part of my life in retirement: the yard and gardens; mowing the lawn and turning the soil; planting and harvesting vegetables; propagating plants and flowers until it's hard to find space for them; feeding and watching a colorful variety of birds that stray into our yard from nearby greenbelts; experiencing the changing seasons each year; reconnecting with family and friends through reunions, e-mail, and other correspondence; watching sunsets from our deck overlooking Barton Skyway and the Greenbelt; pondering Austin's burgeoning traffic and growth; witnessing a proliferation of bees and butterflies during the day and fireflies in the summer evenings; taking neighborhood walks through Barton Hills; and enjoying my solitude and talking to myself—not out loud but within my head, lest some think I'm getting old ... though I am.

Retirement has allowed more time for volunteer service. My longest volunteer effort was with the **CENTER FOR PUBLIC POLICY PRIORITIES** (**CPPP**), originally the Benedictine Resource Center. Helen was its first executive director. When CPPP separated from the Benedictine Sisters' organization and established a separate nonprofit corporation, I served as an incorporator and one of the original board members. I was reelected to serve two more terms before retiring from the board in 2007, pursuant to its bylaws. The mission of CPPP is the improvement of public policies for low- and moderate-income Texans through independent research and policy development, public education, advocacy, and technical assistance. CPPP honored the memory of Helen and the Farabee family at its first Legacy Luncheon on November 17, 2000. I was skeptical about how much

With Mary Margaret and former president Bill Clinton at CPPP Legacy Dinner honoring B. Rapoport, 2006

money could be raised on the strength of our name, but it was successful for the organization ($135,000) and a nice honor for the family. Subsequent honorees include Bill Hobby, Catherine Mosbacher, the Ratliff brothers (Jack, Shannon, and Bill), Bernard Rapoport, and Pete Laney.

I served on the **UNIVERSITY OF TEXAS PRESS ADVISORY COUNCIL**, 2004–2007. Mary Margaret succeeded me on the Council when I declined another term. The UT Press is one of the finest university presses in the nation. It was exciting to be a part of it for three years, and I continue to support its work.

Public broadcasting—radio and television—has been my source for news, music, and home entertainment for years. I recall building a tall antenna on top of my home in Wichita Falls to hear Dallas public radio stations KERA and WRR. Bringing public television to Wichita Falls was one of my most important volunteer efforts. When I moved to Austin, I developed a pattern of listening to **KUT PUBLIC RADIO** each morning and during the drives to and from work. When I was asked to serve on a new advisory council for KUT radio station in 2005, I accepted and was elected chairman of the group. I continue my work with KUT as chairman of its advisory board in 2008.

The Texas Supreme Court appointed me to the board of directors for the **TEXAS EQUAL ACCESS TO JUSTICE FOUNDATION** (TEAJF) in 2003. This foundation, which is funded by a combination of interest earned on lawyers' trust accounts, court fees, and contributions, now distributes more than 20 million dollars each year for legal aid programs throughout Texas. TEAJF supports the programs similar to those I helped establish in Wichita Falls when I was president of the county bar association. The Court reappointed me for another three-year board term in 2006.

HEALTH PROBLEMS are more frequent in retirement because of aging and decreased activity. At age 75, I am much healthier than when I prematurely arrived in 1932 and later struggled through the first and second grades. I discuss this subject for two reasons: 1) the genetic component, which may be helpful to future Farabee generations; and 2) because retirees, including myself, spend increasing amounts of time and money, mostly Medicare, seeing doctors and trying to prolong our lives. If we're lucky, the time and money is spent for preventive care and health maintenance. If we're not so lucky, it is spent for more serious health issues like cancer, heart attacks, strokes, and Alzheimer's disease.

DIABETES is also considered a serious health problem, and about 8% of the U.S. population has the disease. In 1985 I was diagnosed as a type 2 diabetic. I was not overweight nor did my parents or their families have a history of diabetes. I first managed the disease by diet, and later with oral medications (the most effective for me being metformin, which I initially had to purchase in Mexico or other foreign countries, because it was not approved in the United States, as it is now). About the time I retired, I reluctantly took the advice of my endocrinologist and started giving myself an injection of insulin each morning. With the insulin, a couple of pills (containing metformin), some exercise, and a lower sugar/carbohydrate diet, I have managed my diabetes for 23 years and experienced none of the serious physical problems often related to the disease. I suspect that I am healthier because of my diabetes regimen than I would have been had I never had the disease and continued my diet of candy bars, Big Macs, French fries, and greasy enchiladas.

Just before my retirement, in 1999, I discovered that I had only one kidney. This rare congenital anomaly (about 1 in 5000), known as "unilateral renal agenesis," was discovered when I complained to a doctor about pain in my right side, and he ordered an abdominal sonogram. During the procedure, the medical technician seemed perplexed and asked if my right kidney had been surgically removed. I said no, and he explained that the only kidney he could find was the one on the left side. A CT scan confirmed the congenital absence of my right kidney and a couple of other anomalies that caused referrals to my urologist and a vascular surgeon. Case studies indicate a higher incidence of kidney disease and renal failure for those of us with only one kidney; but I have had no ill effects thus far. The condition makes me an unlikely kidney donor (while alive), and hopefully I will never need another kidney—at age 75, the prospects seem good.

My other medical adventures have been for health maintenance and disease prevention: annual checkups by the urologist, dermatologist, ophthalmologist (cataract removals on both eyes), gastroenterologist (colonoscopies removing polyps but not malignancies), primary care/cardiologist (no heart problems), dentist, and most important, the endocrinologist (management of diabetes). All of that and six prescription medications a day seems like a lot; but good health, a high energy level, and productive retirement make it all worthwhile.

INTERNATIONAL TRAVEL

One of my goals in retirement has been to see more of the world—particularly places I have never visited—and to learn more about the people, history, and cultures that preceded our own. I chronicled most of the countries we have visited in Chapter 14; however, we discovered Smithsonian Journeys in 2002 and expanded our travel to Asia, Africa, and Australia/New Zealand.

Smithsonian introduced us to **CHINA** and **JAPAN** in March 2003, with lectures about the history, cultures, and economics of China. Some of the places we visited were: Beijing (Tiananmen Square, the Forbidden City, and touring of one of the few remaining 700-year-old *hutong* neighborhoods); the Great Wall at Mutianyu; Xian (the Great Mosque, Terra Cotta Warriors, museums, and tombs of ancient emperors); Hangzhou (West Lake, Tai Qi exercisers, and a green tea plantation); and Shanghai (the Yu Garden, Shanghai acrobats, the Shanghai Art Museum, the Bund, and the Peace Hotel). We also spent time in Japan, primarily Tokyo. The United States invaded Iraq while we were in China, and we witnessed the early international dissent to our country's actions in the Middle East. We knew that China had the largest population in the world, but we came home with a better appreciation of its global power and one of the world's largest economies.

AFRICA was the focus of our retirement learning experiences in 2004 and 2005. In May of 2004 we saw the southern part of Africa by rail (Rovos Rail's restored Victorian train through South Africa), air (Rovos Air's restored DC-3 and Constellation) to Zambia and Botswana, buses in various parts of South Africa, Land Rovers in two national game reserves, an automobile to a remote village in Zambia over unpaved roads, and boats (ferry from Cape Town to Robben Island, where Nelson Mandela was imprisoned for years prior to the end of Apartheid, and a cruise on the Chobe River in Botswana). Lectures provided information and discussion about Apartheid, socioeconomics of South Africa, the Soweto uprising and its consequences, the South African health system and AIDS, Nelson Mandela,

F. W. de Klerk, contemporary South African politics, and contrasts of Botswana, Zambia, and Zimbabwe. Some of the highlights of the tour included visits to the high-security prison (now closed) on Robben Island, the Cape Peninsula, a penguin rookery, the Diamond Museum in Kimberly, the Apartheid Museum in Johannesburg, Soweto, Pretoria, the Transvaal, the Kapama Game Reserve, Victoria Falls on the Zambezi River in Zambia, and Chobe National Park in Botswana, where we

Poster of Nelson Mandela at National Apartheid Museum, Johannesburg

saw a wide variety of birds and wild game, including giraffes, hippopotami, alligators, zebras, and herds of impala and elephants.

In 2005 (March 1–14), we explored the other end of the African continent—EGYPT. Joe and Carolyn Osborn joined us on this Smithsonian Journey from Cairo up the Nile River to Aswan. Although we learned about the people, religion, politics, and economy of modern Egypt, the main focus was the rich history and antiquities of ancient Egypt. Highlights of this trip included the following: the Great Pyramids and Sphinx on the Giza Plateau; the Cairo Museum of Antiquities; numerous tombs of ancient kings and queens including that of King Tut; the Valleys of Kings and Queens; Temples of Luxor, Karnak, Queen Hatshepsut, Ramses II and Queen Nefertari in Abu Simbel, Horus, and Kom Ombo; the Colossi of Memnon; and the Aswan High Dam and Lake Nasser. We traveled within Egypt by air (Cairo to Luxor and Aswan to Cairo by way of Abu Simbel), bus, cruise ship on the Nile for four days and nights (Luxor to Aswan), and camels. Nine lectures by distinguished faculty persons, including Dr. Zawi Hawass, helped us to better understand ancient, as well as modern, Egypt.

My photograph of the Sphinx and Great Pyramid, 2005

NEW ZEALAND AND AUSTRALIA were our principal international travel destinations for 2006. On February 15–16 we flew to Auckland on the North Island of New Zealand, where we boarded the small cruise ship *Clipper Odyssey* and commenced our journey down the east coast of the North and South Islands. We stopped along the way at Tauranga (Rotorua visit), Napier, Wellington, Lyttelton, Christchurch, and Dunedin before reaching Stewart Island at the most southern tip of New Zealand. We observed spectacular waterfalls as we cruised by the fiords on the west side of the South Island near Dusky and Doubtful Sounds before disembarking to travel to Queenstown by bus. This Smithsonian tour, like the others, provided excellent learning experiences with lectures, visits to museums, nature preserves, and cultural centers. It was an unexpected treat to be on the tour with Frank Kell Cahoon and his wife Paula of Midland, Texas. Frank was a classmate at Wichita Falls High School, and he represented Midland County in the Texas House of Representatives from 1965 to 1969.

At the end of the New Zealand tour, Mary Margaret and I flew to Sydney, where we joined a smaller Smithsonian group to learn about that city in particular and Australia in general. The highlights of this three-day extension of our South Pacific trip included a guided walking tour of the historic Rocks District, tasting Australian wines, visiting the Sydney Botanical Gardens, a boat trip around the Sydney harbor, and a private tour of the renowned Sydney Opera House. We returned to the Opera House in the evening to hear a Mozart concert, celebrating the 250th anniversary of the composer's birth. Seeing the Opera House from the bay, touring its concert halls, and hearing Mozart's music in one of them,

MM and I on a cruise in the Sydney Harbor with the Opera House in the background, 2006

gave me a lasting impression about the importance of creative architecture and the positive impact it can have for a city.

INDIA is the most fascinating country I have visited—its history, people, massive population, architecture, emerging economy, poverty, and government are remarkable. The historian Will Durant characterized India as "the motherland of our race." Albert Einstein said, "We owe a lot to the Indians, who taught us how to count, without which no worthwhile scientific discovery could have been made." Mark Twain observed in one of his travel commentaries, "... India [is] the most extraordinary country that the sun visits on [its] rounds." Our 15 days in Northern India confirmed these rave reviews and more.

We were part of the Smithsonian "Jewels of Northern India" tour from February 23 to March 10, 2007. The group was small (19 tour participants and four staff persons) and diverse—from all parts of the United States, older and younger, with varied professional backgrounds, including two physicians and two lawyer/former politicians (me and former Congressman Bob Livingston of Louisiana, the man who nearly became Speaker of the U.S. House in December 1998 instead of Dennis Hastert).

Our method of travel within India was varied: airplane, rail, chartered bus, jeeps, three-wheeled motorized rickshaws (Tuk-Tuks), and bicycle rickshaws. Travel in larger Indian cities is an experience within itself because of the overwhelming number of people, all kinds of vehicles, animals wandering on and off the streets, and incessant honking. Our rail travel was on the "Palace on Wheels" for three days and nights, with stops along the way. We had a small bedroom and private bath, with a personal attendant in each railcar. I was amazed to meet an acquaintance from Wichita Falls on the train, proving the old adage about it being a small world.

We explored both New Delhi and Old Delhi, visiting its markets, Humayun's Tomb, the Quib Minar, the Indira Gandhi Museum, and the Raj Ghat, which is the simple, yet powerful memorial to Mahatma Gandhi. From Delhi, we flew to the "Pink City" of Jaipur, where we visited a Hindu temple, the City Palace, and Amber Fort; we also had dinner in a private residence. From Jaipur, we traveled to Jodhpur, known as the "Blue City," spending two nights in the Umaid Bhawan Palace which was built by the Maharaja of Jodhpur over a period from 1928 to 1943. Although all of our hotels in India were palatial, the Bhawan Palace was the most grandiose facility I have ever occupied overnight. It was reminiscent of the Texas State Capitol, but larger.

Although 1.13 billion people populate India (second only to China's 1.3 billion), we traveled though areas that were lightly populated and reminiscent of West Texas. The Palace on Wheels stopped in the very early morning near the Ranthambhore, where most of us (Mary Margaret was ill) boarded open-air jeeps and drove through the predawn cold to Ranthambhore National Park and Tiger Preserve. We saw no tigers, but observed many other wild animals and birds. After the tiger "hunt," we drove to Chittorgarh to observe Holi, a festival celebrated across India that acknowledges

Celebrating Holi with two fellow Wichitans: Madav Cadambi and Dr. Ajai Cadambi

the arrival of spring. Although it was Sunday, the celebration was unlike any holy ceremony I have experienced. People tossed henna (brightly colored powder) and water over each other and danced in a circle to exotic Indian music. With a few beers, I joined in the revelry and returned to the Palace on Wheels in my traditional Indian garb, which was stained red, blue, green, and yellow. I was a real Holi Roller.

In Bharatpur, we said good-bye to the Palace on Wheels and visited the Keoladeo Ghana National Park, an internationally famous wetland for migrant water fowl and UNESCO World Heritage site. Bharatpur is a relatively small Indian city with a population of 205,000 people. On a walking tour near our hotel, we visited a typical Indian village. Livestock wandered freely along unpaved streets. We stopped at several of the humble dwellings and went inside one of them. Cooking occurs outside in a clay oven, with heat provided by burning animal dung; there was no running water or indoor bathroom. Despite cramped and Spartan conditions, the older children seemed highly motivated to further their education.

From Bharatpur, we traveled to Agra, the site of the Taj Mahal. We could see the palace from our room in the palatial Oberoi Amarvilas Hotel. Our first visit to the Taj Mahal was late in the afternoon, in order to see the magnificent structure at sunset and in the dusk of early evening. We returned to the next morning before dawn, witnessing its beauty, when the

Farabee 2007 Christmas card with pictures from India and words of Gandhi

sun's first rays wash its pure white marble with soft pinks, blues, and mauve tones. The Taj Mahal is the most beautiful architectural structure I have seen; however, its contrast with abject poverty in India is sobering. We expressed this paradox in our 2007 Christmas card with pictures of the "Taj" as well as one of my pictures of a child begging, together with some meaningful words of Mahatma Gandhi relevant to world policy and war.

The remarkable history of India, its people, their transition from colonialism to the world's largest democracy, stark disparity between massive poverty and the wealthy few, and the leadership and teachings of Gandhi, provide important lessons for the United States and the rest of the world in the 21st century.

We traveled to SPAIN in the fall of 2007 with Jim and Eleanor Cochran. I had never visited Spain, and "Crossing the Pyrenees" with another Smithsonian group was the perfect introduction to Madrid, Toledo, Burgos, Bilbao, San Sebastian, Pamplona, Vielha, Figueres, Girona, and Barcelona. Museums, art, architecture, and history were the highlights of this trip. The museums included the Prado in Madrid, the Guggenheim in Bilbao, the Picasso in Barcelona, and the Dalí in Figueres. I gained new appreciation for the modern art of Dalí and Picasso and the classical of El Greco, Velázquez, and Goya. We witnessed architecture that is art within itself, such as the Royal Palace in Madrid, the great cathedrals of Burgos and Toledo, Frank Gehry's Guggenheim, and Gaudí structures throughout Barcelona. The history of Spain was of particular interest because of its cultural legacy in Texas, Mexico, and Central and South America. The Smithsonian lectures and my observations while in Spain helped me better appreciate how the country lost its freedoms to the Franco dictatorship in 1935 and transitioned into a modern democratic state after his death in 1975.

RANDOM THOUGHTS AND REFLECTIONS

Since I can't return to the past, I have looked back and examined my life in the process of writing this memoir. I have expressed some details about where I came from, what I have done, and who some of the people and institutions are that helped make it possible. Some final thoughts and reflections seem appropriate.

We don't get to pick the time we arrive on earth, our parents, the place we are born, the length of stay, or our date of departure. Changes during my 75 years have been overwhelming. I was the beneficiary of expanding educational opportunities in the 1950's, a growing economy over most of my lifetime, and unimaginable progress in technology, transportation, and communications. Life has not been so good for many during my life time, either in the United States or the world. World War II, the Holocaust, poverty, starvation, HIV/AIDS, and at least two unnecessary wars (Vietnam and Iraq) present sobering realities. Yet, I have been largely unscathed by all of these and other human tragedy and catastrophes.

The odds of my surviving back in November 1932 were unlikely and not much better for succeeding in a life that has turned out to be productive and satisfying—not without some disappointments and sadness along the way. Family, friends, institutions, luck, and circumstance have been very important.

Somehow, I emerged as a leader/achiever type (not necessarily a virtue) from the 1940's to the present. I developed a vision for my life, set goals, and was ambitious about accomplishing them. Over time, the vision changed and was refined and tempered by reality. I married two wonderful women who were also achievers: first, Helen Rehbein and later Mary Margaret Albright. So what did I achieve? What did they achieve? I can't say that I changed the world, but perhaps the small world around me benefited from my efforts. I hope, and think, I left it a better place. The most I can say is that I made some worthwhile contributions along the way, particularly for less fortunate Texans, the legal system, my law clients, constituents, and family.

Most people are cynical about government, politics, and most of all, politicians—not without some reason. At the same time, they are for democracy, which involves debate, push and pull, give and take. When I first ran for office, I proclaimed that I was a "concerned citizen, and not a professional politician." The fact is that if one runs for office, is elected, and then engages in serious legislative work, he/she had better be an able politician, and I think I was—despite my early protestations. Politics is important; it is what "makes the mare go" and the wheels turn—or not turn. The important elements are policy, priorities, and the public interest. Politics has become so bogged down in partisanship, reelection, and raising money, it is increasingly difficult to focus on substantive policies, let alone set priorities or operate in the public interest. Like so many things in my life, I was at the right place (the State Senate) at the right time (the Bill Hobby era) to achieve some worthwhile goals.

Some have asked if I have regrets about my life. The question has caused me to consider various aspects of my life. I have very few substantive regrets, but I can think of many things I could have done better—speeches, letters, trials, responses to others, ad infinitum. This is another way of saying I have been critical of myself in larger and lesser matters—usually after the fact, when it could be argued that it was too late, though not too late for the next time. I have not taken time to bog down in self-criticism, but the process has made me a better lawyer, legislator, father, husband, and person in the many roles I have taken on.

As for bigger items, I regret that I did not spend more substantive time with my children and grandchildren. The distractions of law practice and politics were factors in relationship to my two sons. Geography and the generation gap are my excuses regarding the four grandchildren. In any event, the children and grandchildren have turned out well, and I am very proud of them.

Though no fault of the University, I regret that I didn't get a better undergraduate education. I was so involved in work and activities that I missed

With grandchildren Worth, Sara, Nancy, and Russell
at my 75th birthday party, November 22, 2007

important parts of the cultivation of my mind, which I now consider so important. I regret that I didn't read more books and learn more about music. I wish I had learned to play the guitar better and pick the five-string banjo. I thought about it, but never got around to it.

I regret that I didn't ask my mother and father more about their early life and their parents. Why did my father go to Ranger in 1912? How did Jack and Annie Lee meet? What did they recall about their own families? Did my grandfather Leroy talk about his early life, his Methodist minister father, his beautiful but errant mother Mary Frances, slavery, and his Civil War experiences?

And so it is with most of my regrets; you turn around once or twice, and before you know it, it's too late.

My law partner Clyde Fillmore once told me, "There is no justice." I did not accept his conclusion then or now, 45 years later. Not infrequently, justice is in short supply, but the idea and reality of justice has been and remains an important part of my life as a student, leader, lawyer, and lawmaker. I continue to contribute time and money to causes and programs that work for a more just society.

At a relatively early stage in my life, I discerned that racial prejudice was wrong. It took a few more years to understand the dimensions of segregation, discrimination, and Jim Crow laws, but college and NSA experiences helped me realize how much racial injustice existed around me in the 1940's, 50's, and 60's. I was disturbed when I read the wills of my great-great-great and great-great-grandfathers and saw they were slaveholders, parceling off other human beings, along with other property, in their last testaments. I am thankful that I have lived long enough to witness the first viable African American candidate for the presidency of the United States, Barack Obama. Whatever may happen in the national election after this book goes to press, the Democratic primaries and debates have been historic.

Death and dying are not new to me, but thoughts about the prospect of my own death are new—not because I am ill or diagnosed with any fatal disease, but because I am 75 years of age. When I was in my 40's, 50's, and 60's, I gave little thought to my own demise. As I grow older, thoughts about my own mortality increase because of the death of closer friends and the actuarial facts of life; that is, I am not likely to last many more years—certainly not with the quality of life I have enjoyed. After he was diagnosed with brain cancer and death was imminent, my former Senate staff person, Jim Spearly, observed:

> . . . we live our lives so caught up in our struggles and expectations and trying to get things done on time. All that can drop away, because it is just not important. What is important is you are a human being, you are alive, and there are other human beings around you, and you want to communicate with them, touch and be touched by them, communicate your own human goodness and human dignity, no matter what happens. . . . We have to get things done, but it's not why we're here.
>
> —as quoted from *Nexus, Colorado's Holistic Journal*, November/December 1994

As with so many things, Jim had it right and articulated it well—for me and for all of us.

I am quoted in a book about Texas political humor and on the Web as saying, "I am an optimist. If I ever quit being an optimist, I guess I'll become a Republican." Despite my closer proximity to the Grim Reaper and widespread cynicism about government and politics, I remain an optimist— and a Democrat. After all, I made it through the night of November

With staff member Jim Spearly, in Senate Chamber, 1985

22, 1932, and beyond. I have had a life of wonderful experiences and opportunities, meaningful work, and am blessed with a fine family. Life has been, and is, good.